D1264291

JOURNEY OF AN AMERICAN

Journey

of an American

Albion Ross

THE BOBBS-MERRILL COMPANY, INC.
Indianapolis • New York

Copyright © 1957 by Albion H. Ross
Library of Congress Catalog Card Number: 57-8690
Printed in the United States of America

D
443
. R64

FOREWORD

This is the story of an ordinary Middle-West-out-of-New-England American's troubled pilgrimage through the last twenty-five years of overmuch history and through a great deal of foreign geography.

The viewpoint is that of the small man, neither an outstanding success nor a particular failure at his job, which was, somewhat incidentally, foreign correspondence.

It is the story of an increasing bewilderment, the lot of ordinary men in dynamic times, that became a journey in search of home, that refuge from bewilderment. But the search was, to a degree, high adventure of the sort more likely to be experienced by the dynamic and the confident.

A great many of the people who are met or noted along the way in Europe, the Far East, the Middle East, Africa and in America are ordinary. The story is probably more concerned with their predicament in this age of transition than with the greatness of historic events.

The attitude shown is on occasion somewhat querulous as is likely to be the attitude of the plain man in pregnant and tormented times—a querulousness that is the ordinary mortal's desire for history to let him alone. The perspective is that of one of history's multitude of guinea pigs.

In time it becomes the story of one human guinea pig's journey out of his age both into the past and speculatively into the future, seeking a more homelike environment. From so much traveling comes in time, however, the certitude that there is an essential pattern to the human experience that outlives history.

America, viewed from distant lands, comes to seem a distinctly radical society engaged in an extraordinary experiment. The nation that had once been so familiar a scene, its way of

ALMA COLLEGE
MONTEITH LIBRARY
ALMA, MICHIGAN

life taken for granted, appears to the eyes of the traveler after so many years an almost incredible, incomprehensible exaggeration of the character of the age.

But, from the narrator's standpoint, there emerges evidence that in America also this age of violent transition will pass over. On a new level and under other circumstances America with the rest of modern mankind will find the way home again.

It is hardly important that the teller of the tale himself can find no way out except to bid farewell to the great caravan of history moving into the future, and to seek refuge in a place where the human pattern as it has been through the ages is still in part intact.

Part One

Homeless

1

WHERE the Big Four and the
Erie railroads run through the town of Marion in north-central
Ohio, they use the same double track.

Our back lot on East Center Street was deep. It contained
some ragged lawn and my father's garden. Behind that was a
high board fence, old and decayed, another lot full of brush,
stones and rubbish, and then the railway tracks.

In the night, about the time a small boy is falling asleep, one
night express or another out of the west would whistle for the
crossing down in the business section of town. It sounded very
far away in that half dream before sleeping—a cry in the night
and a summons to something, to something lonely but exciting
and perhaps sad.

There followed the rapid clicking of steel wheels, the heavy
rumble of the Pullmans passing and another long, lone cry far
outside of town at another crossing, as the train fled away
toward the eastern seaboard.

To a small boy East Center Street was a pleasant world of
big lawns, shaded by elms and oaks. Some of the houses were
brick mansions, or so they appeared. Some were fairly humble
frame houses with comfortable front porches furnished in a
disorderly fashion with swings and wicker chairs in need of
repair. The Episcopal rectory, where we lived, was of the latter
class but we belonged, despite the house and my father's eight-
een hundred a year. East Center Street was, within its limita-
tions, democratic and not overly money conscious.

11

Though the Reverend Albion Ross's small son did not know it, he was never to belong again. The house on East Center Street was to be his last real home.

There were other houses. One was on top of a conical, eroded hill in a working-class suburb of Cincinnati. One was on the main street of the little river town of Gallipolis on the upper Ohio. And then there was a dark, narrow house on a noisy street leading downhill to the station from the more prosperous portions of the old town of Hollidaysburg in the Pennsylvania Alleghenies. The church in Hollidaysburg was small and poor and did not do very well by its old rector and his wife.

As time went on, the boy, no longer a small boy, began to come home in greasy clothes from his job in the railway shops in Altoona seven miles away. Then came college, summer vacations, and another summer, after graduation, as an apprentice reporter on the Altoona *Tribune* at fifteen dollars a week.

All through the years the boy had been haunted by the wailing cry of a night express, a summons of the faraway, a sense of exile from he knew not what.

Some devil of restlessness possessed me that autumn and midwinter at Columbia University, where I had gone to take the graduate course in journalism, earning my way through. I was fired as a dishwasher in the cellar of the Teachers College cafeteria and got a job as a doorman, dressed like a grand duke, in front of the Strand Moving Picture Theater on Broadway. About once a week Billie Burke would arrive at dinnertime just after I had gone to work. She would step out of her cream-colored Rolls Royce and hand me a dollar for opening the car door. There are few other memories of that job except that it was infernally cold standing out there on the sidewalk.

I was not living at the University but at Ninety-first Street in a lodginghouse for newspapermen. My protector and patron there was a copyreader with long years in New York behind him. I had walked up to him, a perfect stranger, on the subway station platform at City Hall Square and, in a sudden outbreak of brazenness, asked him if he was a newspaperman.

Tall, cadaverous, somewhat sardonic and carrying a cane, he had looked to me like what a newspaperman should look like. It was the cane that had convinced me. What I did not know was that there were probably not half a dozen men in New York newspaper offices who carried canes. Actually, he had been a college instructor of English and looked, if I had known it, much more like an English instructor.

Still, he *was* a newspaperman. He took me up to his place on Ninety-first Street, a brownstone kept by an Irish woman who looked like the mother in an Irish play.

An odd assortment of single men lived there—unmarried, divorced or widowed. Bill Chase, a music reporter grown gray on the *Times,* had the big room in the back looking out on the little walled area called a garden. Bill might easily have been one of those college deans remembered with nostalgia by campus generations long gone out into the world. We would sit on the floor on Sunday mornings in his room and breakfast at our ease. It all seemed rather marvelous and adventurous to me.

It was not. These were frustrated men. All had wanted to produce out of themselves, to tell tales and write history. All had been ground into submission, correcting other men's work for a living or turning out a daily grist of meaninglessness. They were sad men, and though each of them knew the sadness of the others they did not tell me. I was Youth and some instinct told them that they must not let me know.

In the autumn of 1929 the stock market crashed and the crisis was under way. New York became a worried and disheartened city. The fear of destitution, of uselessness and idleness was taking hold.

After Christmas everything seemed to go wrong. I could see nothing in what I was doing. Was this what life had to offer?

I now knew more of the men in my lodginghouse. They were going to the office and coming from the office and asking themselves silently some question without quite knowing what the question was. Other people went about worrying and marrying and begetting and going from home to office and worrying again. Where was life hiding? It was not here.

I wanted to go home. I was overcome with nostalgia, but home was not the dark little house on the noisy hill street leading down to the station in Hollidaysburg. I didn't know where home was, but I made up my mind to look for it.

At the end of February I sailed for Europe. I had four hundred dollars in my pocket and a third-class ticket on the aged steamer *America*. I had an excuse for going—namely, to learn German as a language necessary for projected graduate studies. It was a poor excuse but it served to quiet any protests my father offered. Also, I had saved the four hundred myself and had paid the fare, not much in those days on that ancient ship.

The world crisis had prepared the way for the success of my rattlepated and irresponsible adventure. Prices in Europe were down to rock bottom. In addition, Mussolini's government, for some inscrutable Fascist reason, was offering students a fantastic third-class railway ticket that took you from the Channel ports round and about through France and Italy for next to nothing.

I could get around and I could afford to stay for some time.

There are various ways of reckoning what year it is. The Mohammedan counts the years from the Hegira, which was the year 622 according to the Christian calendar. There seems to be no sound reason why a man should not choose to count the years of his days according to his own calendar. I reckon that my life began on a morning in March in the year 1930.

I had arrived in Paris and in the early morning had walked by instinct to the Place St. Sulpice, as though under some compulsion. I was standing at the zinc counter of a *"tabac"* with a *croissant* and *café au lait* in front of me when it happened. I can remember nothing very special, merely that things began there and date back to there. I was looking across the Place St. Sulpice at the heavy façade of the hulking church the square is named for. Suddenly the world seemed possessed of many dimensions and I felt dizzy, as perhaps newborn infants do.

In Rome a week later there was a yellow bush blooming on the Palatine Hill in the Italian spring. There were a lot of other things to strike newborn eyes and ears—black-and-white-striped marble in the Italian hill towns and *lingua Toscana in boca Romana.*

Then there was the carnival at San Gigminiano and the affair of the bowler hat. The hat had come into my life in New York just before I had started out across the winter-swept Atlantic. I had gone to the opera. Those of us who knew Bill Chase went to the Metropolitan via the stage door. There was a side row of boxes away up at the top of the opera house where you could see and hear the performance at the risk of plunging into the pit at any moment while craning over the edge of the box. Those boxes were always available for Bill Chase's nonpaying customers.

One night after the performance the doorman at the stage door, who knew me as one of Bill Chase's boys, asked me if I wanted a hat. Someone had left an expensive black bowler hat in the cloakroom some time before. Various people had tried it on but it had not fitted. It fitted me, and I was assured by the hat check girl that it was one of the most expensive hats in New York.

Now, if you have only four hundred dollars and are traveling third class, you do not carry a hatbox. The hat went with me to Europe on my head. Occasionally, along the way, people looked at it with bafflement. The rest of me did not go with the hat. But for all that, I wore it. I wore it to San Gigminiano.

San Gigminiano delle belle Torre is a hill town with a tourist trade because of the thirteen tall towers of now defunct noble houses standing romantically against a Tuscan backdrop. This year there were no tourists. Times were bad. The four thousand inhabitants had the town to themselves. They were having a carnival, not too much of a carnival, just enough for the people in the town.

That night when I stepped out into the jostling carnival crowd in the narrow streets, the old hill town took me to its Latin bosom. My hat was the sensation of the carnival. No one had ever seen anything like it. Girls with laughing eyes snatched it away from me and put it on their heads. Before long I found myself moving arm in arm in a line of singing Italians reaching from one side of the street to the other. I was a personality. I was The Hat. Up little streets as gay as poverty could make them, down again, into the *trattoria* and out again, the night went on. It seemed as if I had lived there all my life and knew all of the four thousand people of San Gigminiano.

Afterward I abandoned the hat. Such is human ingratitude.

I left Italy for southern France and went across to Carcassonne, since the Riviera was definitely too high for my pocketbook. From the walls of Carcassonne I looked out to the distant Pyrenees guarding the frontiers of Spain, and had not the faintest premonition of what the Hispanic pattern of living would later come to mean to me. I went on into the abrupt green valleys of the Dordogne country among the broken, rocky hills, and stared up from a narrow valley floor at the fortress cathedral of Albi. I slept in little hotels or taverns saturated with the fumes of the vigorous wines and strong brandies that had been served to customers for generations.

Along my way I noted with surprise that French-built automobiles behaved very well on the steep grades from the river valleys up into the hills. I was somewhat astonished that Frenchmen could build sturdy cars. I had just taken it for granted that building powerful and durable machinery was an American ability which would be difficult, if not impossible, for any foreigner to match.

Time came for me to move on via Périgueux to Tours, where I settled down for a time to study French.

Tours, France, was full of widows. The Ecole pour les Etrangers, a state-supported institution for teaching foreigners French, was dependent for the success of its system on an abundance of widows. It was one of those direct-method, live-with-the-language experiments where a word of anything but French amounted to blasphemy.

You lived with a widow—eight or ten of you. Ours had a

remarkably cramped, two-story stone house on a street full of cramped stone houses with identical gravel-paved gardens behind and almost identical fruit trees and potted flowers.

Among the guests of Madame, our widow, was a tall, poised young Englishman who had been sent over from Oxford, and who spoke better French than most Frenchmen.

One night the Englishman came home with a bloody face and torn jacket. The trouble, it appeared, had arisen out of a misunderstanding as to the time when a certain husband was expected home. We got a real spate of Madame's French at its shrill best. She bathed his wounds and taped them up, however.

It was in view of Madame's marked disapproval of her British guest's behavior that we had some difficulty in understanding the status of "Mademoiselle, my late husband's mistress."

Madame was well cushioned, more than middle-aged, maternal, sedate and slightly formidable. She had been reared in a convent school and was a sound Catholic. Her husband had been a person of some moderate prominence in commerce and, to judge by his photograph in the salon, definitely bourgeois in the stiff-collar tradition.

She regarded it as her duty to instruct us in the customs of France, or at least those of the provincial town of Tours. One of these, according to Madame, was that no woman of any position went out alone in the late afternoon or evening except to a neighboring shop. She went accompanied by a male.

An hour or two before sunset Madame would take four or five of her young men for *le promenade*. We would walk around the park and sometimes up to the Rue Nationale. Sometimes she would take ceremoniously a *grenadine à l'eau* on the terrace of a small café with her male brood clustered about her.

In the course of such a promenade she exchanged particularly affable greetings with a rather dowdy, if proper, woman getting toward forty or better, who, though probably never beautiful, was still pretty. As was our habit—it was allowed—we asked who she was.

"Mademoiselle," said Madame, "was my late husband's mistress."

There was a shocked silence.

Madame, noting the silence, announced that when we returned home she would explain. Her tone implied that we were in for a lecture on French customs.

Sitting in the salon later, Madame explained. Men, said Madame, are possessed of *la vitalité*, and it just goes on and on. Said *forces vitales* of the male—we stole a glance at the photograph of her late husband—constitute a problem. *Les passions* of women calm down a considerable time before those of men, which, if we understood Madame correctly, do not calm down at all. We began to get a new slant on the gentleman in the stiff collar in the photograph.

Every Frenchwoman, said Madame, must deal in one way or another with the issue thus raised by *la nature des hommes*. Adventures and unfortunate alliances are a menace to commercial credit and to the solidarity of the family. The latter was the important thing. Madame, we gathered, deeply disapproved of scandal.

She, Madame, had accordingly realized that something must be done when she found *les passions* calming down and felt that she no longer exercised to the same degree *l'attraction fondamentale*. There were signs that the inevitable was about to begin. Monsieur had maintained intact his *forces vitales*. We felt that Madame was rather proud of that.

Therefore, she knew that something must be done to prevent *le scandale* so that nothing should happen that would menace *le crédit commercial* and *la famille*.

She had gone out into the town and had made discreet inquiries. She had discovered a very respectable young woman who had previously had an *alliance* with a gentleman of position who had moved away. This respectable young woman worked in a commercial establishment but could live only poorly and save next to nothing. She had, however, a proper little apartment furnished with some taste at the expense of her former *alliance*.

The two women, we had to assume, had a conversation. In any case, the thing was arranged. The still intact *forces vitales* of Monsieur were provided for and all lived happily ever after, or at least until Monsieur had his so sudden heart attack. Both Madame and Mademoiselle were *désolées*.

Mademoiselle, as far as Madame knew, had not made another *alliance*, but she had economized during her period as *la maîtresse* of Monsieur. Madame seemed to find some satisfaction in the circumstance. We felt that it had something to do with *la solidarité des femmes*. Apparently Madame felt that one of the benefits deriving from the existence of *les forces vitales* in men was that it enabled the female to gather a little nest egg for the days when she no longer exercised *l'attraction fondamentale*.

I checked myself when about to remark that being a woman had certain evident advantages. It would have shocked Madame and I had great respect for her sense of propriety.

She was the first of a series of sedate and maternal ladies who were to enlighten me on both the strange ways of the foreigner, and on the view of life taken by their incomprehensible sex.

2

FROM France the warm weather and I moved into Switzerland.

There a touring party of my countrymen was just pouring into a high valley in the Alps. How they came to be touring so prosperously in that spring of 1930 with things so grim back in the United States I did not know. They probably had been

among the sensible ones who had seen the crisis of 1929 coming
or had merely been lucky.

They were in ecstasy over the little chalets, the clean primitiveness of everything in the village where we stayed. Everything seemed to demonstrate to them the bigness of things
American and, by derivation, the humbleness and smallness of
all this. They were not arrogant but they were full of comparisons. Americans were not domineering, patronizing people, so
far as I had been able to observe, but there was something
troubling about their constant comparison of everything with
things in America.

I had never had conscious doubts about America. Like most
people reared in any particular country, I just took it for
granted. However, before I left that other, man-made heap of
mountains, New York, I had begun to feel that the urge to bigness, expansion, to piling things on top of things was somehow
responsible for what was happening there in that crisis year.

For one brief period, back in Altoona during the boom, I had
sold phonographs and the like on the installment plan to people
who could not afford installments. I found only a few happy
people in the big Pennsylvania Railway shops there. Everyone
was being urged by the mobilized sales and advertising power
of a great economy to want things, always things and more
things. I had wondered if discontent was to become a way of
life, a commercial necessity if the machines were not to stop.

Little Switzerland too was suffering from the world crisis and
would suffer more as exports and tourism declined. But it was
small and thrifty. The neat primitiveness in the mountain
chalets was the expression of an approach to life that was
different from ours.

I felt vaguely troubled as I listened to my countrymen then.
For the first time I began to ask myself how much human happiness was a matter of inner fortitude and human intimacy and
how much of it was concerned with what we Americans seemed
to be living about.

In time the troubled moment that my countrymen had
brought with them passed away. High in the mountain meadows

I found crocuses blooming in snow. The bells on the cattle sounded far and sweet from distant slopes. Mountain torrents chanted and the laughter of children rang up from the valley floor.

After a few days, I went on down across southwestern Bavaria to Munich.

The woman who kept the student pension where I found a room was another widow. Her husband had been an officer who fell in the First World War. She was dead set against the French and was sure that the other widow, in Tours, had corrupted not my morals but my political view of the European scene. That you could be a political blank, as I was, did not occur to her.

Most of Frau Major's pensionnaires were German, poor students like me. The Germans who spoke some English were sternly forbidden to use it with me. The first day I sat down at the long boardinghouse table, everyone else had china, cutlery and a napkin. I had nothing in front of me. When I started to ask for them in English, she thundered. I didn't know what she said but I knew I was offside. I began to point. The others, instructed by the Frau Major, chanted *Loeffel, Gabel* and so on as I pointed. I had to imitate them or get nothing. You learn a lot of German in a hurry that way.

It got more complicated later. One day we were walking in the Englische Garten. There was a Portuguese girl staying in the pension—black, sparkling eyes and the rest of the Latin equipment. Everyone knew how far gone I was, but I did not know they knew. She was walking ahead of us with a blond Herr who had passed me in her affections like a sports model passing a milk truck.

I must have been glaring. My companions stopped and began a long harangue in which the constant refrain was the word *Eifersucht*. It means "jealousy." It was the first abstract term I learned and I learned it well.

Down the street from our pension was a brown house on a square. Grown men and a lot of youngsters dressed something like boy scouts, or so it seemed to me, hung around the place.

Little groups of them would march through the streets and occasionally a passer-by would raise his right arm stiffly and say, "Heil!"

It did not mean anything to me. I learned that they were a political party and was told the name but forgot it.

More interesting was the Loewenbraukeller with its arched roof like that of a church, its fifty-piece band roaring and a thousand or so Bavarians drinking their beer at long tables and singing. I would nurse one beer all night but no one seemed to mind. There were other poor students.

The corps or fraternity students had white gloves, but you could wear white gloves without being a corps student. The gloves were part of a ceremony. When the band was roaring its best and the beer mugs were being pounded on the tables in rhythm with a military march, we would all reverse our chairs and mount them like horses. It was a trick making your chair do horsy. Round and about through the aisles we would go, saluting right and left with our white gloves, singing off tune at the top of our young lungs.

There was vitality in these people. I was to learn more about that later—and about the contrast between the German and the Gallic spirit, between innate romanticism and innate classicism. The terms meant nothing to me at the time. All I saw then was that the French were harder to get to know than the Germans. The French nature appeared catlike, self-contained. The German was doglike, friendly and open at his best, fawning or belligerent at his worst. He seemed less reserved and, like us, more dependent on things and circumstances outside himself, and on what the next man thought about him, than were the French or the Italians.

Munich did not have too serious an academic reputation in those days. Too many students chose it for the beer and the week ends. Electric railways fan out from Munich Main Station into the Bavarian Alps, just out of sight over the southern horizon. Early Saturday you drank a boiling hot milk in the Milchstube in the station; then the lot of you, with knapsacks, piled onto the wooden benches in the cars and the train went off.

The Bavarian Alps were the University of Munich's famous *Wochen-end*. No other university in Europe had such a week end to offer.

Sport to the Germans really meant this sort of week-end thing. It might also include competitive games like soccer football, but the American idea of competitive intercollegiate sport meant nothing. Watching one university's athletes compete with another's did not appeal to them. Sport was something you did yourself—mountain climbing, rowing, hiking, perhaps tennis and so on.

To the European or Asiatic, competition may well be a necessity of life but it is not, in the full American sense, the spice of life. American competitive sport on the mammoth football-stadium scale appears to be a religious act. An almost reverent multitude concentrates on the sacred act of competition. I have never encountered anything quite like it elsewhere in the world.

Many years later, in the United States, I took one of those psychological tests for vocational guidance. I was shown a picture of a vigorous man, with an outthrust jaw, climbing a rope. That was all—just one man climbing one rope. The thing to do was to write down quickly the uncontrolled thoughts that came into your mind. A big company used that picture as a vital part of its character analysis for employees. What you were supposed to think to pass the test was that the man was climbing the rope to get to the top ahead of other men.

If you had the right instincts, you just automatically imagined the other men on other ropes and yourself in competition with them. You were then asked if the man in the picture would get to the top ahead of other men. If, again, you had the right instinct, you said yes as you automatically identified yourself with the vigorous gentleman in the picture.

I flunked the whole thing. The only thing that occurred to me was that the man enjoyed climbing the rope. From the standpoint of the testers that response was asinine. Perhaps I had been abroad too long.

Those crisp mornings when we climbed out at some valley station in the Bavarian Alps, buckled on our knapsacks and tramped off along the valley path heading for our mountain, have remained the symbols of my lost youth.

Never, even when I was much younger, had I been so young. None of us had any prospects. After those weeks or months most of us would never meet again. Tomorrow for us was as dead as yesterday. We were not hopeful, for, as things were going, hope was irrelevant.

I had no idea what this feeling, that all moorings had been loosened, was going to mean a little later in Germany. It never occurred to me that we were so young, so untrammeled, so almost senselessly free because for these young Germans around me a world had broken to pieces and they were freed from all bonds because there was for them nothing to be bound to. Kaiserreich, the existing republic, traditions, aspirations had all become a jumble, without significance or pattern or plot. Meaninglessness became an ecstasy.

This moment, devoid of past and future, was sufficient unto itself.

Boys and girls together, we slept in our hiking clothes in mountain huts and smelled one another's sweat. We would huddle around the fireplace as close as we could get to keep away the mountain cold. A girl would laugh in that throaty fashion on the low register that does things to your belly muscles. I remembered in that connection a phrase in a love letter from my New England grandfather to my grandmother, an old-fashioned, honest phrase: "My bowels yearn for you."

There is a type of German girl who is all hard muscles, heavy knapsack and equal to anything and who confused me because she was not feminine in either the daguerrotype or the cosmetics-and-sex fashion but still completely a woman. One in our group was like that. Probably it was because I did not understand her and because she was so different from the girls I had known that I was so drawn to her.

Young men in our Munich student world did not spend money on girls. All of us, boys and girls, were too poor for that sort of thing. We paid our own way singly and nothing was for sale. The crisis, like the mountain cold outside our hut, was setting in hard and fast out there in Germany. It was a bleak world—if we had thought about it, which we did not—and it was good, so good, to be so close together. It was on some nights as if the world out there had sunk beneath a mist of oblivion and we were alone in infinity on our mountainside.

Clearly, so early in the journey I had not found my home, but there were moments when I wished it were so and perhaps the girl did, also. I would bury my face in her hair and she would laugh that lower-register laugh.

One morning from the Zugspitze we watched the dawn wash over the Austrian Alps to the south and the distant peaks of the Dolomites in Italy. We had all climbed the highest mountain in Germany the afternoon before and we were proud of ourselves. You can ride up on a cog railway but we did not have the money and would not have done it anyway. Now we took the more perilous trail down the other side and for a time hung by iron grips secured in the wall above the abyss, inching along the shelf. The girl was quite unconcerned. I have forgotten her name as no doubt she has mine. Pray God that the years have been good to her.

When the semester closed I went north to Braunschweig in the north German plain and found lodging with the family of a solid, rotund Herr Doktor of some science or other.

Probably it was a reaction from those last untrammeled weeks in Munich that opened a new chapter in my life when I met the Herr Doktor's daughter Ilse. She was the type of Lower Saxon *maedchen* of the old long-settled stock who give that golden-halo effect with the sun in their brown-blond hair. She had a sound, comforting beauty suggestive of bright winter days and the open country. Ilse was still moored in a safe but open roadstead of life.

The Herr Doktor and his family were as yet untouched by the loosening of moorings that was taking place in much of Germany. The family seemed moderately well off with a big apartment furnished in old German fashion. They obviously were not living just on his earnings.

They represented a liberal burgher tradition that went practically back to 1848, the liberal revolution which had failed.
They were tolerant, patriotic but not nationalist. They actually
knew their Goethe and Schiller and did not merely keep them
on the abundant bookshelves. There were good eating, sound
talk, quiet friendliness and a spirit of gentle scepticism but no
cynicism in that house.

Perhaps people of that type were too tolerant. The Herr
Doktor told me about the National Socialists in Munich. That
was the party with its headquarters down the street a way from
our pension. They were a little surprised that, although I had
just come from Munich, I knew nothing about the National
Socialists and their leader, Adolf Hitler.

The family did not favor the National Socialist Party but felt
it had something to contribute. They had the idea that the
National Socialists were helping to "wake Germany up." The
"waking up" had something to do with the lost moorings
business I had encountered, without recognizing it clearly, in
Munich. The nation, said the Herr Doktor, was no longer a
nation. It was all divided into classes and parties marching in
opposite directions. What Germany needed was unity and a
new faith in itself. The Communists were a serious problem,
particularly in "red Berlin," although there was something to be
said for them too. Because they were a menace, they forced
those in power to pay more attention to unemployment and the
plight of the poor. Everyone realized that things could not go
on as they were but the world outside did not realize just how
bad things were getting in Germany.

The Herr Doktor did not feel that the National Socialists'
anti-Jewish agitation meant much. He said the real German
Jews were among the most useful people in the country but that
the eastern Jews who had come to Berlin, for example, were
disliked even by the German Jews.

I must have sat there looking blank because I knew nothing
about anti-Semitism and my total intellectual baggage on the
subject of Jews consisted of the idea that they did not eat ham

and that some people claimed you got cheated in small "cheap Jewish shops."

I suppose I equated the Herr Doktor's "eastern Jews" in Berlin with the caste of proprietors of small "cheap Jewish shops" about whom I did not know anything either and let it go at that. The whole thing did not sound very important.

My attitude on the subject of Jews and of anti-Semitism was probably similar to that of a great many Americans in smaller communities. We had not been brought up to be interested in the Jewish question or even to feel that there was a Jewish question. Later I found in the United States that a good many Jews took very seriously the fact they were Jews and often failed to realize that most other people were not at all interested in whether they were Jews or Baptists. Routine American tolerance, which comes close to indifference where it concerns white men of any stripe, is not a bad approach to some things.

Ilse was, in any case, much more of an issue for me than the National Socialists or whether Germany "waked" or not. The far-off mountains in the south and the hard-muscled girl whose laugh did things to me were forgotten. I was even somewhat ashamed of it all. Ilse was sweet and clean like a bridal chamber with white bedspread and starched curtains. It was like breakfast in the breakfast nook, the sun streaming in and flowers outside along neat garden paths.

This Lower Saxon country and the northern slopes of the Harz Mountains had a Hans Christian Andersen character. It was the land of the houses you see in German fairy-tale books, such as the *Pied Piper of Hamelin*. Braunschweig itself had been the seat of a principality and a robust center of war and trade. There was one great market square right out of the old days and they sold Braunschweiger honey cake there, the sort of thing which should be baked by elves and gnomes.

One day as we strode along I very diffidently took Ilse's hand. She smiled at me enigmatically and we walked through the leaf-dappled sunlight in that park, pretending not to notice that we were hand in hand.

Then I had to leave. My money was almost gone and I had a ticket for a boat leaving from Boulogne-sur-Mer. I must see Holland and the towns of Bruges and Ghent in Flanders on the way to the boat. Ilse was all for that. I wished she had not given a hoot about my seeing Bruges and Ghent and had just wanted me to stay as badly as I wanted to stay.

3

I HAD twenty-five cents when I got back to New York. On the dock I motioned the porter aside and tugged my own bag out onto the street and slowly across town to the subway. The twenty-five cents was just enough to get me out to New Rochelle on the electric line that ran up from the Bronx.

A cousin of my mother's lived out there in those days. She gave me a bed and I wrote to my father for a little money.

Incredibly, my friend on the *Times* got me a job within two weeks despite the depression. I went to work on the New York *Evening Post* as a cub reporter. I ate in the beaneries where the unemployed ate and saved every cent. Things were not going well financially on the *Evening Post,* as everyone in the office knew, and I did not seem to get the hang of the job.

There were always rumors that a lot of people were going to be let go, the newest ones first, naturally. The whole city was uncertain and afraid. The great economy that depended on selling ever more things and again things to ever more people had faltered and was breaking down. America had lost the knack of it. The great god Success had failed his people.

One autumn afternoon I rushed up to the financial district from West Street, where the *Evening Post* was located, to look at a mess of blood and hunks of something mashed on the street. It was a broker who had survived the 1929 crash and who had thought the crisis was over and did not want to miss what he had thought was the 1930 upturn. He had come out the window from away up there. They scooped up what they could and washed away the rest with fire hoses.

I had an acquaintance who did night shift at Bellevue Hospital and covered the municipal morgue. Sometimes I went with him on his regular visits to the morgue.

They put them in drawers in the morgue, as in a filing system. Each drawer was labeled and you yanked it open. They were stark naked. A man who has starved to death looks as if he has starved to death. People will insist that it could not happen, not here. The morgue staff knew better.

Still, the crisis had another side. I remember a letter in some publication. A husband out in Texas or Oklahoma wrote it. He and his wife had been prosperous. They had acquired two cars and a new house. He found he had to see a lot of people and was invited to a lot of night meetings. She was pretty occupied herself. They came home at different hours, but then with the new house had come a big bedroom, an extra bath and, above all, twin beds. They did not disturb each other.

Just before the depression hit full force they had everything arranged for the divorce. Then the crisis took the house. When they tried to find a place for each of them they found it was impossible. They could not afford to live separately. The letter ended something like this: "We sold the twin beds and crawled back in together. Thank God for the crisis."

My mother's cousin out in New Rochelle kept her teaching job. Even in depressions children have to be taught. Her husband, who had a job as manager of a low-price chain store in Harlem, was forced, however, to engage in a most peculiar form of dishonesty. He had been told that if his sales went below a certain point he would be fired. So he bought his own goods and concealed the fact from the company. For all practical purposes he was living off his wife to keep his job. I believe the company eventually discovered his dishonesty and fired him for it.

That early in the crisis the Every-Man-for-Himself America of the 1920's was still functioning. There was not yet much evidence of what you could call human solidarity.

For a Christmas present, together with a few other new men on the staff, I was fired. It had not been unexpected. I was glad that I had spent almost literally nothing. You can save quite a bit of money, even on a small salary, in a short time if you do not spend anything at all.

I borrowed—the word is a euphemism—a little money from my patient father and bought a third-class ticket back to Europe. This time he did not protest. Apparently I had a crackpot idea about where and how to get a job. Either he had faith in the idea or he decided my experience had shown you could live for next to nothing in Europe. If he should have to support me, he felt possibly that it would not cost any more there than if I were in Hollidaysburg. There was no chance of a job back in that town or in Altoona. There seemed to be no chance of getting a job in America.

My father loved me. My happiness meant more to him than his own. He had his work as a clergyman. Outside of that and my mother and me, he was no longer much interested in the affairs of this world. He was an old man. The life that mattered was out ahead. He was as convinced as is a little child of its mother's love that sometime we should all be together again over on the other side in the mercy of God in His eternal Household. He never forgave the college professors for the way he felt they had destroyed my faith. All during my childhood there had hung over my bed a picture of Christ as a boy. My father was right. I had lost a great deal more than I had gained.

I sailed on New Year's Day, 1931. Berlin was my objective. Just what my idea was I sometimes wonder now. Somehow I was going to get a job in Berlin. Everyone I talked to about it agreed that it was as impossible a proposition as they had heard of in a long time.

I stopped at Braunschweig en route to Berlin. Ilse was not there. At first I did not ask about her. They asked me to stay over the week end and were obviously glad to see me.

They could not quite make out what I was doing back in Germany. Naturally, they knew about the crisis in America but wondered. America was still the land of opportunity as Europeans saw it. With unemployment rolls constantly mounting, plenty of frustrated young Germans, unable to find work, were dreaming of emigrating to America.

Finally I screwed up the courage to ask about Ilse. Her mother was a little curt and cool. Ilse was away and would be away for some time. I had a feeling, probably correct, that the mother suspected I was much too interested and she could do without young men with no jobs who did not seem to know what they were doing.

The son, about my age and friendly, gave me an address in Berlin that was valuable to anyone in my position. There was a Christliches Hospiz—an Evangelical Student Home—in the poor workingmen's and poor students' quarter north of the Spree where you could get meals for very little and a permanent bed in rooms where several students slept together. Again my allies, the poverty of so many Europeans and the relative strength of the dollar, were going to tide me over.

I had never been in Berlin. It looked menacing on that cold January day when I arrived. The city as a whole was essentially the product of the late nineteenth and the early twentieth centuries. Broad straight streets that seemed never to end were flanked by buildings all about six or seven stories high, solid and depressing. There was another side to it, as I was to find out, but I never quite freed myself from that first impression of menace, grayness and an atmosphere not quite European and not quite anything else.

There was something defiant about Berlin.

Standing in the midst of the sandy Brandenburg plain, the city seemed a little abnormal in its bigness out there beyond the

Elbe where the vastness of the European east, stretching to Asia's frontiers deep in Russia, begins.

The Brandenburg plain had been the East March of the Holy Roman Empire of the German nation, on guard against the east and yet itself, in its way, eastern and with a Slavic undertone. Something of Warsaw was in Berlin, as I was to find later, and probably a touch of Leningrad and perhaps of Moscow.

Was it significant or was it chance that the immense extent of proletarian east Berlin contained a stronger suggestion of the cold eastern plains and of Slavic melancholy? Largely middle-class west Berlin seemed more German and more western European with its café terraces, glass enclosed and steam heated in winter, tree-lined streets that became in places almost Parisian boulevards and finally suburbs full of the villas of civil servants and bank employees and functionaries of the great companies with headquarters in Berlin.

The area north of the Spree was of, and yet not of, east Berlin. Poverty was evidenced by plaster falling off the walls all through the area but there were remnants of middle-class prosperity. Farther out began the "Rote Wedding," notorious fortress of Communism then, grimly and passionately proletarian. Closer in where the Christliches Hospiz was located, in one of those typical inside courts that filled the big Berlin blocks between streets, a certain bohemian feeling existed.

It was, in a way, an odd location for an Evangelical Student Home. Half or more of the prostitutes of Berlin lived in the area. It was dotted with little cafés with heavily draped windows. Inside, dark cloth lamp shades subdued the light and there were *séparés,* booths with soiled and worn red plush seats and a table, where a curtain could be drawn across for privacy.

Illicit passion in Berlin was surrounded by a slightly Wagnerian atmosphere of bourgeois red-plush mysticism. There was a tendency toward nineteenth-century suffering and that grimness and lost-souls feeling that many Germans wanted with their sex.

The area was full of students living as best they could. It had a little of the feel of the Latin Quarter of Paris but it was not very gay.

In the bare Christliches Hospiz they gave me a bed on the vague assumption that I would register at the beginning of the next semester in one of the many institutions of higher learning. I doubt if they really felt I had come as a student, but I was young and poor. They were kind people.

The business of getting ahead in life, of finding a livelihood and a career would have to begin.

Part Two

Europe

4

WHEN she married Sinclair Lewis, Dorothy Thompson had passed on her job as Berlin correspondent of the New York *Evening Post* to a redhead named Hubert Renfro Knickerbocker.

H. R. Knickerbocker had rapidly become the *Post's* most spectacular writer. He was then probably more celebrated than Raymond Graham Swing, who was the paper's London correspondent in those days before he became a great name as a radio commentator in the United States. I had not dared to approach the famous Knickerbocker. After all, I had been let out of the New York *Evening Post*.

For two and a half months I went in and out of the Berlin offices of American newspapers and agencies looking for a job. The whole thing was getting pretty grim.

Then I heard that the woman who was Knickerbocker's assistant had had a nervous breakdown and left him. I got to his office fast. He was cleaning up, getting ready to leave in the morning to do a Russian series.

What did I want? I wanted a job. Did I have newspaper experience? Yes. I didn't tell him how little and he was in too much of a hurry to ask.

I was the only man in town. He could have me or nobody, and he had instructions to find someone in Berlin to cover while he was gone.

He looked at me again. Obviously he had his doubts. I looked young and diffident. I also looked as if I wanted that job bad.

"You go over tomorrow morning to the office of the Chicago *Daily News* across the street and ask Edgar Mowrer what to send," he said. "We'll see how you have made out when I get back. Look around the office and ask me questions if you want."

I was too frightened to ask him questions. Shortly afterward he was gone. I did not see him again until the end of the summer.

The *Evening Post* did not know who was working for them in Berlin. I had only given my initials when Knickerbocker sent off his quick cable telling them of the temporary appointment. They would have jumped out of their skins if they had known Knickerbocker's replacement in Berlin was a cub reporter they had fired last Christmas.

I was the Berlin correspondent of the New York *Evening Post*, standing in for its most brilliant writer. I had not the faintest idea what a foreign correspondent did.

I knew we covered the Philadelphia *Public Ledger*, a morning paper, as well as the New York *Evening Post*, which was an afternooner. It meant I was responsible for news coverage around the clock.

The office boy, a large florid young German with the inevitable semimilitary cap, had been told that I was the boss until the end of the summer. That first day he went home fairly early. In my pocket I had the keys of the office; I was on my own. I sat down and read the back file of dispatches and the old newspapers. Until three o'clock in the morning I read and was down at the office again just after eight the next morning.

The office boy came again and brought the German newspapers and the first of the day's dispatches from the German telegraph news agency. I read them all as if my life depended on it. I still had no idea what a foreign correspondent did. At last it occurred to me that he did not get his news from the newspapers.

About eleven I went over to see Edgar Mowrer, who had a plush second-floor office, deep carpeted and handsomely furnished, with French windows. It was over the Kranzler Café, famous rendezvous at the corner of Unter den Linden and Friedrichstrasse.

Knickerbocker had telephoned Mowrer and told him about me. Edgar Mowrer was brilliant, satirical, editorial in his writing and scathing in his contempt for pedestrian prose. He lived rather luxuriously in a two-floor apartment in the Tiergarten section and was a figure in Berlin. He was later to become a columnist in the United States.

Mowrer knew what was going on and was generous with his help but he was so individualistic that in filing news he was no guide for a young man who had better not try to be quixotic. I was on my own and knew that I would have to use my own judgment and swim as best I could.

I filed my first dispatch and waited for the scream of rage from New York. Nothing happened. They just printed it. For a time I quaked in my boots every time I sent a dispatch off and wanted to rush over to the telegraph office and get it back. Nothing happened. Both papers just went on printing what I sent.

The day came when I could get a solid night's sleep again and could open telegrams from the home office in the morning without a chill of fear.

One day I bought a new suit. In the evening I went to what I considered an expensive restaurant. I had almost never been inside such a place. Solemnly I ate lobster and drank a whole bottle of Rhine wine and went back to the Christliches Hospiz not too steady on my feet. A great occasion had been duly celebrated. The paper that had arrived that morning had contained a dispatch with my name over it—my own by-line.

Meantime the students in the Hospiz, some of them pretty threadbare, had taken up the great debate that was going on everywhere in Germany.

There were students from all parts of Germany, of every political persuasion except the Communist, and some of no political persuasion at all. The debate always revolved around the same theme. Things could not go on as they were. Perhaps because I lived where I did and had been with people outside Berlin, I had begun to see that the Republic was already merely a façade for political and moral bankruptcy.

There is such a thing, in effect if not in textbook anthropology, as the Social Contract. That massive structure, the state and society, is based upon nothing more solid than opinion. A minimum agreement or acquiescence in the matter of what the people want is necessary. The governed will refuse to be governed and the social structure will not be accepted if that minimum of agreement disappears.

In Germany the minimum of agreement was rapidly disappearing, if it existed at all. The Herr Doktor in Braunschweig had been right. The parts were now above the whole. Party and class were coming to mean more than the nation and certainly more than the state. The loyalties of these students were crystallized around parties and political and social programs or slogans but no longer around the whole. Germany was no longer the homeland. It had become an ideological and economic battlefield.

This was revolution in its intimate meaning, the great disintegration before the decision, peaceful or violent. The revolution did not come because of Hitler. It had already happened.

World War I had expedited the liquidation of the old Europe. Neither saber-rattling Kaiser Wilhelm II, nor doddering Emperor Franz Josef, symbol of a whole society in its rather lovable but dangerously ridiculous dotage, had represented anything fundamental in the long-term inner conflict of European society. They had been the failure of the past. The failure of the Weimar Republic was the failure of the future. Collapse of the past will bring sorrow and possible bitterness. Collapse of the future brings frustration. In an individual or, as was to be the case in Germany, in a society frustration leads first to neurosis and then perhaps to insane outbreaks of violence.

At stake was what had long been perhaps the Europeans' essential business, to get on with the job of broadening and deepening the French Revolution. In terms of political propaganda and action the broader movement had taken the form of Social Democracy. Starting in theoretical Marxism and the trades-union movement, it had been pushing slowly toward what its name stood for—a break-through from political democracy to a society that would be democratic, in effect about people, the mass of people and their real needs.

The most decisive enemies of the German revolution were the Communists. The Spartakists, activists in the German Communist ranks, vigorously if clumsily supported by Moscow, had been for several years a real force and menace in the period of the founding of the Weimar Republic.

When Hitler raised the cry of the Red menace later, he was talking about something that was a concrete experience to the Germans. The Communists wanted the "dictatorship of the proletariat" and not a continuation of the French Revolution on a broader front.

Caught between the right wing and the Communists, the revolutionary element in Germany, not very passionate people anyway, sold their birthright for the well-known mess of pottage. They compromised with the right wing.

Friedrich Ebert, head of the state and leader of the Social Democratic Party, made his alliance with the army, which amounted to an alliance with a portion of the Prussianized officer caste. That caste in turn was traditionally linked to the still feudal aristocracy of the Germany beyond the Oder. It was equally in alliance with the hard-faced, capable masters of Ruhr industry grown to greatness in the epoch of "blood and iron."

The Republic, whatever its excuse, cheated, and history can be hard on cheats. Compromising continually and never its own master, it had become shoddy. There are violent revolutions, cruel revolutions and corrupt revolutions, but not shoddy revolutions.

I remember during my first Atlantic crossing a rather poorly dressed, if neat and healthy looking, German of the artisan type sitting on a hatch cover in the North Atlantic cold. To pass the time he had started talking about the days of the postwar German revolution. I was flat on my back wrapped in my overcoat, tasting my bile and recovering, or hoping I was recovering, from seasickness and the cooking smells below. He had talked for quite a while, and it had been good to let someone talk and not have to do anything myself but listen.

Recalling the revolution—I had never thought of that period after the war in Germany as a revolution—apparently served to warm him on that icy day. Perhaps it was also a consolation to him for what apparently had been the rather meager and lonely life that he had since led in his native Nuremburg and in the United States, where he had worked for a few years. Those memories seemed an odd thing to warm and comfort himself with, for I knew and he mentioned that there had been little to eat and much poverty in which he had shared.

But revolution was glorious, he said. He did not talk about violence, in which I gathered he had not taken part. He talked about the way people had felt about one another during the revolution. People felt so close together, he said, and even if you were quite unimportant you counted because people, all those people whom you began to like so much, were going forward. A new day was breaking and you had not lived in vain. You wanted to sacrifice yourself, to give everything to the revolution because you cared so much about all those people.

It was quite an idea and jarred me a little. I could not recall a desire to sacrifice myself for all people or even a few people. But then, I had thought, suppose you are an artisan and life does not involve the idea of success—then what do you live about? It was a troubling thought and I was not then in shape to deal with troubling thoughts.

This was the other side of the disintegration of the past, the revolutionary phase. The feeling which that German worker had talked about was a big reason why a substantial portion of the German people grew so bitter when the Republic started cheating. Revolution, my fellow passenger had said, was like springtime, like sitting in the grass with a girl when the spring has come. You fall in love with revolution, and cheating turns love first to pain and then to hate and then to contempt.

The Social Democratic leaders of the Weimar Republic had kept on cheating, getting less and less revolutionary. The German revolution had gone straight from spring into autumn and then into winter. It had known no summer.

All of these ideas were batted back and forth in the student

Hospiz and elsewhere in my world of young Germans, mostly
rather hard up. I was beginning to discover the pleasures of idea-
mongering. The enjoyment of thinking was a new experience.
Thinking hard had been concerned with learning things, passing examinations or trying to get ahead. Apparently I had grown
to be twenty-five without realizing that you could have fun with
your brains. It was not the sort of thing—so far as I could remember—that would have been tolerated at my college, not in
the 1920's. You were perfectly free to do anything you pleased
but at the price of amiable ostracism if you did not conform. I
always conformed.

5

Out of the ranks of my Ger-
man student friends and their like was to come the force that
would enable an Austrian psychoneurotic to crucify Europe.
The frustrated man with a mind is one of the most powerful
explosives recorded in history.

One day I jumped into a restaurant on Unter den Linden for
coffee. I was full of myself and my job and eager to get to the
office and start producing a dispatch from information I had
been gathering all day. I must have had the confident and
somewhat distracted look of those who are for the moment satisfactorily participating in the world's affairs and whose ego is
purring like a placated tomcat.

At a near-by table was a stocky, vigorous Herr Doktor
in his late twenties. I knew him. He was a rather interesting, leftish liberal, and camouflaged as some sort of journalist
because he had no job and could find none in those times. He

was sitting with a woman in her early forties, neat and competent looking, who may have been a secretary somewhere. When the bill came she took her purse and paid. They had eaten supper. He smiled a little uneasily and seemed to thank her.

Then he looked around and saw me. Rage came into his face. He hated me though I had not done anything except be there. It was the custom for women to pay their own way, but it was another thing for a young Herr Doktor to have a woman pay for his supper and be caught at it. He very possibly would have gone without one if she had not. Berlin was full of mean little jokes about gigolos and the frequent spectacle of the dependent male.

He later turned up as a person of some importance in the Propaganda Ministry under Josef Goebbels.

The intelligent were to be the most potent ally of Adolf Hitler. They would serve in a thousand capacities. From them in particular would come the holocaust of words that would imprison and betray the German people.

Many years later after World War II I read an article about a large New York firm engaged in producing what the headline called "attitudes to order." The article was well documented. Industries and commercial firms had found that attitude was vital to efficiency, both in production and in dealing with customers. It had become necessary to dig deeper into employees' characters and to train their attitudes—which seemed to amount to teaching their eternal souls to jump through hoops. Producing attitudes to order, the article indicated, had become big business.

In a modern society, the attitude-producing industries, such as advertising and public relations, employ today a larger proportion of the "intelligentsia" than does any other branch of commercial industry.

Why is the person who is inquisitive, sensitive, full of ideas and probably to some degree gifted so likely to be found in one of these fields? One obvious reason is that, particularly where liberal education has had its unsettling effect, there are more such people than there are productive jobs for them. The world can consume only a limited amount of the best they can produce and the competition is sharp. Quite commonly they are likely, also, to know a good deal about everything but to have acquired no trade, intellectual or otherwise. Like the girl in difficult times who has no other specialty, they have to do *something*.

Very often they begin with the attitude that their work is a kind of prostitution. When and if they get into the money, they gradually develop the proper "positive attitude."

An equal or actually more potent reason is that they know their own superiority and are tortured with the necessity to clothe it in visible status.

In attitude production Goebbels was as much a master as anyone on Madison Avenue. He understood his instruments, the frustrated, status-hungry personalities of people like my friends. He disciplined those fertile minds into rigidity of purpose but with a variety of expression and invention.

The lame little man used so well the talents of men under an inner compulsion to influence people and be somebody because he was himself a man with a mind who could find no normal outlet for it.

Josef Goebbels' father was a factory foreman in the industrial town of Rheydt, a depressing place on the lower Rhine. His mother was the daughter of a smith.

Prevented by his lameness from entering the army, young Goebbels studied for a long time. Restlessly he shifted almost every semester from one university to another. He was at Bonn, then Freiburg, Würzburg, Munich, Heidelberg, Cologne, Frankfurt and Berlin, returning to Heidelberg to take his Ph.D. His half-philosophical and half-literary doctoral thesis was on "The Intellectual and Political Tendencies of Early Romanticism." He had a thorough and broad education with no relation to earning a living.

He never was to have a profession. He never earned his living in any routine trade or business. For a time he was what is known euphemistically as a "writer." He sold occasional bits and political articles, done on speculation, to newspapers. His trade, which was not a trade, was the lugubrious affair of turning out potboilers. It is a miserable way of earning a living.

Unsettled and insecure, Goebbels wandered from his home town, Rheydt, to Cologne and from there to Berlin and Munich. It was in Munich in 1922 that he became acquainted with the former corporal and small-time agitator Adolf Hitler. The event was of world significance though the world knew nothing about it.

Humbly enough, Goebbels began making speeches at student meetings. The French entered the Ruhr. He went into the Ruhr land as an agitator. In 1924 he became editor of a shabby weekly paper in Elberfeld devoted entirely to nationalist and racial agitation and without pretensions of being anything more than a weekly pamphlet. That was his first steady job and not much of one.

Then he became district commander for the National Social-ists. As the party was starting to build up an organization, he began to earn his way poorly as a regular party functionary.

He had found his calling. In 1926 he was transferred to Berlin to organize and run the party in the capital. He moved on to the job of propaganda chief or campaign manager for the party with headquarters in Munich.

The pure art of politics, the trade of inducing people to act as you wish, became his absorbing passion. It fulfilled his need. Writing of an election before the party came to power, he said, "The election campaign will outdo every previous one. I await it as eagerly as if it were a festival."

Herr Doktor Goebbels had arrived at his destiny out of a con-dition of total frustration typical of that of the German academic proletariat. You could see what it meant to him when he re-sponded to raised-arm salutes as he rode in his big black official Mercedes, flying the flag of his party which had become the flag of the nation.

He represented the class of ambitious young men, the aca-demic sons of the industrious and saving small bourgeoisie. They had an education that separated them from their origins but no "pull." The same class have become in America the most fanatic devotees of what has been called the "great American rat race." To rise in the world has been their own paramount necessity and what kind of a world they made of it has not mattered much in comparison to that necessity.

Josef Goebbels was to be one of the reasons why millions then alive were to die in agony on battlefields or in concentration camps.

He was also a truly cultured man. He understood the arts and had studied fine arts as well as history and literature in his universities. He read Vergil for relaxation and delighted in the society of musicians, artists, actors and playwrights. Socially he had a certain charm although he was perhaps a little overly ironical.

When he came to the end of the road in the Fuehrer's bunker in the Reich Chancellery garden, he made no attempt to escape after Hitler's death. Suicide was the final gesture. He had lived terrified not of death or suffering but of mediocrity. The circumstances of his death should have been dramatic enough to satisfy even him.

He had once said that if the National Socialists had to leave they would slam the door so hard that the whole house would collapse. It was an expression in Goebbels' often highly colloquial language of the Germanic concept of the Götterdämmerung. The house did nearly collapse behind them. Europe stood in ruins and the world would never be quite the same.

It will be a long time before another public relations man equals Goebbels' record.

The predicament of Germany's academic proletariat was, however, only an extreme laboratory demonstration of the issue involved. Education, fortunately, never produced anything in the United States or elsewhere quite so pernicious as the academic proletariat of Germany and its rabid self-destroying protest.

I recall one of the symbolically dramatic events in the months before Hitler came to power. A great throng of students poured into the University of Berlin. A group ran upstairs, pulled in the flag of the Republic and hoisted the swastika flag.

Down in the colonnaded entrance hall and in front of the

48

building the throng began to chant and shout. They screamed in unison: "We spit on this your freedom."

They were not madmen. Germany had not gone that far yet. A good many of them were presumably not even National Socialists. They had merely had enough of the freedom of frustration, barrenness and empty living. They were lost in a world where no connection seemed to remain between the great aspirations of the human spirit and the actual business of living.

The matter of liberal education in its various forms can stand a strong reappraisal. The reality of the contemporary social environment, and the idea-world of the literatures, philosophies and human sciences can seldom be brought together except in the rhetoric of the hypocrite. Split personalities can become a dangerous affair for the rest of the people as they did in Germany. The ordinary American's distrust of the egghead is not entirely unjustified.

6

THE GERMAN financial crisis of 1931 was a brutal assignment for a young man still not too sure of what a foreign correspondent did for a living. The world's high finance was in it up to its neck. Short-term foreign credits fled homeward; gold and exchange reserves dwindled; foreign exchange rates did dizzy swoops; credit became paralyzed; the German economy sighed like a dying horse and lay down.

Multimillionaires and those whose business was other men's millions conferred in closed committee rooms and issued incomprehensible communiqués. The other European offices of the New York *Evening Post* kept telephoning me to ask esoteric questions because the German crisis had all Europe agog.

I remember nearly getting knocked out because I had my elbow on the table and was resting my chin on my fist when Reichsbank President Luther, sitting at the other side of a large table surrounded by correspondents, hit the table so hard that my fist stunned me. "You cannot draw blood from a stone!" shouted the Reichsbank President.

Germany could not pay its foreign creditors. That was clear enough. All sorts of financial institutions and businesses could not pay various people either. That was clear. The why and how of it all was anything but clear and changed from hour to hour.

In the midst of all this Knickerbocker finally returned from his Russian trip having turned out a series of articles that gave the *Evening Post* the last boost in circulation it was to enjoy.

My heart went into my boots when he walked in with a stout young man from New York whom he had picked up, I believe, in Vienna. Knickerbocker used that cold friendly voice which was as near as that freckle-faced Texan with the slight drawl could get to the executive attitude.

I did not know then that he was incapable of being an executive. He could never think of people as things. He either hated people or liked them immensely.

What he had to say on that occasion, however, was alarming enough. The young man would compete with me for the job. At the end of the month Knickerbocker would decide which of us would remain. I did not say anything. I was all choked up. Really, I had tried so hard and done pretty well.

As his later career as an author was to show, the stout young man could write like an angel. He was friendly and would turn over his copy for me to see. I wanted to tear it to shreds. All of it was colorful, chatty, warm, without a wasted word. Ira Wolfert was a born feature writer. I lost all hope.

I had been planning to buy some new clothes for I was getting by on the one cheap suit that I had bought and my other, which was ragged at the cuffs and too shiny to be decent. I dropped the idea and began to save every pfennig again. Apparently life was always going to be like that.

I had to leave the Hospiz about that time. It was by now quite evident that I was not a student.

I got a room back in a courtyard with the family of a proprietor of a cheap restaurant and arranged to have my meals there. Even though I was accustomed to coarse food the stuff he served was really terrible, but it was cheap. The customers were wretchedly poor people who wanted grease and soggy bread to make them feel they had something in their bellies.

As the month went on things seemed to get steadily worse. That accursed young man just wrote better and better. It was hard not to like him. He was a roly-poly, cordial creature who told me all about himself and made it seem as if we had been friends for years instead of competitors for a job that to me, at least, meant everything.

Knickerbocker was ill at ease. I think it occurred to him suddenly what a situation he had created. Probably an executive would either have been amused or he would never have thought about the feelings of the two things in the outer office. But Knickerbocker was not an executive.

The papers had come containing all the dispatches I had written while he had been away, and I presume he talked to Mowrer, that patient irascible man. He finally screwed himself up to it. He told the other man that I had the job. The other fellow actually had probably never had a chance—not because he was not the better man but because Knickerbocker could not bring himself to do it to me. He was no executive.

My relationship to my boss became almost legendary. A photographer who turned up in Berlin and lived there for a while wrote an article on correspondents for *Outlook* magazine. I was mentioned as resembling the then famous phonograph trademark, the Victor dog which sat listening to its master's voice.

Knickerbocker is gone out of this world now, and I am not ashamed to say that I, who had never had a brother, loved him in those years as one can presumably love only a brother.

He sometimes drank too much. Then he would come by at night when I was working on stuff for the *Public Ledger* and would be rather belligerent and more the boss. At such times he was rather dull witted. Alcohol was to mess up his life later. After wandering around the office and asking rather pointless questions, he would remark that he did not feel too well.

I would remark, as icily as I dared, that I had noted it. He would look at me with a partly amused and partly ugly expression and shrug and go off. The next day he would be exceptionally kind.

Those nights when he drank nevertheless upset me. The trouble was that I worshiped the man.

A year after we started working together he showed me a jocular letter from a friend in New York charging him with having gone to seed and claiming that I was getting all the by-lines in the paper. He acted as if it were a triumph for both of us. Yes, I think for a short time he loved me as a brother loves a brother.

I hope so. It is a comforting thought to carry into the years.

Of all human relationships, friendship has a quality quite its own. There is no element of imposed obligation as in the relationship of parents and children, or of contractual and social and legal compulsion as in marriage.

I remember that once my aging father spoke of my mother as his closest friend. To a boy it had seemed at the time a rather cold thing to say about one's wife. Perhaps it was quite the contrary.

I once saw what the friendship of a man and a woman can become. One Christmas vacation I stayed up at college. It would have cost too much to go home. I got a job as substitute for the boy who was handyman around the rather decrepit colonial frame house of a retired professor and his wife. They had sent out into the world the usual northern New England flock of children and were now alone in the college town where they had spent most of their lives.

On a snowy morning just after Christmas I had been all over the house stacking wood in the boxes next to the stoves and cleaning the central hall. The hall lay between the professor's study in a corner of the house on the ground floor and the rest of the house. I knew that the white-haired old man had not been out of his study for at least three hours and that his wife had been for an equal time up in her second-story sewing room at the other end of the house. There she could not see the side where the professor's study was nor hear anything that went on there.

She was as New England as a daguerreotype. Around the house she wore a light-gray starched dress that reached to her shoes and had a little lace collar at her throat. When she wanted to make some particular request, she blushed. It was a lovely thing, that flush of youthful color in those old cheeks.

That morning, when I went into the sewing room finally to tell her that the wood was all in, she made a request. Would I go down to the professor's study and help him hunt for his glasses? He had lost them. As usual, she blushed a little, in that old-world fashion of hers.

I went down, and there was the professor stumbling around, diligently looking in all the places where he had not put his spectacles. I found them, gave them to him, was thanked and went back upstairs.

I had to ask. She had been in the sewing room all morning and the professor in his study and I had been the only other person in the house. How did she know that the professor had lost his glasses? She had never asked me to help him hunt for them before.

She looked baffled and a little annoyed and then she blushed quite furiously and looked away to avoid my eyes. She said, "I don't know, Mr. Ross."

She always addressed students as "Mister," probably because she regarded them as young gentlemen who should always be given an example of good manners.

Blushing more furiously than she, I withdrew, not sure if I were a young or any other kind of gentleman. I had glimpsed an intercourse that went far beyond anything the word usually refers to. Over the years the two of them had come to look in a subtle fashion alike. There was a peace in that house and also a mystery that had something faintly supernatural about it.

Later, when I had seen many of the great works of art, I felt there was a kinship between them and whatever it was those two had done. When you sat in the Louvre or the Prado or in the Vatican museum, the thing you felt was more than you could see or comprehend with the mind. It was whatever it is that the artist brings back from the infinite. That feeling always brought me the memory of the professor and his wife.

With them love, as the hot blood of youth interprets love, had withered away through the years and had become friendship. That friendship, at the portals of eternity, had produced a strange flower for which there is no name. A Michelangelo or a da Vinci in the full ecstasy of creation would have understood what had been achieved in the somewhat dilapidated old house in that quiet town.

7

THE GERMAN financial crisis was eventually solved by agreeing to freeze remaining credits and by other short-view arrangements. Unemployment shot up to percentages hitherto unachieved. Chancellor Heinrich Bruening continued his economically sound, financially intelligent, politically disastrous policy of deflation.

It should be recalled that the whole crisis had started with a French maneuver that made insolvent the Austrian *Kreditanstalt*.

France had so arranged things that the planned German-

Austrian customs union project had been effectively checked by the Austrian and German banking crisis. In the course of the settlement of the German and Austrian credit and banking crises, the customs union project had been dropped. For France and the Little Entente the proposed customs union had been a flat challenge. Now the Germans had been taught a lesson. Only they had drawn the wrong moral from the lesson.

The moral was supposed to be that they must be good little boys in a continent dominated by France and her allies. The conclusion that the Germans actually reached was that without force they would never get anywhere and would suffer chronic unemployment and economic strangulation. This was not fully accurate, but Hitler and Goebbels screamed its seeming self-evidence from the housetops.

By now Communist and National Socialist gangs were constantly clashing, with a steady roll of dead. The police, armed with remarkably effective rubber clubs, were maintaining public order by carrying on continual street warfare.

Communism and National Socialism between them, plus the heavy-witted German Nationalists under Hugenberg, kept any effective majority from being set up in Parliament. Democratic processes of government as applied in Germany had made democratic government impossible some time before Hitler came to power. Germany was being governed dictatorially by a democrat, Chancellor Bruening, for lack of any other way of carrying on the government.

One night I went to the Prussian Landtag. Keeping order in Germany depended to a great extent on the Prussian administration which policed and governed directly the most important areas of Germany. I went into the press gallery and sat leaning on the balustrade with my head on my arms. One of those interminable debates was going on about who was responsible for killing whom in one of the recent clashes. The Nazis and the Communists were exchanging many accusations with little evidence. Between them sat the other parties with the Center Party itself, symbolically, squarely in the center of the chamber.

Tired out, I fell asleep while the debate droned on. Suddenly I awoke but was obviously still in my dream because a chair was right in front of me up in the air. It crashed to the floor. All sorts of missiles were flying. A violent battle was going on in the chamber.

The predicament of the Republic was symbolized when a Nazi hurled a desk drawer across the chamber at the Communists. It struck a deputy of the Center Party square in the head and he collapsed bleeding. There were others bleeding.

I snapped out of my comatose state into the full jubilation of having a wonderful story. Turning to an old reporter of the German Parliamentary Press Service who was standing next to me, I announced breezily and joyously, "What a story!"

Tears were running down his face. I looked at him, dumbfounded. I must have said stupidly, "You're crying."

He looked at me and said, "Young man, you are very young. You are not German. This is not your country. This is the end of democracy."

Remarking that it was still a wonderful story, I rushed to the telephone and put through a first call to Knickerbocker at the office. No other newspaper or agency had a man at that moment in the Prussian Landtag. The final editions of the New York *Evening Post* would have a scoop. Let democracy take care of itself.

When it was all over and Knickerbocker said he could not use any more details, I walked back. The old reporter from the Parliamentary Press Service was still there. He had filed his routine report to his service. He looked gray and old and somehow afraid, as if he had seen a vision. As we sat together he prophesied to me a great deal of what did come, including, I believe, war. There would be a lot of people who would go to prison. He might be one of them. There would be much suffering.

That troubled me. I had never quite connected politics with suffering individual human beings. Politics was news stories and something you talked about and got excited over and left you full of ideas. I had never actually thought of it in terms of the one thing that to me was concrete and real—the happiness or contentment or misery of individuals.

The German reporter was wretched because his people, the

democratic people, had been such fools to let the National Socialists and the Communists, democracy's enemies, participate
in government. Now it was too late.

Eating a lonely meal in a half-dark little beer hall afterward,
I felt depressed. For the first time I began to understand Edgar
Mowrer's so-called editorializing in his dispatches. He had been
warning and again warning. I had disapproved. I was very
proud of writing just straight news. Let the reader work out
what it all meant.

But if my German reporter-prophet was right, if this was
about something personal, about suffering, then people should
understand, be made to understand, what can happen to a
democracy.

Here in Germany an example of one of the basic problems of
the democratic form of government was shown to other nations. Two totalitarian parties, the National Socialist and Communist, had been permitted under the constitution to enter
Parliament, both with the intent of destroying parliamentary
government itself. There could be no democratic government
because they were persistently engaged in sabotaging it.

The issue is whether a man who wants to vote against democracy, wittingly or unwittingly, has a right to be represented
in a democratic government. Admitting right or left totalitarianism to a parliament is much like inviting a man to come and
live in a house when he has announced he intends to burn it
down.

Possibly there is a higher liberty which justifies giving the
enemies of the democratic form of government the right to plead
their case for its removal. I am inclined to believe there is. It is
another thing to place them in positions where they can sabo-
tage the functioning of democratic government.

In the United States after the war there were to be excesses in
the search for Soviet sympathizers in the government. However, what happened to Germany and to the world as the result
of letting the enemies of democracy participate in the democratic process was a much more important object lesson than
the injustices later committed in the United States.

You cannot play under the rules of the game if there are

players on the field who refuse to accept the rules. You can either cease playing altogether, which, if the game is carrying on government, is impossible, or you can play according to their rules, or you can kick them off the field and lock the gates.

The latter course is not very palatable to the liberal. But there is a liberalism for liberalism's sake that tends to make the liberal an actual ally of the enemies of his own freedom.

I had learned a great deal that afternoon at the Prussian Landtag. Nevertheless, I remember feeling rather angry at that confounded old man. He had spoiled a wonderful evening, a personal success. We must have made at least two editions in New York because the stuff was moved fast. Why did that old fool have to go and get me depressed?

It must have been about that time that my youth or perhaps my childhood began drawing to an end.

Life had always been somewhat on the difficult side for me, but it had been my private affair. Now I began to have this feeling of being linked with the unhappy affairs of other people. It was not a pleasant feeling.

I began to lose something—a little of my verve and freshness. It is part of the strength of youth that it is so naively and unconsciously cruel.

8

IN THE spring of 1932 I started to look for another room. Among the advertisements in the papers was one that said that a "foreigner" was wanted and hinted at some sort of advantageous terms. I was getting a very modest monthly salary and advantageous terms, whatever it meant, interested me.

The building near the Kurfuerstendamm, the gay boulevard which was the center of Berlin night life, struck me as being impressive. Still, I went on up in the elevator.

A maid in uniform opened the door. I was ushered into a salon with Chinese silk tapestries hanging on the high walls. It was immediately evident that these people were not renting the kind of furnished room that I was interested in.

Two men, almost too perfectly dressed, looking like businessmen, came into the room. I got up and told them I felt I had made a mistake, I could see that they would hardly be renting the kind of cheap furnished room in which I was interested. Would they please pardon the interruption? I would be going.

Talking all the time, they gently forced me to sit down again. I could see now that they must be brothers. They asked me if I was a foreigner. I said yes, but that I would be going now as it had just been a misunderstanding.

Whom did I work for? I said I was employed by an American newspaper.

Answering questions, I granted that I was an American citizen and that my organization in Berlin did not sell, buy or transact any other business. I had no relatives in Germany or in Europe.

They began to get excited. It was perfect, they said, and beamed at each other.

They divulged that they wished to rent the apartment: salon with Chinese tapestries, dining room, complete furnishings, linens and household equipment. I was just what they had been looking for.

Coffee in a silver service had been brought in by the maid, but I got up and started for the door, explaining hastily once more that it was all a mistake and said that unfortunately there were poor Americans and that I had been looking for a cheap— I almost shouted the word—single furnished room.

I bade them good-by and found myself gently installed in another chair with the coffee table in front of me. I was getting alarmed.

Then they explained. They were Jews with a prosperous textile business in Berlin and another small establishment in Paris.

They were leaving for Paris. Adolf Hitler was coming to power, they believed. How long he would last they did not know. Anyway, they had reasons for not giving the impression that they were abandoning Berlin for good.

The housekeeper, of whom they were fond, would stay at their expense, care for the apartment and cook and serve my meals. They wanted very much to have a foreigner take the apartment, one who would not be too greatly inconvenienced if it were necessary to give it up quickly. I was perfect for their purposes. The rent of a cheap furnished room, they presumed, was about so many marks. I nodded agreement. Good, for that sum they would rent the apartment to me on a monthly basis, two weeks' notice either way.

There were more expostulations on my part which were quite insincere and more assurances from them which were now unnecessary. "Shake hands" all around and *"Vielen Dank,* Mister."

A week later I moved in. The gray-haired, starched and motherly housekeeper, told that this was indeed "all" my luggage, hung my three suits, including the one with the ragged cuffs, on three of the many hangers in the big closet. My underwear and shirts occupied half of one drawer in the battery of big drawers.

Since the maid had been dismissed, the housekeeper brought in coffee and little cakes on the silver service. As I sat and tried to look nonchalant, a gold-embroidered Chinaman on one of the tapestries leered at me.

That apartment had a temporarily disastrous effect on me. I bought another suit and now had three pairs of shoes, granting that one of them had slightly cracked tops. I started spending every cent and dropped in on all sorts of fancy bars on the Kudam. There was one across the street from the apartment that I considered ultrasuave.

The bar girls in those days wore very décolleté evening dresses and their conversation was on the dubious or just plain bawdy side. The smart installation of such places dated from the prosperity in the late 1920's but drinks were dirt cheap for the depression was at its worst. The dollar was still the Hoover dollar and that helped for I had few of them. I began to get shadows under my eyes and was proud of them.

Berlin was corrupt. Coming home late one night from working for the *Public Ledger,* I decided to have a *Glühwein,* hot wine, to ease the pain of a sore throat. I turned into a place with a lot of lights out front and a stairway to a setup with a long bar, a dance floor and a band.

I sat at the bar. The barmen were boys in pages' uniforms, who seemed young for the job. They all had a sort of dewy look.

After ordering my hot wine, I turned to look at the dancers, watching especially the women in long evening dresses. I was thinking what a weird-looking lot they were when someone started caressing my hand. Twisting around, I looked into the face of a bar boy.

I grabbed my hot wine, downed it so fast it scorched my throat, took my check and got out of there. Now I knew what was the matter with those women on the dance floor. They were not women.

Up on the west side was a place that I came to visit on nights when I worked late. I had discovered it by chance. It was a restaurant and bar with chintz curtains at the small windows. According to the menu outside they served an inexpensive Hungarian goulash. Nothing is better than a paprika-loaded goulash on a cold winter's night.

When I went in, the proprietor bustled out from behind his counter most cordially. He sat me square in the middle of the room, directly under a lamp. The rest of the place seemed to be all corners. The architect had been a specialist in corners. Peering into the darkness, I could see that couples were occupying the corners, snug and cuddled up.

I was thinking something benevolent and trite about love and being young only once. Then I noticed that all the couples were girls. My first thought was of leaving, but the goulash was first class and the proprietor had brought me, free, a big glass of very sound wine. So I stayed. At any rate I could not be corrupted there. Nowhere in the city was a male safer.

The attitude of the proprietor puzzled me. He was so cordial. I understood when a policeman looked in. He saw me, registered surprise, shrugged and walked out again. I turned and smiled at the proprietor. He smirked back. For a while I made a habit of going in there for the extra-size goulash and my free wine.

After I had got well settled with Knickerbocker I went down to Braunschweig to visit the Herr Doktor's family. Frau Doktor thawed remarkably when she heard I had a regular job.

Ilse, too, was friendly but there was no longer that comradeship of the first summer. I felt resentful. I was working hard now at making a career for myself and was well dressed for the first time and she was not interested. I tried to impress her with stories of Berlin and the bars and what I considered to be its sophisticated life. She appeared only puzzled and not overly impressed.

Then I got my big chance. She told me that she was coming up to visit friends in Berlin for four or five days. I had never told them in Braunschweig about my luxurious apartment.

The Americans in Berlin almost to a man were self-proclaimed experts on European women. Remembering their conversation I decided that probably Ilse was not interested in me any more because she considered me a milksop. European women, it appeared, regarded an absence of boldness in a man as an affront.

Now Ilse was going to be up in Berlin alone and the issue in my mind began to be: was I a milksop or was I not a milksop? I invited her to come to tea, and the fact that she willingly consented to come alone fitted in superbly with my American acquaintances' revelations on the subject of European women.

There are painful scenes in young fools' lives and this was one of them. She was not shocked. She just looked first perplexed and then amused.

She said finally that I was being vulgar and that I should stop pretending to be whatever it was that I was pretending to be. That was the gist of it. She wanted to know if the foolishness were over. If so, she would stay for a while. If not, she would have to go.

She also got the explanation of the apartment out of me and laughed. She saw that I was miserable, but told me again that I had merely been silly.

She acted as if I were having some kind of sick spell and was clearly in need of an aspirin and a good night's sleep. I felt that next she would be counting my pulse and popping a thermometer into my mouth. For a young and coming Don Juan it was a big letdown.

I blurted out that I honestly loved her. She said she wouldn't pretend to feel any strong affection for me but that we should be friends. She was full of solicitude and sure that I would get a hold on myself and, so to speak, live to a ripe old age.

She went back to Braunschweig next day.

I had learned a good deal about sophistication in that afternoon. Some people were born with it and it certainly had nothing to do with décolleté bar girls and late hours.

After a few weeks I wrote her a careful little letter suggesting that I stop for a few hours in Braunschweig en route to some undisclosed—in fact, nonexistent—destination. She replied that everyone was home and I should come to visit them.

Her attitude had changed again when I arrived. Gay and comradely, she acted as if we had a special joke in common. She wanted to know if I were still seducing young ladies in my luxurious chambers. At last I could see that the whole thing was quite funny and we laughed over it together. It was, however, with somewhat mixed feelings that I learned what had saved me on that unpleasant occasion. Ilse had not been shocked at my advances because she simply did not expect sensible behavior in the man-woman relationship from an American. She had taken it for granted that there was in me an element of clumsy adolescence, something akin to small-boy nastiness, that was inseparable from my citizenship. I was just part of the spectacle that has been providing an endless source of amusement wherever people in foreign countries discuss Americans— the spectacle of a man who lets his womenfolk get the better of him.

9

Meanwhile the months passed with leaden feet for a prostrate nation. In the Reich Chancellery Heinrich Bruening, the democrat, had been replaced by Franz von Papen, third-rate intrigant and puppet of von Schleicher, the political general who had the ear of President Fieldmarshall Paul von Hindenburg.

Some forty per cent of the workers *ging stempeln,* lived by getting their dole cards stamped to draw their hunger ration.

It was one night during this time that the body of a poor man was brought home to Wedding in North Berlin. The episode mattered little to the foreign press and there will certainly be no mention of it in history. But I shall remember it for the rest of my life.

In the Rote Wedding were crowded Berlin's most profoundly Communist proletariat. The roughly paved streets stretched interminably between gray, featureless tenements. Most of the famous Red proletariat lived around the dank paved courtyards that filled the big blocks.

On that night humanity flowed steadily out of those dwelling places with an increasing fury and despair. The throng moved silently and stank of old sweat, for soap had become a luxury.

A Communist, working as a porter in a west-side building, had been killed by a National Socialist gang. His body, wrapped in the red flag of revolution, was being brought on a cart through Wedding, to be burned in the crematory.

The streets were empty of vehicles. Travelers were avoiding Wedding that night. The police stood drawn up in strong squads here and there against the walls, three and four rows deep, tense. They did not dare to venture out of the formation which was their defense.

You could hear the wheels of that wagon coming, bumping and grinding over the paving. The throng became a solid sea of heads in all the streets around. You could not move and the acrid stench of the people was in your nostrils. You felt through your body the threat of pent-up violence.

Not only the dead man coming, but all life seemed at an end. There was hunger and sickness and there was no hope of redemption. These masses, like the infuriated students at the university, spat on "this, your freedom."

Now you could see the torches borne by the mob around the wagon. It was a scene out of the French Revolution. The immense, pressing, sodden throng was silent, but you could hear those around the wagon cursing bitterly.

The wagon came nearer, rolling toward the square where the mass had become impenetrable, crushed together around their leaders who stood on a rough low platform. Other torches were lighted. The throng stirred a little as if every part of it had moved for long blocks back into those endless, dreary streets.

The wagon came out into the square as the impenetrable mass somehow gave way. Now you could see the wagon in the dancing, flaring light of the torches. The body, wrapped in the red flag—a symbol to these tortured people of the only human hope—seemed to rise as it responded to the lurching movement of the wagon.

Then the convulsive thing came into that throng that had to come. Women began to moan. Tears streamed down men's faces. Out of the distance, sounding like the sea in storm, a cry rose out of those streets: "Revenge, Revenge, Revenge."

The German word *Rache* is all one harshness and hoarseness
as if there were blood in your mouth, a word like the sound of a
strong young man fighting for his last breath.

"Revenge, Revenge, Revenge!"

There was no end to it. It seemed as if they would never tire
of it. All around me people strangled and gasped and wept in-
sanely.

They wanted their due from the bitter, hateful world for that
dead thing on the wagon, for that symbol of themselves. They
wanted revenge for the dead who had gasped out their last in
the mud of France in the long war years ago; revenge for the
republic of faith and hope that might have been; revenge for the
lost dream of a new road.

Though I was no partisan of the red-shrouded figure, it was
too much for me. This was no longer a political demonstration.
This was man groveling in agony before the wretchedness and
the meanness of life, before frustration and the dead-end horror
of the empty years.

All of us were mingled in the common stench of poverty and
desperation.

That suffering mass hurled back in the face of God its un-
wanted immortality. They cried out for annihilation. They
seemed to long to die in pain and bathe in blood if only they
could take with them into a common grave all that had been or
would be in such a world as this.

Afterward I bathed my face in the washbasin at a beer hall,
straightened my clothes and rode back to the office in the under-
ground. My nerves were still taut but in the calm after the emotional storm I began to feel somewhat of an ass. However, I was
to pay no further serious attention to efforts toward saving that
hopeless regime, the so-called republic.

Man had timidly questioned fate at the end of the First World
War. It had seemed as if a new start might be made. I understood now what the German worker on the ship had meant on
that cold day when he warmed himself with the memory of what
he had called the postwar revolution when he had cared so
strongly and so much about all those other people.

Now for one moment I had felt my flesh mingle with the flesh of others in a common frustration and a common pain. I had seen the wretched jouncing thing wrapped in red cloth as the symbol of myself, as the pitiful symbol of all of us who cannot find our home in this world.

And I knew also that I was a little nearer home for having lost my identity though so briefly, believing for a flickering, blind instant that there are no men but only man in his agony.

Berlin was a city of immigrants. They had come from towns and villages all over Germany and adjacent Eastern Europe. They lived out their lives in those gray, long streets that were all alike, the *Steinmeer,* "stone sea," as the Germans called it.

The *echte Berliner,* "the real Berliner," meaning the workingman, had a tough hide and a crude fatalism. He fed on that coarse and often much-to-the-point sarcasm of his. He helped his working-class neighbor, his comrade, but he expected and gave little quarter in life. He died as he had lived, anonymous and rather sullen, but tough to the end.

Yet he had and still has a reputation for humor. It was brutal and it was *Galgenhumor,* "hangman's humor." It was the humor of hopelessness, concerned with the ridiculous struggle of little men to escape from the trap. The humor of East Berlin was self-mockery and there was an ugly element in it. Failure fascinated those people for it was the stuff of their lives.

Very popular was Karow's Lachbuehne, or Laughing Theater, deep in working-class east Berlin. People came from all over the city but it was chiefly a workingman's beer-hall theater. You sat with your beer at heavy wooden tables, beside stout, muscular people who munched pretzels, filled the air with pipe and cigarette smoke and guffawed loudly.

The rough farces that Karow staged on his successful Lachbuehne were original compositions, half sketch and half drama. They were monotonously alike.

The favorite scene with the audience was usually in the grand finale when Karow, having portrayed a man who had failed at everything, would be found in a kitchen with his weeping or infuriated wife and screaming children. Half-drunk, he would be in a rage of frustration as he careened around the room. The kitchen shelves were full of crockery and there was usually more furniture, cabinets and the like than you would really find in an east Berlin kitchen.

Gone berserk, Karow would start in on everything in sight. He would smash all the crockery amid screams and bitter imprecations from his wife and children. He would smash chairs, overthrow cabinets, tear the stove loose and finally hurl through the window chests, tables and anything else he could find. Between the man's bellows, the woman's fury, the children's screams and the smashing of crockery and furniture the uproar was deafening.

The crowd would choke itself laughing, upset beer all over the tables and applaud vociferously.

There was a link between the hysterical weeping, the howling rage that had swept away the normal sullen fatalism of that Wedding throng at the sight of the dead man on the cart and the nightly bellowing laughter in Karow's Lachbuehne. These people, peasants and small townsmen, had come out of the old Europe, where along with the poverty had been at least intimacy and stability. Now they lived lost in a sprawling city, one of the largest in the world, in an economy that neither they nor anyone else understood.

In them was the neurosis of the modern world, the hidden hatred of a fate that made each one's life an empty existence as another face in an anonymous mob. Rarely did the dark powers well up and overflow.

Years later I thought of that when I flew over Mount Etna as it was erupting. An incandescent chaotic mass streamed out of the bowels of the earth down over the gray fields of dead lava, and clouds of nauseating gas billowed upward. It occurred to me that one might compare the society man was building with the planet he inhabited, a crust around a seething, boiling heart.

10

It was urgent curiosity that, a short while later, sent me off in search of peasant Europe. I wanted to know where the people came from who inhabited this swollen, artificial city, Berlin, especially the area north and east that seemed a vast brick and stone encampment of the uprooted.

I knew that the majority of these people came out of Germanic or Slavic peasantry. To the east and southeast of Berlin lay the states of the Poles, Slovaks, Hungarians, Croats, Slovenes and Serbs—names that were synonymous with peasantry.

I had drifted into reading Slavic authors who wrote about peasants and I had seen the peasants of Italy, of France, of western and southern Germany and of Holland. But I knew that I had no real knowledge or understanding of them for they are a fundamental ingredient which is absent in the Anglo-Saxon community. This circumstance warps the perspective of people living within the framework of Anglo-Saxon civilizations and therefore limits their comprehension of the world as it is and as it has been for so long.

It is natural for man to consider the place where he lives as the center of the world, or to regard the impermanent residence of power and wealth as the center. But if you take as the center of humanity the place where the majority of human lives are being lived, and if you take the way of life of that majority as the predominant one of mankind, then the picture changes.

More than half the world is a peasant world. Contained

within the vast lands of Asia and its eastern European fringe are
the populations of the Far East, southeast Asia and the Indian
subcontinent who, with the Middle Eastern and the Slav, constitute the human majority—the mainstream of humanity.

Beyond Berlin and Vienna, on the eastern edges of Europe
proper, begins a continuity of peasant life that links the peoples
of eastern Europe to the Asiatic majority of mankind.

I was spending many long winter evenings in Berlin reading a
book called *The Peasants* for which the author, Wladyslaw
Stanislaw Reymont, a Pole, had in 1924, a year before his death,
received the Nobel prize for literature. Published early in the
century *The Peasants* was required reading for German officers
who had to deal with the peasantry while stationed in Poland
during the First World War. Called in German *Die Bauern,*
the book consisted of four thick volumes. Reymont had spent
five years of his life writing it.

He had been in no hurry as the peasant is in no hurry. Breeding and rearing generations of men and livestock are not done
in a hurry.

Reymont has been duly labeled a realist. He gave no idyllic
charm to his peasants. They blundered through the affair of
living, quarreled, suffered, felt good or had trouble with their
bowels and stank more or less from hard work and not overmuch bathing. But their lives had concrete meaning.

I wanted to go and see if it were true. The world into which
I had been born and reared had grown completely unreal. Millions of men were being left without any function. Letters from
America, the news reports in the New York papers and the daily
grist of German news said the same thing.

The common fear of those times hung over our little office.
Our papers, in New York and Philadelphia, were doing badly.
At any time I could become unnecessary. Men in offices in
West Street, New York, or at Independence Square, Philadel-
phia, could decide at any moment that my participation in hu-
man affairs was unnecessary. It did not depend on how well
I did what I did.

Years later, on the wall of an old house in the cathedral close of a green, English lowland town, I saw an inscription over a sundial. It read: "Man is as a shadow walking."

In our life man had become the shadow, large or small, of his function. In the world to which I belonged we were our jobs. We were respected and welcome because of our jobs or a subject of contempt and indifference without them. If you just had work of some sort, work without much importance to you or anyone else, your shadow would be only a faint suggestion of something on the wall. You would be nothing, no real personality, because what you were doing left no imprint. The crisis in the industrial civilization blotted out men and exposed the irrelevance of the individual in our modern world.

I wanted to go to Reymont's peasants, to the ancient life pattern. I wanted to know why it was durable and if it was real. As an excuse I invented the idea of getting a Polish Christmas story and also some dispatches on the Polish political and economic situation.

After I got permission, I selected a spot on the map out in the plains of Poland and took off in its direction.

Christmas Day was about to dawn freezing cold over the plains of the Vistula as I clambered down the steps of the train which stopped only a minute or two. All I knew about the place was that it was a big village and completely Polish and peasant. The station clerk went back inside to sit next to the stove.

There was an empty space beyond the station, snow covered now, which may have been intended as a square or just for grazing. A few stores were scattered along the road that came to the station and farther up at the corner of another road was a garage and a gas pump. What looked like an eating place was near by but everything was closed.

Beyond, along other roads, were a few frame houses and then what appeared to be scattered log houses. There was a big, barnlike stone church.

I went into the station and sat next to the stove. The clerk said nothing. He just stared at me, rather incredulously. To him I did not make sense. I asked in German if there were many people there who spoke German. He said yes. That was all he did say. It was true though about the German. It turned out that many of the men spoke it, though rather brokenly. I never found out why.

The cold outside began to hypnotize me as it apparently hypnotized the clerk. His attachment to the stove was almost neurotic. I wondered if I would sit there all Christmas or until another Warsaw train came.

As the day cleared, a few men arrived at the garage. I roused myself and went across to it, shivering.

A fairly thin young man with a moustache, who seemed to be one of the owners of the garage, such as it was, had a high-wheeled mud-spattered Ford. A deal was made. For a small sum, which would go on the expense account of the Polish Christmas story, he would drive me around all day and we would visit houses. The "village" seemed to include every point within twenty-five or thirty miles.

I mentioned that I would pay for the midday meal at the eating place, which was still closed. He stared at me. We would eat where we were when mealtime came, he said.

Then he paused and pondered and looked me over again. I had struck an intelligent guide. That young man understood that I came from behind some sort of curtain, from another world. He leaned against the door of the garage and explained.

This, he said in effect, was the Polish countryside. You went into a man's house and you sat down with him. You did not have to explain why you had come. When his people ate, you ate. It was like that. It was not like Berlin.

We climbed into the car. The customary cold morning's battle between high-wheeled Fords and the human will took place with the usual snorting, jerking, thumping from the machine, and the usual administrations of boiling water.

Without warning, in the familiar alarming fashion, the Ford backed abruptly into the rutted road, as of its own volition. I felt right at home. My father once owned one of these machines that had retained some of the characteristics of a horse.

We lurched and hammered along for two or three miles. I could see now that the houses were built of logs stripped of bark and cut square. Often gayly painted, they stood near the road which had no very definite borders.

We jammed to a stop in front of a log house painted blue. A man and some children crowded into the doorway and we walked in without a word. We sat down on a bench. There were a table and two or three chairs, benches, some burnished kitchen utensils and various crocks, a brown clay-plastered oven, bunks built against the wall and a door into another room at the far end.

There was also an old man, wrinkled and solid, and a younger man and two or three women and the children. The description is generic. I do not remember each house we visited very clearly. There were always more people than space, it seemed.

It was hot inside. Maybe it was always hot or perhaps it was kept hot to celebrate Christmas. Tea in mugs appeared and a big plate of varicolored cakes that were spicy. My young man with the moustache made a few desultory remarks in Polish.

Finally the old man spoke to me in broken German. Was I a German? I realized with a shock that apparently not a word had been said by my driver about what I was doing in their home on Christmas morning.

The old man's German was understandable but he was having difficulty with mine. My driver, in a distracted, an almost indifferent fashion, broke in with a most confusing mixture of Polish and German.

Out of the welter I understood that they were asking if I wished to stay for Christmas and overnight. I bogged down and asked the driver to please say it all over again. He stopped being distracted and explained once more.

He was only beginning to get the hang of me and my odd way of looking at things.

I had told him, he said, that I intended to stay around over the Christmas days. He had mentioned that. They naturally wanted to know if I wanted to stay with them. Nothing could be simpler. He looked at me with the expression of an indulgent father explaining to his small son that A comes before B and C.

I explained to them in German that, of course, as a complete stranger I could not impose on their hospitality, particularly during a family holiday, et cetera. The driver did a more or less simultaneous, tired interpretation.

They looked at me like children watching a man at work. It was evident that they felt this was some sort of verbal setting-up exercise that I was going through. It had no relation to them. They just smiled.

The driver sucked on his tea and listened. He was clearly bored. He was getting used to me but was not much interested in my congenital incapacity, as he evidently saw it, to give straight answers to straight questions.

He asked did I want to stay there the night or did I not? I said that I thought we should be visiting some other places. He told them so briefly that I was not staying that even I understood. They smiled, shrugged and pushed the plate of cakes at me and more tea was offered.

I rose, bowed and went into a thank-you speech. My friend the driver rose also and watched me like the rest. I went over, bowed and thanked profusely the old lady who I assumed, possibly correctly, was the number-one woman of the house. There was always in those houses such an old woman.

For a moment everybody looked alarmed. Then they saw that whatever it was I was up to was harmless. My memory is that the old lady smiled at me a little mistily, looking as if she expected my trainer to come in at any moment and put me to jumping through hoops.

Everyone was pleased. I did not make sense. That was clear. But they evidently felt that whoever had taught me my tricks had done a good job and that it had been a good show all around.

The driver was downright enthusiastic. He beamed at me as we walked out to the car. While the driver again went through the ritual of inducing the Ford to start, children from near-by houses came running to the house where I had been. I could see that they looked at him reproachfully. Why had he brought his Christmas treat to that house and not to theirs?

As we visited around, my reputation spread. Children would

come crowding into the house expectantly. I was now under an obligation to go through my act. The driver expected it and, while I was engaged in thanking whoever I assumed to be the lady of the house, he nearly took a bow.

Now the roads filled with women and girls in richly colored peasant costumes. They were going to Mass. Their menfolk were less colorful but in their gala dress.

All the feeling of those first cold dawn hours when I had secretly wondered what I was doing in that Godforsaken place was gone. It was a wonderful Christmas. It was all the little boy back in the American Middle West could ever have dreamed a Christmas to be.

From a distance the clusters of girls going to Mass seemed like the russet and gold displays of foliage and flowers at an autumn garden show. As you came nearer you could see their bright ribbons fluttering in the wind. The rare bursts of sunlight sent crystalline showers, like handfuls of jewels, dancing over the snow.

We turned back with the others to go to Mass. The church was so crowded that the driver and I had a hard time squeezing in but we got inside, somehow, pressed in the throng.

People looked around at me and whispered. The girls smiled and their eyes laughed. The word had got around. The driver stood next to me like a man with a bear on a chain.

We could all barely kneel together when the time came, we were so pressed together. The high altar was ablaze and the congregation a mass of mingled colors like a Persian carpet. Sonorous Latin syllables filled the nave. Incense rose toward the clerestory windows.

The church hushed before that mystery. We were silent in the presence of that sublime human parable of the little child born of a virgin woman, the son of the Living God, who came into this meaningless world to give it the assurance that its meaning was that God is love.

Throughout the Christian ages peasants had died with lips pressed to the crucifix, to the agonized body of the man who had been that Christ child and who died so that man's life should not be an empty and senseless thing.

The feel of those bodies pressed together was like a benediction. Peace came on me as it had seldom come since I was a little child. The poisoned agony of my aloneness, of which I was only half aware, became suddenly real and then slipped away like the end of pain.

When we left the church, the driver must have felt that something had come over me. He was aware of things in his own way. We drove far out to a distant hamlet that was part of the village. He was no longer distracted. His German was quite good when he wanted to be understood, and he explained things to me.

I mustn't thank people so much and make those speeches. If I wanted to stay, I could stay. If I didn't, I could go on someplace else. He had lived briefly in Warsaw and knew that city people were different. These people were peasants, his people. They did not ask questions. If you came to their house, it was the will of God and you were welcome. There was food enough.

I had read sufficiently to know that not all peasants were just like that. These people were also Slavs. There was something of the Tolstoy soul in them.

We stopped for a time at another place and then went on to a somewhat larger house where the men spoke quite tolerable German. It was time to eat. No one even asked us. We just sat down with them. It was an enormous meal but I was hungry. The women were pleased that I ate so much. One of the men had explained in an embarrassed way that their food was different from what I was used to and maybe I wouldn't like it.

It was late in the afternoon when all the dishes were cleared away. Probably because he spoke better German than the others had, one of the men was able to explain that they really would like me to stay overnight with them. The driver agreed readily to call it off for the day and come back in the morning. He left.

The men stripped off their upper clothing and their boots and sat in their underwear and pants. They looked at me and I did the same. It got rather stuffy in there with the oven going but I didn't care.

Reymont had written of the four seasons and had followed his peasants through spring, summer, autumn and winter. Doggedly I began to question, following Reymont, who had been an encyclopedia of peasant thought, prejudices, passions and customs.

The Germans' idea of forcing their officers to read Reymont had not been so bad. Those men began to take me seriously. I had met their immigrants in the railway shops in Altoona, in the slums of New York and the crowded emptiness of east and north Berlin. Detail by detail, I learned of the traditions, the faith, the fears, the loves.

Cold food and hot tea were brought in and the women disappeared again beyond the wall. The men talked.

Life was hard and there was not enough land for the young men. They went to the towns. There was jealousy, meanness and ignorance here, but the details of working and living were warm and strong in them. The cattle and the horses and the crops, the village and the households and the priests were the lived drama of life. The word "we" was with them all the time— we the peasants, we the hamlet, we the village, we the family with all those relatives, we the parish.

I settled back with a sigh of relief. Life was not meaningless. Reymont had written that it was sometimes bitter, ugly, painful but he had not lied: There was no emptiness.

We all went to bed in those bunk-like beds but I do not remember any embarrassment. The children had been put to bed and were sound asleep all over the place.

The presence of the children was good. It was good as was the taste of that hearty dark peasant bread and the warmth and smell of the cattle in the stalls where I had gone with the men.

There were a lot of people in that room and I was glad of it. You needed people close up to you. Outside the ice cold of the Polish plain in winter had settled down with the night.

It had been a wonderful Christmas. The picture of Christ as

a boy that my father had hung over my bed came back to me.
It was mingled with the vision of the church and the high altar
and all of us kneeling pressed together.

I know that I slept fitfully at first but not because I felt it was
a strange place to be. Nothing was strange but that the search
for humanity, the conquest of self, the long voyage home,
should be so difficult.

11

I WENT BACK to the peasants
once more in the following spring. Deep in Eastern Europe,
straddling the Polish-Slovakian frontier, is the High Tatra range
with the lower portion of the Carpathians running eastward into
Ruthenia. I had decided to hitchhike in a circle around the
Tatra through the villages in the Slovakian valley to the south
and the rolling hill country that falls away toward storied Cracow in Poland to the north.

The time was right. South of the Tatra, protected by the
abrupt peaks etched against the blue veil of the northern horizon, the orchards were in bloom and around to the north the
buds were just breaking open and wild flowers appearing hesitantly in the wet grass.

In the vicinity of the Tatra you could pay for a night's lodging
in a peasant house. It was tourist country and the villagers were
accustomed to occasional hikers.

It was the pagan period of the year, the period of resurging
fertility when the earth opened under the plowshare and pregnant peasant women showed in their bearing that certain pride.

Life itself, its creation and nurture, vegetable, animal and human, is the peasant's function.

One day I found myself sitting on the high seat of a wagon bumping along a road behind the Tatra Mountains. The peasant sitting beside me driving was in late middle age, strong and markedly Slavic, with high cheekbones. He spoke fairly good English. He had worked in Chicago and some other places in the Middle West, but after staying there for twelve years he had decided to come back to the country under the Tatra.

I wanted to know about this man and how he had found his way home. He was content. America had taught him to get things done and keep his eyes open for the main chance. After he came back he had prospered and was glad he had been in America. But he had not wanted to stay there. He had found it was not homelike in America. People were kind enough, he said, but you never really knew anyone well. Everybody seemed to be always moving away. You wouldn't have grandchildren, they would all go away and be strangers. He said that what you did in America did not seem to get you anyplace even if you got prosperous and bought a house. The house would be sold by your children and everybody would forget about you.

Later that evening I studied the old people sitting on a bench in front of the thatch-roofed house where I had found a bed in the village. I noticed that the young ones going by all waved or nodded to the old people and said something in greeting. I thought of the flesh of your flesh going on from generation to generation and that you did not die because your grandchildren and great-grandchildren did not become strangers. That peasant had said that what you did in America never seemed to get you anyplace. Was it the absence of the future, not of the past, that plagued us? Was it that our grandchildren and great-grandchildren would be strangers and because of that we were really only strangers in this world?

But it was down there in Slovakia that I also came in direct contact for the first time with the political priesthood and the intolerant nationalism that came to play such a dubious role in Eastern Europe.

The peasant was both jealous and credulous. It was the unhealthy, neurotic side of him. The Slovakian peasants would talk by the hour about their enemies—most of them imaginary ones. The Slovaks were anti-Czech, anti-Hungarian (remembering the Magyar magnates' rule in the past) and against the Carpatho-German villagers in the region.

Angry, arrogant little politicians, ambitious lawyers and—unhappily—bigoted and bitterly narrow-minded priests summoned up like sorcerers suspicions in those people. Peasant folklore is full of stories of the powers of darkness and of things that move in the night.

The people trusted little beyond the boundaries of their village fields. Whatever you told them about life outside was somehow twisted around so that it became negative and menacing. They were drawn in on themselves and defensively hostile toward the outside world; the basis of that hostility was primarily fear.

They needed education. How were they going to continue living in a world where everything new and everything strange was rejected or feared just because it was different? The problem was how to give men education without tearing them up by the roots and launching them into that meaningless wandering away from the village community with its humanly adequate life.

Yes, I thought that these Slovakian peasants were unbelievably credulous. They believed in all manner of pixies and phantom creatures. But then I was to have an experience to take me down several pegs in my college-educated self-esteem.

At the eastern end of the Tatra I stayed one night in a village on a hillside that was one big orchard. A brook plunged down through it and the air was scented with blossoms. The thatched houses nestled in fairy-tale disorder along footpaths winding through that picture-book scene.

All day I had dawdled among flowering trees, climbed up mountain paths to watch the smoke from cottages drifting up through the white mist of blossoms, and sat half awake and half asleep by brooks, listening to the water. Everything began to seem unreal, and I found myself drifting off more or less into a dream living.

When I finally got settled with my supper in me, it had become night. Across the road was a little river, and beyond that a steep hill loomed up in the darkness. Up there, some distance from the village, was a ruined castle.

The place was haunted, I had been told. What self-respecting ruined castle is not? This one was favored by the ghostly presence of a witch or some sort of old phantom crone. What the ruined-castle industry would do without Americans, I cannot imagine. Anyhow, I was true to type and, stumbling over rocks in the dark, I dutifully set off up a twisting path to fulfill one of the obligations of my citizenship.

It was deadly still up there and dark as pitch. I stumbled through a gate into what seemed to be a courtyard, where nothing could be seen but the faint light of the sky above, and got out through a breach in the wall onto a battlement that jutted out over an abyss.

I saw no reason for staying there in the dark. Then something breathed harshly behind me. I did not turn. I did not dare. Maybe it would go away. But it might also push me into that abyss. I turned around.

There was no point in disbelieving the evidence of my eyes whether this was the twentieth century or the fifteenth. The thing there was a witch. It stared at me from haggard eyes. Unkempt, matted hair hung over its shoulders and its hands were claws. It moved noiselessly. Summoning all my will, I moved toward the breach in the wall. The thing moved to intercept me and croaked something. Behind me was that abyss. I moved, sweating and trembling, to try and get around it, but again the witch was in front of me. I could step back into empty air at any moment and be crushed to death below. Maybe others had and it had been called an accident.

The awful thing was that the phantom made no sound when it moved. Otherwise I would have heard it when it came.

Desperation got me. I plunged past it and through the breach in the wall. I could not find the place where I had come into that courtyard and, looking around, saw that the thing had followed me. Then I saw a gate, apparently the main one, under what looked like a tower. I rushed headlong, nearly breaking my legs on the rocks in the courtyard, and made my escape.

Right outside the wall there was a light. It made me terribly happy. Someone had come who could help me. I looked closer. The light came from the window in a little mud hut against the wall. The fear cleared out of my mind.

The old woman came out the castle gate. Of course she was barefoot. She looked dreadfully poor and pathetic in the light from the window. I gave her a coin and slunk off down the path.

The maternal side of my family was Irish. If you are going to live with yourself, you have to blame a moment like that on somebody. Why not on the Irish?

The next day I got a ride on a truck into Nowi Targ, the big market town in the south of Poland. I had no Polish zlotys. You could use the last of your Czechoslovak money right at the frontier, but I had spent mine and would have to cash my American Express travelers' checks.

The banks in Nowi Targ were polite but firm. They would not accept dollars. American dollars were no good.

The impression in Nowi Targ was that the dollar had gone to pieces and the United States was bankrupt. Southern Poland was full of emigrants' dollars that were hidden away like gold and now came pouring out. There was something like a panic. Dollar trading had been suspended.

For a couple of weeks I had not seen a newspaper and no one had told me anything about the dollar going off gold. With no reason to change money in Czechoslovakia, I knew nothing.

I was destitute. There was no way to reach an American consulate and no money to telegraph, telephone or travel. The police, to whom I appealed, did not understand and said to come back in a few days.

By late afternoon I was ravenously hungry. What was I to do? Suddenly I remembered that I was well away from the mountains in peasant country where they did not know about tourists.

I went out to the edge of town on the road to Zakopane, the Polish mountain resort, and got a ride in another truck. A fair number of miles out in the open countryside I got out and struck into a side road. After about a mile I saw a hamlet. It was suppertime. I walked up to a house with a bench in front and sat down showing in every way I could that I was tired. A man appeared and spoke to me but in Polish. Then he motioned me inside. I went in and we sat down at the table and ate. They talked to one another and paid little attention to me.

After supper we just sat around. A place was made for me to sleep on the floor on a sack. I smiled wearily and they smiled back. I lay down when they got into bed.

The great god dollar was dead. I did not know what was going to become of me. My job must be gone. The paper could not keep its foreign bureaus if the dollar were gone, and from what I had heard in Nowi Targ there must have been some sort of financial breakdown in the United States.

I looked at the people sleeping around me. It was a very poor house. They had appeared to be dull, heavy people. Certainly they were not my sort of people.

I had never been so homeless in my life. There I lay among peasants in southern Poland with no idea what my future would be. But they had taken me in. Those clodlike people, coarse and clumsy, had shared with me what they had.

The aloneness that was in me, the baffled searching feeling, was quieted in spite of all the anxiety. Remembering that night later I knew that, though I might never find my way home, home is there all the time. I knew that it was a question of whether men wanted it or chose to go on wandering in the night.

The next morning I got a ride up to Zakopane. A good many hotels were open. At the Cooks Travel Office I got straight what had happened and relaxed. They changed some of my travelers' checks, and I got a room with a bath, inexpensive as this was the off season, and luxuriated in hot water and soapsuds.

A few days later I went back to Berlin.

12

ADOLF HITLER had at last come to power. The story of Adolf Hitler is familiar in all its aspects of horror, terror and peril. The record of his years in power reads like a libretto from a lesser Wagner in which a grandeur of sound could not redeem the posturing and pretense—the almost *opéra bouffe* effect—that made more ghastly those myriads of deaths. Even now it is hard to believe Buchenwald. Hitler owes his probable position in history to the circumstance that he was a failure. As we know now, he exacted revenge from the world.

All through his humiliating, hungry young manhood he had accumulated resentments, laved vanity with self-pity and nursed the golden, twisted dreams of the hopeless failure. He even appeared somewhat pathetic. He was essentially the figure Hans Fallada's novel, *Little Man, What Now?* described with such acuity and understanding of failure. Hitler may be charged with enormous crimes, but he was not the creator of the evil he symbolized and served. He infected nations with one ancient sickness of man, and the strain he spread threatened all men. Germany, like much of the rest of Europe between the wars, was full of failing men. People who before the first war should have led lives that made sense to them and accomplished something in their little spans, now lived failure. They festered in mediocrity—a relative term most nearly descriptive of the condition.

The so-called little middle class with their ambitions, continual butt of the sarcasm of both the privileged and the less ambitious rank and file, suffered agonies of frustration. But the thing was not limited to them.

A society had been built up where life was intolerable without progress. And neither Europe nor the German heart of Europe was moving forward.

The golden age of Europe was waning. The ambition-ridden Reich, since its creation in 1870, had been haunted by the knowledge that it was almost too late for a new great power to take its place in European history. The Germans were the central people of Europe but they had remained disunited too long. By the time they came of age, the unquestioned primacy of the European was ending. They had not taken part in the great European explorations overseas. The pageant of the expansion of Britain and the Iberian Peninsula had passed them by. Their galleons had not ridden the Spanish Main bearing treasures from the Indies to the courts of Castile. Their flag had never floated over headlands and exotic ports around the world as had that of the greatest of empires where princes and peasants paid homage to Queen Victoria.

Germany since 1870 had developed in the fields of education, commerce, industry and the sciences, had become surcharged with diligence and brilliant creative capacity. It had then been led by political incompetents into the dead end of the First World War.

National Socialism, when it came, was not a program. It was a neurosis. Germany, or rather a varying mass of individual Germans, had been sick since the final year of the First World War.

Other countries at the beginning of the 1930's were also caught in stagnant hopelessness. The crisis was world-wide. But to the Germans that crisis brought a complete nervous breakdown. Their feeling that it was too late became intensified. Their world fell to pieces around them in an irrational hodgepodge of resentments, hatreds, fears and delusions.

I felt that I understood these people, perhaps because of a growing lack of confidence in my own world. I had also been very close to young Germans. I felt the sense of failure that was in them, their fear of being just another formless inkstain on a blotter, of having lived to no particular purpose. All of this drew them to one man—Adolf Hitler.

They flocked to him because he alone could give relief to that unbearable strain of frustration that they were living under. He could do it because he was more than half mad.

I must have attended at least two hundred of those ritual-like meetings where Hitler spoke. The drama usually began with the throng pouring into a huge hall, filling all corners. They looked tired, the drawn, drooping tiredness which comes not from working but from not getting anywhere.

Band music is a good antidote for that feeling. A big band began to play joyously with rousing solid brass and plenty of drumwork. The crowd began to cheer up. Messengers ran back and forth, and officers in full regalia appeared, importantly doing unimportant things. The National Socialists always built up expectation carefully.

Then it came. The central doors at the rear of the hall swung open. A solid phalanx of gold-fringed swastika banners was borne down the center aisle. The band music, triumphant and powerful now, raised people out of their seats. Thousands of arms rose in rigid salute.

Massed banners again appeared in the doorway, along with *Schutzstaffel*—the SS troops—in black and silver uniforms, followed by high party functionaries also in uniform.

In front of the glittering, impressive array walked that rather pathetic figure in the familiar simple coat and dark pants, looking depressed and distracted.

You wanted to see him as the crowd saw him. You had to if you were to understand. This man was you in your mediocrity, your depression, your wishing that living were about something important. He was you in the midst of this magnificent display and roaring march music, you in the burgeoning of hope and gratitude, you in the midst of the cries of *Heil!* rising to ever more maddening crescendos.

When he finally rose to speak, there was that hoarse self-pity in the voice that was you in your weakness. The words came.

First there was the long complaint; next the sounding of a note of confidence; then in turn rage, contempt and finally that calm pride, the arrogance of a master of men and overlord of history. That was you—triumphant at last.

Hitler was not the Rooseveltian or Churchillian orator. They were aristocrats. This son of a bastard father and a servant-girl mother reached deeper. Out of his own sickness he fed the sickness that was in the people and granted them salvation from self. His strength was that any faith is better than no faith at all.

He liberated those people from the burden of frustration that oppressed them; he gave them confidence in tomorrow, a reason to live and a reason to die. No one can give more. And so a great part of the population of one of the best educated and most industrious nations took voluntary refuge in the mad dream-world of a sick man.

Once I took a German girl in her late twenties to one of those affairs. She had never heard Hitler because she was a declared opponent of National Socialism, calling herself a Social Democrat. She was not an intellectual, and my interest in her was not in her intellectual attainments. But she did have a good head on her shoulders. She could explain why she was against National Socialism and it added up.

After the meeting was over I first telephoned my office and then went across the street to a restaurant with the girl. We had had no chance to speak to each other during or after the affair.

While I was studying the menu she remarked with no apparent relevance, "He made me think of my childhood in the village in East Prussia, of Sunday mornings and the green fields, the good German earth."

I peeked over the menu to see if I had perhaps sat down with the wrong girl. Nothing had been said in the hall about East Prussia, green fields or, even by exception, the German earth. But it was indeed the same girl and her eyes were shining.

Morally a bit on the shabby side, she had looked the part. Now that was gone. She looked healthy and resolute, mistress of herself. She said something to the effect that her life was a mess and she was, if I remember correctly, "unworthy of Germany." She added that she was going to get herself a real job and straighten out.

As the expression goes, you could have knocked me over with a feather.

She did what she said she would do, too, although oddly enough she never became a National Socialist. But she always spoke of Adolf Hitler with respect, and claimed that he was too good for the gang around him—a proposition that was highly improbable.

Of course, she could not have found a job and straightened herself out before Hitler arrived on the German scene. There had been no jobs.

The Weimar epoch had made confused efforts to accept the fact of German defeat in 1918. With Hitler the effort to compromise with life ended. Depressed, isolated individuals and families changed before your eyes.

The awakening of that nation might be compared with a military display I later saw one morning. It seemed that morning as if the troops stretched for miles. Most of the units were sitting around in disorder. They were waiting for the only thing in their lives that ever changed anything—orders.

Finally the commands rang out, starting from up among the staff officers and ringing down from unit to unit, echoing and re-echoing. The sharp notes of bugles sounded. Bands swung into formation. New commands rang down the files. Flags unfurled. Tanks and artillery wheeled into position. Faster and faster came the commands. The pattern emerged. Far away you could see the guidons fluttering.

A final staccato barking of commands and the gray mass moved with rigid precision as the bands began to play. You could see in the men their pride in this instrument of power surging forward at the word of command.

At that point in German history the ordinary men, who had been sitting, staring blankly into nothing, or wandering, neurotic and bewildered, stood up to the emotional orgies which Hitler and his like put on. Shoulders went back, eyes cleared. There were jokes and occasional singing.

There was work to do. A man was needed. People were glad to see him coming for a job. A man's wife spoke with that old tone of affectionate respect for the breadwinner and head of the family. Father was somebody again.

I saw the rising of a nation from dead rot and despondency. It is hard to give the devil his due, but if you saw it, you saw it.

The catastrophe of the Hitler regime was an extreme and warped example of what the dynamism of modern society can incur. The circumstances in Germany were extraordinary and the principal personalities psychopathic, but they were the product of an approach to life in which the emphasis is on doing, not on being. That approach is the basic attitude of modern man.

The Hitlers or less vicious equivalents will keep cropping up in modern society as long as unemployment remains a danger for the individual. Job security is the urban equivalent of the security of land tenure in the peasant environment.

Our industrial society, because of the complete interdependence of its members, leaves only one kind of security, namely the smooth functioning of that interdependence. In consequence, modern industrial society is the most intricately organized society that has existed. It has formed the mentality of men out of its own necessities. It must move as its planning staffs dictate or fall into chaos. It must move with precision and as an army moves or it cannot move at all.

The driving force of all the vibrant activity that is the rhythm of the modern world is an incessant stream of commands coming ceaselessly down from above. Ours is a society fashioned on obedience.

What had been lacking in Germany during the confused Weimar epoch were words of command. With the combination of mass unemployment and the lack of a guiding authority, all issues changed. Life simply became intolerable. Faced with an existence as living corpses without function in life, people ceased to give a rap about freedom. Freedom is a value of the living, quite meaningless to the living dead.

During the 1930's Germany and the other highly industrialized nations all wrestled with the same issue of government planning versus the individual's freedom to choose his place in life. Germany could produce no rational solution. The German social order could have been made to function by orders from above, by dictatorial control. By permitting open enemies of democratic government to participate in its processes, the German Parliament of the Weimar Republic failed to assume dictatorial authority over the German economy.

There was no solution left but the wrath of God, through the voice of the demagogue.

Hitler came in with a minority in Parliament and only three National Socialists in the cabinet. He was considered in those days the prisoner of Hugenberg's heavy-witted Nationalists. Given the circumstances, he had to have absolute power or let the agony of the economic crisis continue. That authority was procured by the introduction of terror.

This was the first revolution I had seen. I began to understand both the function and the atmosphere of terror. Terror frees the revolutionary regime from the paralyzing pressure of opposition. The terror started with the Jews. It was a seemingly irrelevant but actually quite practical place to start. An undefended minority, once isolated by determined, hostile propaganda, is useful. It becomes the medium through which the method of terror can be introduced and spread.

My first personal encounter with terror took place when a boycott of Jewish stores was staged in Berlin. With the unsound idea of being guinea pig, I saw fit to enter a large department store in east Berlin about which a cordon of young Nazis was strung. I made some small purchase and came out with it openly displayed under my arm. Before I knew what was happening, blows were raining down on me. I ran. They followed, beating me over the head and back. One of them yelled again and again, "Dog head!" Why this name, I don't know.

They only followed me to the end of the block where, apparently, their jurisdiction in the matter of beating up "un-German Germans," as they called them, ended. I was sore all over from the pummeling but glad that I had not tripped and fallen. A group in the next block started toward me, grinning unpleasantly, and I got out of there fast.

Elsewhere the terror was going on in earnest. "Beating" stations had been set up by the Storm Troopers in their local headquarters throughout the city. Jews, notably eastern-looking Jews, were dragged there and beaten unmercifully. The police did not intervene. The news got around and people began to understand that this was not a change of cabinet that could be reversed. Getting this point across is a function of terror in a revolution.

I went one late afternoon to a humid courtyard in east Berlin. In a room opening onto the courtyard was a little synagogue. Next to it was a dark, cavelike room where a middle-aged Jew sat in bed in his night clothes. Propped up with pillows, he half sat and half lay. He could not lie down entirely for he was too bruised and broken. He was a thin man. He coughed incessantly and spat up blood.

A doctor was there and had given him injections to lessen the pain but that was all he could do. They were letting the man die at home. He had been beaten unmercifully, and there were so many things broken that it would have been torture for him to be moved.

The man was weeping. There were children and they kept coming and pulling at his nightshirt as if to keep him from going away.

13

M<small>Y CHIEF</small> and friend, H. R. Knickerbocker, left. He accepted a fancy contract with the Hearst organization and turned his job over to me. At the ripe old age of twenty-seven I was sole correspondent in Germany for a New York and a Philadelphia paper. Doing the work that two of us had done previously kept me hard at it for a while, but it was not to last.

The New York *Evening Post* collapsed and was sold. The foreign service was temporarily kept up by the Philadelphia *Public Ledger,* but in May that too ended. I was out of a job.

With the telegram from Philadelphia, telling me that it was all over, in my pocket, I went downstairs to walk in Unter den Linden and try to collect my thoughts. On the street I ran into Frederick Birchall, former managing editor and then chief foreign correspondent of the New York *Times.* He told me to come around and see Guido Enderis, head of their Berlin office, and himself. To my incredulous relief they fixed me up with a new job.

When Birchall was in Berlin—which was most of the time— he and Guido were inseparable. Birchall was British. He had spent most of his working life in America but had remained loyal to the Crown. He was short, rather bald and wore a white Vandyke. His ideas on the female as a phenomenon were exactly the opposite of those of Guido Enderis. All of Guido's efforts could not down Birchall's conviction that women had a great future and there was also considerable to be said for their past and present. The two men quarreled steadily about it.

Frederick Birchall had never mastered either journalese or the use of the typewriter. He wrote interminable dispatches in lucid English prose that was a delight to read. He wrote them in longhand, patiently working hour after quiet hour.

In the Berlin office with Birchall, Enderis and the indefatigable Otto Tolischus, who was actually the backbone of the whole operation, I had a problem making a place for myself. The adjustment was not easy.

I was no longer living in the luxurious apartment near the Kurfuerstendamm in Berlin. The Jewish owners, safe in Paris, had finally decided it was not practical to maintain a Berlin residence.

Once, around three in the morning, there was a hammering

on the door of my new quarters. A stentorian voice shouted, "State Secret Police. Open in the name of the German Reich!"

I was by that time thoroughly involved in the not exactly legal activities of the anti-Nazi Confessional Church group. Shaking a little and sweating in spite of the cold, I opened the door.

A man in plain clothes and two SS men in uniform marched in. Another in the hall looked at me coldly. The three went into the bedroom and turned the mattress upside down. They went through all the drawers and closets, looked under the table in the living room and inspected the bathroom cabinet.

In the living room was a pile of National Socialist Party instruction books and manuals, including material I had obtained with some difficulty from the Party because it was confidential. I wondered if they were going to make trouble about that. Otherwise there was by chance almost nothing in the apartment except my clothes, toothbrush, shaving kit and, on a table in the hall, a pile of *Angriffs,* the National Socialist afternoon paper.

The Gestapo men came out into the hall and beamed at me. Raising their arms in the Hitler salute, they boomed: "Greetings, Party Comrade. Pardon the interruption. Heil Hitler!"

I made a little wagging movement with my hand which could be taken for the Hitler salute and they tramped out. As I closed the door I felt that my role in the affair had been somewhat less than heroic. And I was to feel this even more strongly.

A long line of trucks stood out in the street and people were being loaded into them. Armed SS troops stood guard.

I put on my pants and a shirt and went into the outer hall. The SS man in the hall saluted, "Heil Hitler, Party Comrade." Again I wagged my hand. The neighbors across the hall, gathered in their doorway, looked at me as if they were seeing a ghost. I smiled feebly and went downstairs.

There was another SS man in the downstairs hall and the one on my floor yelled down, "Is good. The Herr is a Party Comrade."

A group of frightened people in the hall stared at me apprehensively. I felt a horrible sense of self-importance. These people were obviously afraid of me. It made me feel good in a way. I believe that I had the decency to blush inwardly at that thought.

An SS man took the arm of a man in the group to lead him away. His wife started to cry and cling to him. She was shoved aside and the man was taken to the trucks for a trip to the Gestapo prison. Everyone there moved away from the woman as quickly as if she had leprosy. She stood alone in her night clothes with the tears smearing her face and looked at me imploringly. I could see she was thinking that as I was a Party member and lived there perhaps I could help.

I scuttled up the stairs, closed the door and sat there feeling like Judas Iscariot.

I had to get dressed though and find out if there was a news story. Back down at the trucks my "party comrades" told me that a seditious publication was being put out clandestinely by a resistance group somewhere in the block of apartments. They started to ask me if I knew anything but I moved away quickly. Fortunately, commands rapped out at that moment and the whole column with its prisoners got under way.

I thought of a certain girl whom I knew rather too well, who danced occasionally on the stage and had a good apartment because of her previous excellent relations with a banker. Suppose they raided her place some night?

In those years she was giving shelter to a homeless old Jew. She called him father.

She was what the Nazis called pure Aryan and had a perfectly good Aryan father and mother who lived somewhere in east Berlin. Since she was not exactly a good girl, as such things are understood, she did not see much of them.

The old Jew was quite alone in the world. He had once had a small but fairly prosperous technical publishing house. The crisis had come. The business got in trouble. He had held onto his old employees too long.

His wife was no longer interested after he lost his business, and in the divorce settlement she got their house and just about everything else that was left. He had thought he could get going again, but then the National Socialist regime came. He was destitute and dependent on Jewish charity.

He lived in what had been the maid's room in the girl's apartment. She had known him in his more prosperous days when he was a business acquaintance of her banker. After a while he began to call the girl who had taken him in "daughter" because she called him "father." You felt it growing on him and on her. He was a gentle old man and had never had children.

He would sit reading under the lamp in the living room of an evening, and then the two of them would drift into conversation. He would scold her gently, for she was extravagant and had little money, and she would try to justify herself just as gently.

One evening he went out for a walk with the Pekinese. A woman friend who had dropped in took up with us the matter of how dangerous it was for an Aryan girl to be living alone with a Jewish man in the apartment.

The girl was shocked and looked a little sick. Knowing them so well, I felt a little sick myself. She said that everyone knew it was not like that, and that the old man was her second father— no, her real father now.

The woman said that everyone knew but the Party might not look at it that way. Under the law, having him in the house that way could be construed as a crime for a single girl. The charge of *Rassenschande,* "race shame," was a serious business. There was frigid silence. The subject was dropped.

I remember a New Year's Eve, cold and clear. As I had been working, I got to the girl's apartment just before twelve. She had a bottle of champagne and a small supper and was wearing a party dress. The three of us were alone, the old man and she and I. He looked at her with that funny proud and worried look. She was lovely that night in that dress. Earlier she had been out to a party and was a little excited.

When we had drunk to the New Year, she put her arms around my neck and kissed me and said things she may or may not have meant. When she had gone out for a moment, the old man leaned over and said that I should try to learn to love her.

He never mentioned the matter again. Probably it was the champagne and her mood that evening that made him speak, for he was a very discreet old man.

One late afternoon I found him badly upset and with a bruise on his face. He had gone to the government's public assistance office to see if he could get aid. He had been ill and wanted to pay the doctor's bill.

In the First World War he had been on the eastern front until the collapse of Russia and had been wounded. He had received the Iron Cross. He cherished it and kept it in its box in his table in the maid's room. He had pinned it on when he went to ask for help, thinking it might count against the fact that he was a Jew.

After he had filled out the usual documents a young Nazi listened to his request.

According to what the old man told me, the young man then stood up, his face red with fury. He seized the Iron Cross, tore it off and threw it on the floor. Then he struck the old man in the face and demanded to know why a "dirty bastardly Jew" dared to come in wearing the Iron Cross.

The old man had asked to have his Iron Cross back and was told to get out before he was thrown in a concentration camp.

All afternoon he kept on mourning for his Iron Cross. He had been a good soldier, he said, and had been badly wounded and he wanted his Iron Cross back. He became very pale and agitated and cried out that Germany was his country; he loved it and had fought for it and they should give him back his Iron Cross.

Some years later his "daughter" got him out of the country and they went together to London. The outbreak of war caught them there. They had passage overseas but could not get away under wartime regulations.

That last letter told me that they were living in great poverty and that the old man was dying. I heard nothing further. I can imagine that the old man may have died in her arms.

They had been going to one of the far British dominions to

found a new home when the war and death intervened. I have often remembered those two so different homeless people sitting in the lamplight of an evening, drawn together under such strange circumstances.

14

SOMEHOW I wangled a longish leave from Berlin and went down to Marseille to catch the French vessel that sailed weekly for Tangier and Casablanca.

"Monsieur," the purser greeted me, "you are probably the only passenger in the first class who has paid the full fare himself." The ship was full of people: *fonctionnaires* going back to Morocco and the members of some veterans' group on a government-subsidized tour.

I felt left out of things, being the only passenger so naive as not to know how to avoid paying the full fare. But I did not know somebody who knew somebody in France. Americans in Europe, even old-timers such as I was becoming, are always paying the full fare. It is a national vice. Apparently we are not an economical people.

I had not had Latins around me for some time and that familiar relaxation set in. The French are a nervous people. Even they, however, relax you. Their way of talking with gestures is part of it and a good deal of it also is the use of the bon mot. Words go together in sudden patterns that dissolve again in a constant effervescence to make way for new ones. This game of skill played with sentence structure and shades of meaning is refreshing, like taking a sort of mental Bromo Seltzer.

It was also relaxing to get away from the fraudulence of the slogan-filled atmosphere of National Socialist Germany. The French are pessimistic belittlers, but they do not have the German *Weltschmerz,* that wrestling with life which exhausts everyone but a German.

On the ship was the *"culte de femme,"* that awareness of women, the constant awareness of their exciting quality, with which only Latins succeed in spicing the menu of everyday.

The whole business of there being two different kinds of us seems to have taken on a special meaning among the Latins. It is sharpened into an irony, an intoxicating irony. Few of the Frenchwomen I have seen have been glamorous. I did not move in the more fashionable circles. American women are probably more beautiful and they certainly have longer legs, a matter Europeans always mention with approval. But with American women you just do not have that feeling that there is something seductively ironical about their being different from men.

A *fonctionnaire* going to Morocco again, who had known fairly well the American colony in Paris, got into conversation with me on the subject. He thought that American women had all the separate elements of charm but that they were like a young wine that has not yet become a palatable beverage. We let it go at that. I was no authority.

The trip down to Morocco and southern Spain was a voyage into the unknown. I did not know what I was sailing into, nor did I foresee that it would forever haunt me a little like the sharp minor song of reed instruments.

The Arabs call the Barbary lands in the western half of the north coast of Africa, between the sands of the Sahara and the waters of the sea, the Djezira-el-Maghreb, the Western Isle, rightfully feeling that anything that can be reached only through the wastes of the desert or by the sea, is an island.

I was to come to Spain from the Western Isle as the Arabs had come in the Middle Ages. It gave Spain a different meaning.

Morocco was then still the Morocco of that first French resident general, Lyautey—a feudal kingdom with a civil engineering veneer. There were nationalists and accompanying issues even then but I knew little about them. After the coming World War there would be great changes and conflict in Morocco, but that was a long way off.

In Spain there was a republic at that moment. It did not matter. There was always something political in Spain that did not matter. I am not sure even now that anything political in Spain ever really matters—Spaniards themselves remain unchanged.

This trip was an escape from issues into reality. Issues foreshorten reality. They turn the world into headlines. Life is not about headlines. It is timeless or it is nothing.

I spent a night in the *quartier défendu* of Fez, an ancient Moroccan city. They let you in the little gate in the wall, one by one past the French sentry. If you were a soldier, you had to have a ticket to prove that it was your night to sin. To the military there was nothing improper about sin—but it must be on the night laid down in the orders of the day. The French can be very meticulous.

Inside, the streets were narrow and the houses more or less alike. Most houses had a large room in the center with tables. In the corner on cushions sat an Oriental band made up mainly of black men. Commonly they sat stripped to the waist with their instruments in front of them, and sweat rolled slowly down the creased fat on their shining bellies.

Around the central room were little rooms with curtained doorways. Men got up with women and went into these rooms.

You did not have to. The houses were also what would be called café concert in Europe. It was the place to hear Arab music. Possibly a majority of the customers came actually to listen to the music, excepting naturally the soldiers who had their tickets and, so to speak, an obligation.

In the place where I went with an Arabic-speaking acquaintance from the hotel, the Negro singers and musicians were halfway through a long, anatomical description, set to music, of some Arab's beloved. You needed an interpreter to get the idea. It started, I was told, with the lovely locks of her hair and her rosy toenails. It went on and on about her ankles and the mole on her throat, alternately. The longer it lasted the shriller it got with a grand resounding of cymbals at the end. Arabs, I was to discover later, are like that. The Freudians say everybody is.

Having done the singing commercial for the house, the musicians turned to music.

That night they sang the old Moroccan songs of longing for the lost land of Andalucia beyond the great strait to the north. The Moors had not forgotten Cordova and Granada, the seven hundred years of Arab speech and Moorish rule in Spain. I was to find, in the hot streets and little squares of Seville and in the countryside of Andalucia, that southern Spain had not forgotten either.

The question of whether Africa begins at the Pyrenees as the French say or begins gently as you come south through the Iberian Peninsula is a difficult one to answer. Arabianized Africa has certainly left a heritage in southern Spain. There are no courtyards quite like the Moorish or Andalucian courtyards, no fountains as refreshing as these here, objects of the water-worship of men from arid lands. The gardens, with that walled-in stillness and hushed light, filled with flowers and fragrant shrubs and the murmur of moving water, are a refuge from the world. The Arab had brought to the Western Isle and to Spain the desert's desire for rest from the heat of the day.

With the Arab had come also the melancholy, minor-key music of the East, with its sense of anxiety, its rhythmic monotony and its mood of remembered despair. The passionate tremolo song of Andalucia, artificial and exotic, could only have come from the Arab, out of those seven hundred fantastic years when the crescent flew from the towers of Spanish cities and muezzins called to prayer.

Black Africa is present too in this meeting place of Africa and Europe where the tidal currents of human migrations have mingled. Moorish sultans had ruled in Timbuktu. The common bond of Islam had brought Negro clans from West Africa into Morocco and there had been many slaves. The word "Moor" to old Europe meant a Negro. His link to the mysterious area of the West African kingdoms, to the sultanates out on

the desert and on the distant Niger, had added something inexplicable to the Moor and had its influence beyond the Strait of
Gibraltar.

In Rabat I saw for the first time the high-stepping grace of
the true Negro when the Sultan's resplendent *guardes noires*
marched. I did not understand what I was to half-comprehend
later: these were men inwardly free of the burdens of freedom.

In Fez I saw that where the French system of the *ville neuve*,
the isolated French colonial town some distance away from the
Moorish city, had left old urban Morocco largely as it was.
France had an archeological respect for what it had found in
Morocco. Lyautey, founder of the French regime in Morocco,
had set up a system of co-existence that did not shatter Islamic
tradition and the old arts of living.

Even in these times Fez was still a secretive city, hiding its
charm behind blank walls. There was an inner wall around the
bazaar. The palace of the sultan was another walled-off domain
within the city. Nestled up against it for protection and likewise
defended with walls was the Jewish quarter. At night most of
the gates were closed and you could enter or leave only in the
presence of guards.

Fez lived the old life. In mosques the rule about taking off
your shoes or covering them with cloth slippers was strictly
enforced. There were a few houses, their interiors resplendent
with mosaic tile, which you could visit, but only when accompanied by some official or guide.

The hotel of the Société Trans-Atlantique at Fez was a former pasha's palace on the hillside just outside the city walls. I
felt that I had never before seen a real garden when I saw the
terraces there. They were full of orange trees and fragrant
shrubs and flowers in disorder, a massed mixture of colors.
Water fell from basin to basin with a chanting, metallic sound.

In the distance were the flat roofs of houses where people
lived in the early mornings and late afternoons, and the minarets
of the mosques of Fez. The singsong of venders in the narrow
streets came softly as from a long way off.

When the day came to leave, I had to be almost dragged away
from a seat on the corner of the terrace looking down over all

that. When boyhood is gone and youth is beginning to pass away, you do not like to leave such a place on a clean-washed morning for you know that you will be tormented with memories. It is perhaps better never to have truly lived but to exist immersed in the routine of the years. Remembered peace can be great bitterness.

Cádiz is a tight, closely built-up island in the sea linked to the Spanish mainland by a long sandspit. People live on balconies and in open windows and in intimate little squares among the streets. It is like seeing a play, for everyone seems to have just room enough to move around within the confines of the stage. Nothing is concealed and everyone seems to be looking into everyone else's windows as if the stage had been set so that no one would miss anything.

There was not too much to visit except a few altar pieces in the churches and the historic hall where the Cortes of Cádiz met in a troubled moment in the history of Spain. For the rest of the time it was good to sit with a cup of black coffee at a table in front of a café, feeling like a walk-on extra charged by the stage manager with nothing more important than looking wise and a little debonair.

The principals in the play were fishmongers, market women, street gamins, officers very much in uniform, lounging soldiers and dark-eyed girls wearing shawls who walked the way all women should walk to make life more exciting. Occasionally young men in groups played guitars.

After watching the drama in one of those tight little squares, the atmosphere further heightened by the nice stage work of ships' lights bobbing about in the great bay of Cádiz, you went to sleep in a high old Spanish bed and presented in your dreams your own version of *Carmen*.

The most practical man I had ever met was my friend, the doctor in Seville. I had become badly sunburned and was laid up for several days under his care. He was British, had taken a medical degree, done a successful internship in a London hospital and was ready for a proper career in the fogs of London. Then he went to Seville on a vacation.

He told me that upon his return he had sat down and given serious thought to what mattered in life. He had evaluated success, what you could buy with money in London, family connections and so on. All those things were impermanent. In a very businesslike fashion, as he described it, he had decided that sunshine mattered.

He had wanted to be useful, not a parasite, and in any case was under the necessity of earning a living. He had, fortunately, a profession useful anywhere. So he settled in Seville and launched into his lifelong affair with the sunshine.

The sun had not abandoned him and presumably would not. In the course of events he had acquired a Sevilliana as wife and the Sevilliana had acquired a family. The Sevilliana apparently shared him with the sunshine in a slightly polygamous arrangement, emotionally speaking, but was not jealous, which is unusual for a Sevilliana.

She was in fact better off than many of her sisters. The doctor had the passionate vocabulary of a Don Juan but his only mistress was the sun.

Otherwise, he was not the passionate type but a solid, neatly dressed and graying medical practitioner, very prompt with his bills and sure of what he was doing. He had a proper and encouraging but not particularly sympathetic bedside manner.

It is, when you think of it, odd that the American businessman considers himself, and is considered by others, the acme of practicality. His wife is the most expensive woman on earth. He is hagridden by ambition and prepared to sacrifice health and happiness to bigger and better thumbtacks. He is adamant, however, on how practical he is and on how impractical people are who go at life differently. Between better thumbtacks, that family of his and his famous civic or similar obligations, he comes close to being a martyr without a crown—and he says he is being practical.

The better I got to know my doctor the more I became convinced that he was just the dry, practical man he looked. He merely knew what being practical means.

The doctor's son and I took off in the latter's rather rickety car for Cordova, passed under the tower, La Calahorra, onto the Moorish bridge leading into the town and ended up in front of the largest of all mosques, started in the eighth century and completed in the eleventh. It had been transformed into a cathedral. Inside we got lost, as nearly everyone does, among the 850 pillars and in the 48 aisles. The original edifice had occupied nearly the same area as St. Peter's in Rome.

Cordova had been the seat of the western caliphate and once was the most learned and civilized city in Europe. This immense mosque of the Ommiad Dynasty had been built to make Cordova a greater religious center than the cities of the eastern caliphate.

We went down the next morning through rolling hills covered with gray-green olive groves, past towers perched on jutting rocks and through the dusty poverty of pueblos into the *vega* of Granada and saw on its high hill the Alhambra of the Moors, last stand of the crescent on the soil of Spain.

There in crenelated stone against the distant line of the Sierra Nevada was one of the reasons for the nostalgia of the Moorish songs for the lost land. That forest park with the water rushing down, the courts and the pools of the Alhambra, the gardens of the Generalife were not real. They had been built in unreality when the caliphate of the west was gone and the Moorish empire was fading into extinction. But, for all those who have been there, it is something good to remember when the emptiness of the years fades into the unfulfillment that comes to by far the majority of men.

We went from Granada through the wild high country to the ridge above the Mediterranean where the last of the Moorish kings had turned to look back into his lost kingdom, and then we continued down the precipitous highway into Málaga and so to Gibraltar.

That evening the doctor's son went back to Seville and I sat in the garden of the hotel on the Spanish side of the bay at Algeciras and watched the light fade from the great rock. The ship would sail for Marseille tomorrow.

There come those moments when time moving on is an intolerable burden and you do not want tomorrow.

That was what the doctor had found. He had rid himself of

the need for tomorrow. It is part of the bigotry of the dynamic society, of the cult of success, to deny that those who do not need tomorrow can feel the need to work, to participate, to produce. I knew that I had no desire for idleness but at that moment I was soul-weary of tomorrow and wondered if I had not learned something quite important about life. Perhaps we shall not come home until we are weary of change and have given it a proper place as a secondary matter. Change has become an obsession and a new morality. Change has become a moral imperative, a primary virtue in itself.

The doctor had found the sun, his work and his patio in Spain. I coveted that peace. The sense of something close to desperation came over me with the doubt that I should ever find peace for myself.

The P and O liner that sailed the following day was outbound from London via Gibraltar and Marseille for Indian ports.

I remember little about that fast passage up to Marseille except the matter of the cream-colored suit.

After stowing my small bag in the cabin, I went down to the first-class dining salon to reserve a seat at a table for dinner. The chief steward put my name on a list. Then, since my cabin steward had been off duty when I came on board, the chief steward asked when I wanted my clothes laid out and my bath drawn. I said that I had my clothes on.

We paused. The chief steward, I could see, was struggling. Our minds had not met.

What he meant, he explained gently, was when did I want my dinner clothes laid out? There was emphasis on the dinner clothes. I responded once again, as I remember, that I was wearing them. The chief steward became unhappy and looked at me closely. He said that what he meant by my dinner clothes was my dinner clothes, and presumably I wanted them laid out. He evidently felt that this statement was clear enough for anyone and should clinch the matter.

There was nothing for it but to explain. The cream-colored suit with chocolate-colored dots which I was wearing was all I had taken to Morocco and southern Spain and I had nothing else with me. I had been banging around in autobuses, the kind where natives rode on the roof and people put chicken crates in your lap.

He wanted to know how I expected to dine if I had no clothes. I repeated that I had clothes. I had them on. He granted that but countered that in order to dine you had to have dinner clothes, did you not? He now felt he had solid ground under his feet and said that, lacking dinner clothes, I should of course dine in my cabin. It being a small cabin and hot, I said no, I would of course dine in the dining salon.

The chief steward was still thinking this clearly impossible and I was continuing to be stubborn about it when he suddenly remembered something. There was a colonel of the Indian Army on board who had no clothes. I said that seemed interesting as I had never seen a colonel of any army in the raw.

The chief steward looked increasingly British. Apparently he felt that the booking office was getting unduly careless. He pushed on and said that the colonel ate behind a palm. I was shown the palm behind which a small table had been hidden. That night the colonel and I ate shamefacedly, hidden from the sight of the more fortunate passengers.

15

IN A SUCCESSION of letters to my parents I had claimed to be incredibly miserable by myself in Berlin and hinted that I was going straight to the dogs, which, defined in terms of my father's New England morality, was perhaps not so far from the facts. The letters finally had the desired effect. Because they felt that I must be in a bad way, my parents came over to Europe.

Several months before they made the long trip, my father had been retired. I had known what this would mean to him. My father was at heart very much the modern man. Success was not his deity but neither did he value life for its own sake. Living was doing. It is a characteristic of the modern man.

My mother, at the moment of my father's retirement, did the one cruel thing of her life. The rector of a fairly large church in a Pennsylvania city had asked father to live there and help with various duties such as visiting the sick, celebrating occasional early communion services, and so on. It would have been difficult for my father with his miniature pension and only a little help from that parish, but he longed to do it.

My mother would have none of it. She owned a little house in Lynn, Massachusetts, opposite the house where she had been born. Though they would be strangers in Lynn after all the years, she sought security in that little house. It had become the passion of her life.

Convinced that the longer my father stayed away from Lynn where he had nothing to do, the better off he would be, I had described my aforementioned circumstances. And so they came, though rather with the air of doing something completely daft.

My father had always had some difficulty in getting through to adults, but he had a miraculous way with babies, an old man's affinity for those small creatures who have come so recently from another shore. His long ear lobes were a professional asset. When he was presented with a sprawling infant to be baptized, the baby would take a look at those ear lobes, grab hold of one and lie there in his arms, gurgling contentedly through the ceremony.

I shall always remember him standing in the light from stained-glass windows in his black cassock and white surplice with a child in his arms. He would look into the infant's wide lovely eyes as though searching for something. A man of child-like faith, he was perhaps seeking some knowledge of the land from where he believed they came and to which he believed that he was traveling.

My father was firmly against alcohol, but I had acquired in Europe the habit of taking a glass of wine with my dinner. He noted the fact after he arrived in Berlin. It did not make him happy but he did not openly object. I was a grown man. Then at dinner one evening I saw a wine glass at his place. He took the wine bottle, poured his glass full and slowly drank it. I could see he did not like it but he drank it down. I smiled for I understood, though I doubt if he and I were thinking of the same thing.

Once a story had been told to my father by his own father, a man firmly convinced of the actuality of brimstone and hell-fire. It was the story of another man who was of the same stamp and fully convinced of the reality of heaven and hell.

That man had two sons. They had led evil lives that scandalized the whole town but their stern old Puritan father had loved them. He would not ban them from his house as he had been advised. Both of them died—in the vivid language of that sternly righteous community—full of iniquity. Soon afterward the old man himself felt death approaching. To the shock and horror of his fellow churchmen he plunged into a senile and debasing career of what he fully conceived to be mortal sin. He did not last long at that rate. In his death agony he babbled that he must go to his sons for they were in torment. He had given what he had left to give, his immortal soul.

My father had used that story in a sermon and had, perhaps unwittingly, been most unorthodox, for he had said that God the Father would have found the sins of that old man more precious than all his life of righteousness.

In my father's eyes the wine-drinking was certainly not a very serious matter but he still felt it was a little wrong. He drank the stuff because he was not going to watch me do alone something that was not quite right.

In Berlin he found the American Church closed. He opened it and was quite happy for a time, then handed it over to a young pastor. Later he heard that the American Church in Florence,

Italy, had no pastor, and my father and mother went down there for the winter. When I went to Italy in the late spring for my vacation, the church in Florence had finally found a younger pastor and my parents left with me to visit Rome.

By then my mother knew the city of Florence and its famous galleries by heart but my father had seen none of it. He had been completely wrapped up in his church work. He said little, but he was all broken up because he had to leave. It was the end of his work, the burial before the grave. He still wanted to participate.

The years of my father's waiting for death taught me the price we have paid for the passing of the old world where the generations lived united and families earned a common livelihood. The aged are the outcasts in our modern world. Unless they have made their fortune and have purchasing power to contribute, they are only tolerated in the dynamic society. They have no part in movement, change and tomorrow and therefore no part in life at all.

In the weeks before his death, when pain had undermined his will and his natural reticence, my father told me frankly what those years had meant. From him I learned to hope that I would be spared old age or would find some means of escaping from the brave new world, the dynamic society, before old age reached me.

Even after returning to Lynn my father kept busy somehow. At the age of seventy-five he built a garage and I received a harassed letter from my mother saying that he was up on the garage nailing down roofing. She concluded abruptly that she was going out there to stand underneath because "the old fool will fall off and bust like an egg."

But Lynn was never home; I wonder where home was for him.

Before they returned to America they had spent some time in England. I had paid for a Cook's Tour for them against the violent expostulations of my father. His Yankee independence had rebelled against taking something from me that he could not afford himself. He was silenced by the argument that my mother had a right to see England. And my mother's few protests were silenced by the argument that my father, as an Episcopalian clergyman, should have the opportunity to see the English cathedrals.

They left Paris bound directly for Canterbury. The channel crossing was rough and my mother was most unhappy but she kept her Irish humor. She wrote me that at the worst moment, when she was quite ill, she found herself firmly gripped in the strong left arm of a deck hand who inquired, "Would you care to use this basin, Maudom?"

She said it would have been discourteous not to comply and she found it helped. She took the incident as a striking example of British good manners.

When they got to Canterbury, they were taken by Cook's to a calm inn out on the edge of the cathedral city. According to my mother, there was a bright fire in the fireplace and the room was cheerful and intimate in a very English fashion. Through the big bow window you could see the green lawns and, despite the rain, the towers of the great church in the distance. My mother wrote they were tired when they arrived and so were glad to be where it was quiet and restful.

But my father wrote one sentence on a card: "It is good to be home again."

I did not know quite what he meant. He was the first member of his family to visit the British Isles in the two centuries or more since his forebears had sailed for the New World. Also, he never indulged in anything poetic or strange. From what he told me afterward, he had written the message almost without knowing why, almost as if someone had been guiding his hand.

Perhaps he was not alone in that "home again" feeling. We Americans have made great sacrifices to keep alive the European civilization of our forefathers. We are proudly tough-minded about it now. We need Europe, we say, to aid us against Russia. Are we hiding something from ourselves?

We, the North Americans, are a migratory people. How much of the notorious nomadism of Americans within the continent is a restlessness, a seeking for something we cannot quite find?

Also, there has never been anything in the history of travel like the great annual American trek to Europe. The largest ships and the greatest air fleets in the world cannot cope with it. I wonder if historians one day will not find this phenomenon intriguing.

Returning to Germany after my parents had left, I began to feel that it was impossible for me to stay there. Germany, this drugged and herded mass of people, fanaticized and hypnotized, was becoming unbearable. The pattern was now clear. Hitler had to go on. He started with Austria and the *Anschluss*. Then he went to work on Czechoslovakia's German-populated Sudetenland.

It was at this time that Herbert Hoover came to Germany on a European tour. With him was the editor and general manager of the San Francisco *Chronicle,* Paul Smith, then about twenty-nine years old. Because of his hard work the conservative *Chronicle* had waked up, and he had also found time to come with Hoover to smooth out the former President's public relations. It has never been a secret that Herbert Hoover had trouble with public relations.

I had known Paul rather well some years before when he had lived for a time in Berlin and had hung around Knickerbocker's office a great deal. It was the only case I can recall of two red-headed, freckle-faced people being attracted to each other.

During the Hoover visit Paul and I talked about my going to work for him in San Francisco. My final decision to accept his offer was made on not very rational grounds. It was influenced by such things as INS correspondent Pierre Huss's account of drinking long cool glasses of fresh orange juice under the oaks at his parents' home in Palo Alto. I accepted, with the proviso that I first go to the Far East on my own.

Possibly I wanted to get settled in life. California out on the west coast of the United States was not within the territory which I regarded as "back there" and would just as soon not see again.

The idea of "back there" had come to have a fairly precise

definition in my mind. It was not the whole country—America. "Back there" was roughly the area north of the Mason-Dixon line and east of the Mississippi River. "Back there" was the northeastern and north-central industrial and commercial heart of the nation; it was the country where I came from. "Back there" was the country where they took the joy out of life, the place where everything went wrong, where you suffered and were humiliated and from which you strove to escape. The rest of the United States was not part of "back there." It was "out here."

A professor teaching contemporary cultural anthropology or sociology could have told me that "back there" was the world's most intensive and vigorous center of ultra-modern industrial civilization in combination with the free competitive economy. It was the supreme symbol of and, as such, an exaggeration of modern Western man's concept of life with its scale of values and a related system of production and distribution.

I, in my blindness, thought of its people as stodgy. Youth tends to think of anything familiar as stodgy.

Only slowly through the years, as I became aware of the pattern of human experience over the milleniums, I began to understand that circumstances had combined to produce in the people "back there" one of the most remarkable groups of human beings that had existed in the seventy centuries of recorded history. The conviction, long difficult to accept, grew on me that, as placed against the perspective of the human story as a whole, the people "back there" were both outrageous and extraordinary, that they were radical and in their way fanatical. Their conformism, which I mistook for stodginess, was an aspect of that fanaticism, or at least very definite radicalism.

They were the members of the free competitive society in the form it had taken in the greatest of the purely immigrant societies. Their history began little further back than with the beginning of contemporary Western civilization, the epoch of the industrial revolution and the merchandizing age.

Whole libraries would be written about them. Their idiosyncrasies and astounding accomplishments would fascinate generations of men. I should come to see that they were possibly quite mad and certainly inspired.

But a conservatism, of which I was only slowly becoming aware, made me doubt the validity of the pattern of living into which I had been born.

My parting from Berlin after those many years was brutally informal. I felt nothing. Finding that my total belongings went into two bags, packed in one hour, I rushed for the train.

I was going through Prague, Budapest, Belgrade and Sofia to Istanbul and then, via Athens, across to Alexandria and would pick up a Japanese liner at the Suez Canal. Between trains at Budapest I sat on the terrace of one of the cafés by the Danube in Pest and looked across at the massive pile of the Hapsburgs' imperial palace and the old royal town on the high rock of Buda.

Europe was still at peace. The café orchestras were playing. Hungarian women were still the most voluptuous that Europe had to offer. They dressed with a flair for the dramatic that possibly only the women of Budapest ever achieved in quite that way. The coffee made all other coffee, except for Arab black, just a brown brew in a cup. I began to wonder what on earth tempted me to leave Europe.

There was just enough time in Belgrade to discover that it still could not make up its mind whether to be an overgrown Balkan village or the capital of a kingdom. Sofia, capital of Bulgaria, was still a Turkish provincial town with Mid-Victorian ambitions.

Toward the end of that long trip there was only one *wagon-lit* and one faithful diner left, shifting from one local train to another, and two other passengers. One was a fat man who looked so much like a smuggler that he could not possibly have been one. The other was a nondescript woman who could sleep longer than any mortal I have ever seen outside of a hospital. Like the dormouse of *Alice in Wonderland,* she slept through the entire Balkan country. So we rattled on toward Istanbul.

A couple of days later I stood aboard the little Rumanian steamer which plowed down through the Dardanelles and across the Aegean to stop at Piraeus, where we stayed all day.

Then, with the sun sinking in the west in a storm of brazen color, we headed out from the Athenian coast south toward Alexandria. I looked back to see Piraeus and Athens mixed with the shadows. The silhouette of the Attic ranges became only faintly visible. But the last of the day centered and lingered on the Acropolis. The columns of the Parthenon were bathed in long streamers of light from the west. How could one better bid Europe farewell? There is no nobler symbol of Europe's eternal verities than that arid hill in Greece.

Part Three

Far East

16

In a small hotel at Port Tewfik at the southern end of the Suez Canal, I met the first officer of a sea-going scrap heap that sat in a dry dock at near-by Suez. He told me about life on that boat and invited me to come along for what turned out to be the hottest meal I ever sat through. The boat was a Red Sea tramp.

The vessel's engines were old. Her officers, all British, told me the temperature in the engine room went to one hundred and thirty Fahrenheit. With the noonday sun beating down on the concrete dry dock, the temperature in that tiny steel mess-room where we ate rose to a hundred. Through much of the meal I was fighting to stay conscious.

The men on the ship were "out East" people, the Conrad types. I discovered what "East of Suez" meant. Britain still ruled the great semicircle drawn from Australia up over Malaya and India and down the African east coast to the Cape of Good Hope. Hard living breeds men and they were the Empire, they and their like ashore. They had worked all manner of shabby country ships up and down the coasts of India and out Singapore way.

What struck me was that they were not rough men. They did not speak English with the Mayfair or Oxford accent but still they bore themselves with that shoulders-thrown-back air of a Guards officer. They wore clean uniforms and were clean-shaven.

They knew all the Arab mares that ran in the races in Cairo,

117

and I gathered they all had the same inordinate capacity for whisky as the first officer had shown in the hotel. Blithely they referred to natives as "niggers," by which they did not mean blacks. They knew the old saw about the British colonel's saying that "the niggers begin at Calais" but did not subscribe to it. On the other hand, although they had been so much about the world, they looked blank when I brought up that other old one about the London *Times* headline that said "Continent Isolated" when there was a big storm in the English Channel. From their standpoint, the continent *had* been isolated.

What is striking about the British out in the world is how British they are. They carry their home with them. Home, to the British, is an attitude. It is a discipline, knowing precisely what you don't do and sometimes what you should do.

An American once told me about the British crews of the desert pumping stations on the pipe line that brought Iraq oil to the Mediterranean. They were completely isolated without a woman of their breed within leagues. But every night they bathed, dressed in formal dinner rig, stood about having their before-dinner drink and dined in their barracks as if they were in one of the best London clubs. The American said it did wonders for his morale.

The British have been able to carry home with them all around the world because home was something one worked at, a daily ritual which resulted in ever more solid tradition.

I had a feeling that tradition was even stronger among those men on that rust-eaten hulk trading to Red Sea ports than it was in the industrial towns of England. They seemed even more British, even more profoundly at home.

A ship is a protection against the too-many-ness of us going in so many directions that makes the world unhomelike. After I got used to the sea I felt a sense of moral security on a ship. The Japanese use the word *Maru* as part of the name of all their ships. Also referring to walled castles, the word means a thing closed or completed within itself.

One of the best cures for loneliness is a long sea voyage. You feel lost when you finally go on land. You do not get that feeling of security, however, on one of those monstrous ferryboats that make the five-day haul from New York to Cherbourg and Southampton and back. I don't consider them real ships.

I had ships on my mind at that point, for I had come to Port Tewfik to start a long sea voyage.

When I climbed up the ladder on the side of the *Terukuni Maru* it was with a sense of going into a friendly house and closing the door happily behind me. And I felt a vast sense of relaxation when I saw her sailing notice from Port Said still hanging at the purser's office, saying that the *S.S. Terukuni Maru* was sailing for Colombo, Singapore, Hongkong, Shanghai, Kobe and Yokohama. It would be a long trip.

Weighing about 12,500 tons, she was not a large vessel but she was a well-built full liner. She flew the flag of the commodore of the Nippon Yusan Keisha's European service, for her captain was the senior captain of the line.

The captain, a Eurasian, was nearly as round as long. His father had been a British marine engineer who had married into a good Japanese family. I believe it was one of the families that founded the line.

A very orderly man, he would get down on his knees, fat as he was, and run his finger along under the bunks on inspection, something few ship's captains must consider part of their duties.

In the monsoon, which we hit as soon as we came out of the Gulf of Aden, he made a rather grotesque picture as he stood on the bridge snipping at his dwarf pine tree. He had been brought up a proper Japanese and had an affection for that little tree such as only a Japanese could have. Balancing his bulk and swaying in the roaring monsoon, he would carefully snip here and snip there with his shears until he was quite sure the tree had had a proper haircut.

Sailing in that infernal monsoon was like being locked in a rolling steam bath; I got outrageously seasick. One of the things that depress you so when you are seasick is the healthy brute who goes swaggering around the place on his sea legs. My captain was very Japanese. He sat down next to me as I was lying on a sofa in the ship's lounge and commiserated with me, saying that he did not feel very well and never did in the monsoon. Then he rose and went to play his game of ping-pong for a couple of hours with his customary vigor.

I recall one other non-Japanese passenger on the ship besides myself. He was British counseler to the line, married to a French woman, and occasionally referred to as white Japanese because he had been out in Japan so long. Also on board was a Japanese writer, a neat little man who looked like a rather dry lawyer but who was actually an expert in the field of child psychology.

Younger children on the boat, I had noted, seemed to run around quite wild. Older children were impressively subdued and proper.

The Englishman and my writer friend explained that this was the traditional system. Everything changed at the age of puberty. Children were then forced into their obligations to society with a rigidity which Western young people could not have tolerated. Much later in Africa I found that same sharp emphasis on the age of puberty where it is connected with the most important tribal ceremonies and is considered the great moment, the fundamental turning point in every man and woman's life.

The young savage is given time to work off his normal antagonisms, rebellions, dislike for restraints and so on. When restraint comes, it encounters a personality ready to emerge from the child's world of fantasy and disordered emotions and able to accept the fact of society.

To an Occidental suddenly thrown into a small, purely Japanese shipboard society, the spectacle was quite miraculous. Young children were completely unrestrained, and what kept them all from jumping overboard, except a remnant of common sense, I do not know. Older children, getting into or beyond puberty, were perfect ladies and gentlemen, rather painfully so.

The old Japan was a peculiar civilization, my two friends said. It was a highly developed society completely rooted in primitive custom and experience. The Japanese had gone one better the British traditionalism which carries elements of feudalism and other older societies right into the ultramodern world. The Japanese had brought with him his entire history, including primitive man himself.

I learned another thing about the Japanese social system, this time by experience.

There was a couple on board, about thirty years old. They came from fairly high Japanese society. The young man was connected with one of the principal Japanese banks and the wife belonged to a very influential family.

I got enthusiastic about both of them. The husband, like many passengers, was generally engaged in an interminable game of Japanese chess, and the wife, accordingly, had more time to talk. She had had a first-class education. The two of us took to walking around the deck, now and then passing through the narrow doors in the partition that separated the first-class deck from the second.

One day as I was resting in a deck chair the husband came and sat down next to me. He looked unhappy and did not speak for a moment. Finally he said that I had been walking around the deck a great deal with his wife. Both an icy feeling and a flush of embarrassment went through me. To be suspected of being more than friendly with his wife was awful. And how did you explain that it could not possibly be so without making things worse?

The husband went on to say that the Japanese people on board had noticed something that was embarrassing for his wife. I wanted to crawl away somewhere. What could I say?

Then he came out with it. It seems I always stood back and let her go first through those narrow doors. This was quite proper as I was Western, but there were many older Japanese men and women on board and since his wife was a young woman of good family, he asked me as a courtesy to her to walk through doors first. This ship, he said, was like a part of Japan and that constant breaking of tradition on the part of a Japanese woman jarred people.

After that, out of courtesy, I strode through the doors first and let her trail behind in accord with tradition.

For a man brought up in the great American matriarchy, the experience was embarrassing but there was also a certain satisfaction in it. I had been a minister's son and as a boy had lived with a man and woman who had been haunted by female tyranny.

My father's happiness and our livelihoods depended on the women of the parish. It was their attitude toward the minister's personality that decided whether the parish was a success and whether we stayed or moved on. There had always been a string of them, Mrs. So-and-So and Miss Such-and-Such, who threw a depression over our mealtimes. In every parish they were at work. The expression "able mind," usually referring to a big-busted vigorous woman who wanted to boss the parish, was one I heard regularly. My gentle father, already aging when I first became aware of such things, for I was born rather late in his life, was harassed by the determination of women to rule. In my little boy's world of images they became dragons.

On the ship, as I went striding ahead through those doors, followed by that young woman, I think the little boy took a shame-faced, peek-over-your-shoulder satisfaction in at last finding himself among people where women knew their confounded place.

Something else crept up on me during that voyage. I found myself trying to imitate the Oriental custom of bowing, the depth of one's bow indicated by the relative status of the other to oneself. The feeling for their eternal kowtowing got into me. They would keep on bowing, the lesser in age or status bowing a little lower than the other. They kept it up, one, two, three, several times, until they had satisfied all obligations of courtesy.

They used a little of that ceremonial language with which they normally regulated their own human relations in greeting me or talking to me.

This feeling for formality, the clearer recognition of people's relative status, was another thing which had been learned by peoples who had brought all their experience along into the present in one form or another. The British had it, too, as had the continental Europeans.

The first-person, "Hi, Joe" attitude toward the boss had always appeared to me to be a piece of blatant hypocrisy. All it does is leave you naked in your actual relation to the boss. "Hi, Joe," is the jerk's democracy. Authority and relative rank are facts, ever present and compelling. I found formality in such relations refreshing because it is honest and comforting and because it places you on a solid basis of reality.

In most European languages there is another device that is important—the intimate form of the pronoun "you." It permits people to establish the relationship of intimacy, of personal friendship, where it actually exists. The other, more common form of the pronoun prevails as between people who are not intimate. English no longer makes such a distinction and is to that extent an inadequate language.

It was typical of the jerk's democracy that so many Americans in war and occupation times later picked up the intimate form of the pronoun. They used it where there was no intimacy and created the impression that they thought they were talking to inferiors.

Possibly it was my father's influence that made me sensitive to those things. He belonged to another America, the more honest one, before the phony folksiness appeared as an opiate against the actual impact of hierarchy in the modern business and public bureaucracies.

You could hardly imagine my father saying "Hi, Joe" to the bishop. When he spoke to someone in that way it was a warm and real thing.

I remember that when I was young my father told me with considerable emphasis, so that I would remember it, the classic story of Thomas Jefferson's raising his hat to the slave who had raised his own hat to him and Jefferson's remark that he did not want a slave to be more of a gentleman than he.

Japanese, as I was to learn later when I studied the language, had developed a whole complex of grammatical usages to be employed between people of different status. That was the other extreme from jerk's democracy. It went too far and was even then being simplified.

17

Flagged gallantly, despite the rain that was like a darkness over Kobe, the *Terukuni Maru* rode into the harbor, her siren bellowing, for on the bridge they could hardly see. Rain rolled down on us in waves of wind-driven water. In the semidarkness the ship thundered again and again her warning to small craft. A fleet of tugs and launches gathered around her and signals flashed from the shore out of the gathering night. She was home from the sea.

Employees of the line telephoned me from the dock that they could not reserve a room in the hotel up on the hillside above Kobe where I had meant to stay. I took a rickshaw, which was a stupid thing to do in that rain, and started off up into the city.

It was late at night. When I saw what was obviously a railway station, I made frantic motions to the rickshaw boy and we pulled in there. I did not know how to tell him to take me to a hotel anyway. What I could do was get a ticket to Osaka, a city farther east.

That rain made me a little dizzy. There had never been such a rain. It was like a bombardment. The city shook under it and water was running right into the station.

In Osaka there were hotel porters in the station who spoke English, and I was soon tight in bed in the New Osaka Hotel listening to that unbelievable rain and glad to be out of it. The next morning I learned there had been a tremendous flood in Kobe. A dam in the hills behind the city had broken. A wing of the hotel where I had meant to stay had been swept away.

All connections with Kobe were broken and rescue columns were fighting through oceans of mud toward the central section. Hundreds had been drowned. A good many had died trapped in the subway tunnel. The porter who had brought me to the hotel told me that my train had been the last one in. After that the tracks had washed away.

Japan was a land of catastrophes of nature. It lived from earthquake to earthquake, and villages and towns were constantly being swept away by storms and floods. The violence of the forces of nature may have helped to keep alive that primitive nature worship which presented the world with the strange spectacle of an industrialized, intensely modern state still living inwardly in primitive times, adoring rocks and trees, dedicated to the sun goddess, Amaterasu Omikami, and making no essential distinction between the living and the dead. Japan was populated by a spirit world of men and things, of benevolent and malign forces, going back to the most ancient forms of human experience that elsewhere had faded from the minds of modern men.

Once in Tokyo I went with four or five executives, well-tailored, efficient, busy men, to a shrine on the roof of the large establishment which they directed and from which they did business throughout the world. The shrine was, as I could understand it, one of the occasional dwelling places of the spirits of the founders of the firm, or at least they could be reached there. These very modern, crisp gentlemen went up there to report certain measures that they had taken. They clapped their hands to summon the spirits and then told the founders all about it, much as if they had only retired and now could be called on at their club. There was no evidence of exaltation or anything strange about it. The founders had a right to know and might be troublesome if things were not explained to them, and so a report was made as part of the day's business.

Osaka was rather a shock to me. It is one of the world's big cities. The morning after I arrived I went up on the roof of a fairly high building. As far as I could see there were smoking stacks of factories. In the center, streets were paved and there were main arteries leading to various districts, but elsewhere a crooked network of unpaved lanes and roads twisted through a debris of houses, small factories and sheds that looked like packing cases thrown into a huge junk yard. Canals were everywhere.

This ancient city was a frontier town on a huge scale, the frontier of the industrial colossus out of the west in the old Orient.

Osaka was not exactly my idea of Japan. I went up to Nara.

Ancient Nara had been one of the shifting capitals of the early kingdom in the days of legend and for many centuries a sacred place. A town snuggled under the lee of a broad plateau or terrace that was one great lawn crossed with occasional paths and bordered by a low range of wooded hills. In the hillside forests were the temples and the shrines, hallowed places dear to the spirits of the ancients. Some dated back to the eighth century.

Deer browsed on the greens and you could, from certain vantage points, look down into the plain that swept away toward Osaka. In the evening when I arrived, the lights of the temples were just coming on in the forest. It was quiet and deeply restful, but the distances were considerable and I decided to go back down to my inn in the half-hidden town.

It was a Japanese inn, and for the first time I slept on the floor mats and slept better than you would think. Before that, I had my bath sitting on a stool while an old woman scrubbed my back. She seemed to think she ought to and I had been told about that sort of thing.

A young man from the inn went up with me very early the next morning to the great sweep of lawn where the deer browsed. The rains had ceased a day or so before. The sun broke through a mist that rose from the plain.

The morning was hushed as if waiting. Then we saw coming up a path from the plain a body of priests, Shinto in pure white with strange high headdresses and Buddhist in darker robes, and a long line of troops. In the center between the marching files came other soldiers each bearing a square box. The boxes contained the ashes of soldiers who had died fighting in the war in China. The families of the dead marched behind.

We went and stood off to the side as the priests, troops and civilians took up their formation on the lawns facing the hills, the forest and the concealed shrines and temples. Smoke from breakfast fires drifted up lazily from the clustered roofs of the town below. Silence fell over the throng and they bowed low toward the sacred places and the boxes were lifted a little as if in offering.

The Shinto priests stood forward, clapped their hands to summon the spirits and sang out into the hushed morning. My young companion translated. They told the ancestors, the ancient ones, that the sons of the riceland, of the land of the many gods and the sacred places, of the soil and the waters, had come home again. I do not remember all of it and I did not fully understand. But all of that was of home, of the legendary islands in the sea and of the hoary story of the birth of the race lost in the shrouded past. They spoke to the long dead as if they were there to be seen where the forest began. All of it was full of the conviction that men in generations are as a river flowing, a current in the abyss of time.

They had come home, the dead, to those islands where all was home and the centuries were mingled in the stream of one common life until time was no more.

I felt a sense of desperate aloneness for I could never be part of such a living together that knew no boundary between the living and the dead. This was pagan, primitive and complete. Here the rocks and trees had life and the generations spoke to one another as if yesterday and tomorrow were all mystically today and forever. This was an intimacy, an incandescent concept of the great family eternally at home such as I, an Occidental modern, had never encountered. The muffled strokes of the temple gongs sounded.

I shall not forget that homecoming of the newly dead to the pagan islands in the western seas.

The urge to leave aside today's issues took hold of me and I avoided the new Japan. Issues would become faded headlines in newspaper libraries and clipping morgues but this came out of antiquity. This was Man as he had been through most of the human story.

At Ise in groves not far from the sea are the Great Shrines of Imperial Shinto. The more sacred of the two is dedicated to the sun goddess. The shrines have been rebuilt of Japanese cypress every twenty years since ancient times. Some call them austere and bare, but three or four million Japanese come every year to visit them. These people, the peasants in the thatch-roofed villages, were pagan. They were both pagan and Bud-dhist—eclectic is the heavy technical word.

I had gone down to Ise seeking contact with the pagan spirit. From there I brought away only an awakened sense of the sig-nificance of stark simplicity, but all pagan Japan was open before me. A journey or detour into another reality began. Those days are not entirely clear to me. They were time out from one's self.

There were holy places deep in shade and sacred waterfalls, simple shrines beside woodland roads and glimpses of the house-hold faith. I came to inns like those in Japanese prints and gardens that were paintings, whole landscapes of exquisite un-reality. I do not remember how I came to enter those private gardens in Kyoto. Someone must have taken me. But who?

On the coast there were some little islands cast together in a design without design. To the Japanese they were something of great beauty and inexplicably significant; and I found myself feeling the same way about them. A pantheistic insight into the personality of the inanimate got into me. The world around became oddly homelike, though a little alarming.

There were rooms, their walls of unpainted wood, with noth-ing in them but warm woven straw mats on the floor and one small vase of flowers arranged with traditional skill. I did not want to leave them and I did not know why. I came to a painting that was nothing but a single dead branch on gold, and I sat and saw no point in going on again until evening.

The effortless simplicity of that beauty which is nothing but proportion, unadulterated, undramatic and alone, possessed me. I do not remember just what I was about in those days.

Somewhere in the Izu peninsula there is a deep gorge with precipitous sides and a river roaring through. Perched on either side are inns where Japanese go to bathe in the hot-springs water. It was silent in those inns where we all walked in our stocking feet or *tabi*. I heard the far murmur of the river and pushed aside a screen of the parchment wall and there was a garden with nothing but a stone lantern to one side. The position of that lantern on the lawn was a masterpiece of pure design.

I bathed naked in steaming pools after the bath boys had scrubbed me to a glow. In the baths, soothing sunlit rooms, were both men and women as naked as I and it did not matter. Along the way the burden of self had abandoned me for the time.

A small girl came and gazed at my abnormal whiteness of skin and touched me and laughed, and then I laughed for I knew I was a strange creature and it would be better to be nearer the warmer and richer color of yellow bronze which was the color of her body.

Fujiyama's white cone rose in the distance. The plum rains returned one day. Another inn on the black, rocky shore across the little bay was first hidden and then revealed in the rain as were the flowering fruit trees in the garden, and I pushed aside the wall and walked naked across the grass terrace and went into the sea. I had not known that I could swim so far and so long. The rain sang the rain song and the cool sea stirred in its sleep and mine.

A fisherman in a boat with a high prow and stern sat all afternoon fishing off a headland clothed in dark pines. On the shore I sat alone and learned at last to be still for hours at a time. The goodness of that patient stillness became part of me and part of a silence that is a voice without words.

The little maids in bright kimonos piled up mats very high to make my bed at night for they knew in the inns that I was strange and needed ever so many mats. They laughed a small laugh in unison like little bells chiming, for everything amused them in the bounty of their youth. It was such a joyous thing, the matter of the mats.

I learned to cherish the hot green tea that was always there to be poured into a cup without a handle from a pot with only a suggestion of a design on its glazed surface. It warmed and comforted after a long walk in the rain along rice paddies and down narrow paths into hidden hamlets.

White rice steamed in the bowl in my hand, and I reached with the slender sticks for a little of this and a little of that in the many small dishes on the round table close to the floor. Places with chairs and great gawky high tables began to appear absurd. The way to live was on mats, straw mats, with only a scroll on the wall, a few letters in fine, firm brush strokes. After a time I did not want all those mats at night and I could put the lacquered wooden headrest under my head and lie quite still, feeling the hard resistance of it until sleep came. The household gods kept watch over me in the night in their small shrine in a corner of the inn.

At Kyoto I had bought books on Shinto and its legends and beliefs that had not been available on the ship. In an inn beside an orchard above the narrow lanes of a seaside town I sat down to read myself deeper into all that. I knew after a time that I must stop. There was no escape from what our world had made of me. These were fantasies of a child.

Our truth was no truth either but it had destroyed all this. The old gods slept and we were alone in an aloneness that the pagan had never known.

That disordered voyage of escape from shrine to shrine and into the old Japan had landed me up the Tokaido road near Hakone. I went on up into a volcanic hot-springs area to a modern hotel, possibly with the idea of shaking myself out of whatever I had got into by meeting foreigners again. As it happened, except for a couple of the silent, pipe-smoking variety of British, there was not a foreigner in the place. However, I had fallen out of my trance and found myself in conversation with a very modern, businesslike Japanese, an engineer.

He suggested we bathe together and continue the conversation. He said that he wanted me to meet his wife and children. He was rather excessively modern, for normally the wife, "the honorable inferior," was not dragged into social relations between men.

When I went down to the bath I found that I had lost most of my indifference to human nakedness which I had acquired during my journey through old Japan. My Occidentalism was catching up with me again. I again felt embarrassed at being unclothed in public and hoped there would be no women.

The engineer, still businesslike but naked, struck me as a bit funny when he came prancing across the room to greet me. He swung me around and I found myself in front of his wife and a string of sons and daughters, nice people but stark naked.

I bowed a bit confusedly to Madame, smiled faintly at the daughters and tried to think of some theme of conversation other than the irrefutable fact that nobody there had any clothes on. I could not seem to get that detail out of my mind.

After a bit of rather heavy going, the engineer and I got two little stools and sat down in front of a steaming pool to soap ourselves before getting into the bath. Fortunately, the rest of the family gathered happily around the other pool, lathering themselves vigorously.

18

POLITICAL Tokyo was depressing after being outside in the old Japan. The Japanese Foreign Office and most other political Japanese had a favorite theme when talking to Americans in those days. They claimed that if the New Order, their name for their brand of imperialism, did not succeed, China would become Communist and the whole Far East would be threatened with Communism. They harped on the fact that about one third of the former Chinese empire was under Soviet domination. Probably that was true, but the circumstance made less impression on visiting foreigners than it might have since it referred to such improbable places as Outer Mongolia and Sinkiang. Japanese insistence that Chiang Kai-shek was incapable of checking the Chinese Communists also seemed rather beside the point. He had been fighting the Chinese Communists for almost ten years, while the Japanese themselves, at that moment, were bogged down with powerful forces in Chinese Communist territory and were fated to stay down.

I went about wanting to get straight what the Japanese were trying to do. The simple assumption was that they were trying to conquer China. They said they were not. Foreigners who had lived their nearly all their lives seemed to agree with them.

I recall one of the old-timers who said quite seriously that the Japanese just wanted the Chinese to see things their way and be friends with them and that they were going to keep on beating up the Chinese until they got friendlier.

Gradually it became clear to me what they did *not* want. This was an age in which a lot of people seemed to know better what they did not want than what they wanted. They did not want strong Communist influence in China and Soviet predominance. They did not want a westernized China under the influence of the great western powers. They did not want a united strong China.

There is a trick to the Japanese mind. I had a rather close Japanese friend in college and later studied Japanese language, culture and institutions at the University of California and therefore know enough to suspect that I know nothing about it. Still, I think there is a trick to Japanese thinking that is associated with their capacity to be Buddhist, pagan Shinto, Confucian and what not all at the same time. It is their eclectic mind. They do not exclude things because those things do not make sense when put together with other things. Probably for that reason they have brought their whole history with them from primitive man all the way down.

That trick got into every conversation on politics. I started out on the assumption that certain things excluded certain other things, but they did not. Their language is eclectic. The written language is a combination of Chinese ideograms and a phonetic or alphabet system combining two principles that seem to be mutually exclusive.

The Japanese have an inborn horror of the simple declarative sentence. Things are referred to in passing, you beat around the bush and it is not fair to mention what bush. It is like the custom in villages where houses actually have only one room. The well-bred visitor comes in. His host is dressing. The visitor sits down a few feet from him and stares dreamily into space. His host, having finished his toilet, gets up, walks around the room and comes over to greet his guest effusively, among other things inquiring when he arrived though they may have been sitting next to each other for a quarter of an hour.

Slowly I came to a conclusion in regard to what the Japanese called the "China Incident." They wanted an independent China under Japanese hegemony on terms of equality. That in fact is about what they said in many public declarations. Certainly, one of the principal purposes of their invasion of China in the minds of many Japanese was to liberate China from foreign domination.

I had begun to realize that if something did not make too much sense to me it probably came nearer to Japanese reality than if it did make sense to me. The representative of one of the great American banks was leaving Japan about that time. He had spent over a quarter of a century in the country. Every year or two, he told me, he had been back to the United States and each time he addressed a high-level bankers' luncheon in one of those luncheon clubs up in a Wall Street skyscraper.

The first year he returned he made a lengthy speech. He confessed that it had been a good speech. A lot of busy men had stayed over their allotted time to hear him out. Each year, however, he had found that he had less to say. The last time he had simply told them that having lived a quarter of a century in Japan he had decided that he knew nothing about it.

Gradually I became aware of two obvious developments.

One was that the Japanese habit of dragging all their history with them was bringing back the shogunate, the feudalistic rule of the warrior caste. The shogunate preceded the Meiji Restoration of the last century which was in turn followed by the introduction of parliamentary government. The military were now in the process of actually taking over the authority again.

The other development was that their paganism had gone dynamic. They had succeeded in combining that deep, primitive sense of home and of the unity of the generations with modern dynamism, resulting in a roaring nationalism. The desperate restlessness of modern man had them. America had its part in that.

Commodore Matthew Calbraith Perry and the squadron of American "black ships" had forced Japan in 1854 to abandon isolation and open its ports to the world. After that America had made a great educational effort to wake up the Japanese. We and other Occidentals had convinced them that eternal change, bustle and push was the way of the world; we had half-imposed on them a Calvinist belief that progress was righteousness.

Japan had to prove in the modern competitive fashion its superiority which until then it had taken for granted. It now had the competitive spirit, the desire to show the world. Amaterasu Omikami, the ancient sun goddess, had become in a peculiarly Japanese fashion the spirit of get-up-and-go.

The Occident was about to reap what the Occident had sown. Japan was far and away the most westernized of Asiatic nations. The Occident was going to reap a lot more of what it had sown as all Asia awoke, for the Western spirit of progress was also the spirit of turmoil.

Obviously, the thing for me to do at that moment was to go to Manchuria and North China where the new shogunate and the new Japanese Babbittry were in full flower. Things were happening there. Besides, I was set on seeing Peking before somebody modernized it.

On that trip down the Inland Sea and out through the Yellow Sea to Dairen, the port of Manchuria, I bumped my head until I wanted to take it off and leave it in the cabin. The ship, small but fast and modern, had been built to carry Japanese. They are a foot shorter than Europeans or Americans, and the top of me kept colliding with the tops of doorways. That liner in miniature proved very practical, though, as it slipped down the narrow route through the islands.

The Inland Sea of Japan is one of those places where you want to jump off at every island and go fishing. You nearly could. The channels between the islands seem at points like the canals of Venice. Nature was having a day off from the serious business of geography when the Inland Sea archipelagos were created or else the cherubim had leave to amuse themselves. It is a whimsical, child-sized ocean, never really in earnest.

Occasionally I saw a sacred torii and a shrine perched amid rocks in the forest near the water. A flowering tree stood by a single house in a small bay. Fishermen's boats were drawn up on shore and yellow-bronze children ran naked along the strand while others, snug in their kimonos, sat on rocks and observed these matters with elfin solemnity. A fisherman slept in his boat offshore, rocked gently by the tidal current.

If you had at last learned to live untormented by the image of your status in others' eyes, it would be hard to think of a better life than as a fisherman in a village hidden in an island cove down in that Inland Sea.

Night came. The waters turned black. Ashore, tiny lights could be picked out here and there appealing to the traveler outward bound.

Then one by one the shore lights went out. The ship moved silently through islands and passages, only the sound of the wind in the trees coming over the water. I thought of the yellow-bronze children who had run on the shore and now slept clustered in their quilts near that body that had borne them in the peace of the womb.

Off to the east I could occasionally see the glow of lights from a city on the coast. One of those cities must have been Hiroshima.

19

THE American-built stream-
liner that raced north out of Dairen over heavily ballasted track
toward Mukden and Hsinking was the first I had ever seen.
Such trains were a new thing even in the United States.

Through the window I saw what seemed to be the American
Middle West flashing by. The contours of the plains were those
of the deep interior of the North American continent. The fields
were the same vast expanses of cultivation with the suggestion
not of peasant husbandry but of machine or labor-gang agriculture.

Seen at that speed, the settlements that came up out of the
horizon and disappeared gave the appearance of the thrown-
together, boxlike communities that one glimpsed for an indifferent moment from the windows of an express running somewhere between the Mississippi and the Rocky Mountains. Only
the heaps of huts in the plain were strange. They housed seg-
ments of the horde of refugees who had been pouring for years
into the country from hunger-stricken, overpopulated China.

The train rushed past a steel mill blazing and smoking beside
the track. On a long curve it swung near nondescript wooden
houses on cinder-blackened expanses of bare clay, cut through
a few broad barren streets and ran alongside a group of factories
built of clean new brick and with sparkling windows.

Japan was building a new America in the great plains of Manchuria. You could feel in the businesslike-looking passengers
the spirit of competition and the desire to risk, build and progress. This spirit was a challenge to all the Orient.

Most of the passengers were Japanese and Manchuria seemed to have a special effect on them. They looked a little flushed. Some had the brand of success on them, a certain vigorous confidence, and others were taut as so many Americans are taut. They may have felt good or felt strained, but the content seemed to have gone out of them. Manchuria was not home. It was like North America, vibrantly alive, but, in a fashion you can better feel than explain, divorced from reality, divorced from permanence and life as a value in itself.

The Japanese were always being scolded by their press and by their imperialist leaders for failing to emigrate to Manchuria, or, as they called it, Manchukuo. Japan was incredibly overcrowded—some eighty million people in a country with about the same amount of arable land as there is in California. Looking at Manchuria, I thought I understood why they did not come, I who had been born in such a land as this. For it was clear to me that such lands as mine and as this could never be home, in their sense, for anyone.

In Mukden the hotel was a bad imitation of one of those square structures in American trading centers of the prairie country. The Japanese version was equally impersonal and had the same overdose of cold concrete and tile.

In the center of the city was a sprawling walled arsenal, a military town, once the seat of power of the Chinese war lord, Chang Tso-lin.

Broad and badly paved streets cut up Mukden into big squares each containing a disorderly collection of more or less Chinese buildings. The city did not seem to have any physiognomy. You could not make out what it was meant to be.

The next day I went to stay with a hospitable American oil company representative who had not even heard of me five minutes before he asked me to be his house guest. We lunched with the official representative of the United States and later went to a formal dinner given by the local chamber of commerce.

Various foreign representatives were introduced. That created a problem. The American was in theory accredited to the

Kuomintang government in China, if to anyone. America did not recognize the "sovereign state" of Manchukuo. They got around it rather nicely. Wreathed in benevolent smiles, the chairman introduced the American as "the Honorable Private Gentleman from the United States."

In Hsinking, made by the Japanese the capital of their puppet state, heavy-bodied Manchurians, reportedly much addicted to the smoking of opium, were going slowly through the motions of self-government as if they were doing setting-up exercises. They lived surrounded by a host of Japanese counselors and experts who could have accomplished their job of administering Manchuria far more efficiently if they had not had to engage in the mummery of governing through the oxlike Manchurian excellencies.

My impression, hopelessly superficial, was that the Manchurians were plain stupid, far too stupid to do anything with what is probably the most valuable piece of real estate in the Far East.

It is orthodox Far Eastern policy to regard Manchuria as the strategic key to the Far East. Lying between Soviet Siberia, China and Japan, it holds a formidable position of leverage for whoever controls it. Its mineral, agricultural and forest resources, combined with the fact that it is a relatively virgin country, make it the natural area for the development of a fully modern economic and power center.

One of two dynamic forces could take root in Manchuria—modern, industrial and large-scale agricultural capitalism or modern, industrial and large-scale agricultural communism. The Japanese, with their borrowed pioneering spirit, were at the time introducing the former at a tremendous rate but, as it turned out, were in reality clearing the ground for the latter. The deal at the end of World War II by which Manchuria was in effect turned over by the United States for Soviet occupation sealed the fate of China.

When it finally halted in the station at Peking, the locomotive that had hauled the groaning train down from Mukden to Peking over Chinese-built lines gave a long drawn-out sigh of relief. So did the passengers. We were covered with dust and soot, tired out from trying to sleep braced against the incessant jerking, and sick of battling against the flies that parked in small armies on the tasteless food in the dining car.

I went to the old compound of the British Embassy. There was no one there but the British guard unit, the too perfect Chinese personnel, a language student in the British diplomatic service, and Jerry.

Jerry was a young diplomat, very Mayfair and tennis rackets. He had lived in an apartment across the court from me in Berlin. On boisterous occasions, as late as four in the morning, he had dropped galvanized iron washtubs from the top story into the paved courtyard below.

He was temporarily in charge of His Britannic Majesty's Embassy in Peking. The actual embassy was down in Hankow with Chiang Kai-shek. The North Chinese government, installed in Peking by the Japanese, sat under a distinguished old Chinese, Wang Keh-min. Jerry was not accredited to this government.

The whole position was anomalous and nothing could have pleased Jerry more. He carried his then junior status like a flag. He and I, with the language student, appeared one night on the dance floor of the Grand Hotel singing a roundelay requesting the girls of someplace or other to consider something that perhaps proper young ladies should not.

As "friends" of Wang Keh-min, the Japanese wanted to confer seriously with His Britannic Majesty's representative about all manner of things. Most of them were matters that His Britannic Majesty was in no position to consider seriously unless he were to break faith with Chiang Kai-shek. It turned out to be extremely difficult for the Japanese Imperial Government's representatives to deal seriously with a young man who went about singing improper roundelays in conspicuous places and who apparently could not concentrate for more than two minutes on anything.

But Jerry was neither a fool nor a flyweight. He had a talent for nonchalant eccentricity and he was using it.

While I was there the Japanese placed a sentry in front of the British compound gate to make the British lose face. It was quite an issue for one must not lose face in China. The rumor got around that the sentry would be shot dead by the British guard at high noon on Jerry's order. Although no one could claim solid evidence of his intention, the idea that Jerry might do it came to be taken seriously in the Japanese Embassy. As the Japanese were not sure that Jerry was not completely hare-brained, they withdrew their sentry.

Jerry was on excellent terms with people with whom he was officially on no terms at all. But he was so systematically scatterbrained about it that even the most subtle Japanese lawyer could not interpret any of it as recognition of the puppet government. In his private quarters, with the doors closed, he worked hard on his reports and looked on occasion a little harassed.

I was living now in a compound bungalow. Sometimes during the day I would go off in a rickshaw prowling around old Peking and suddenly make up my mind to go back to the compound and cool off for an hour. It was usually hot and dusty. At the door would be waiting my Chinese boy—no more a boy than I, actually—and a bath would be drawn, fresh barley water would be at hand and clean clothes laid out. I never found out by what mysterious telepathic process he knew that I was coming back at that particular moment.

He made me understand why people insist on using the adjective "bland" to describe Chinese. His calmness was more refreshing than the barley water or the cool bath. He was calm about something that I did not grasp and anchored in something I could not see.

After a while I began to learn more about Peking. Even here in the turmoil of China one was aware of the generations, the river flowing. Peking was a city of family compounds. Quarters of the city were made up of more or less interlocking compounds, the residence of what amounted to a clan of people interrelated and responsible for one another.

This was the most ancient of civilized societies. You could

understand why people believed almost passionately in the mission and the message of China. That civilization had risen time and again to new heights and fallen once more into disorder. The story was so long that the lifetime of my country covered only the period of one of many episodes in China.

I went to one of those interminable Chinese plays that spread over hours. The audience wanders about and drinks tea and eats and goes out and comes in again. The play also covered, nonchalantly, a few hundred years of Chinese history. Recurring periods of disorder were presented with a certain ritual monotony. Everyone on the stage was fighting.

These episodes were terminated by a great crashing and clanging of bronze off stage and the new emperor and his people, glorious in silk robes and strange headdresses, would appear. The squabbling horde would slink away. The glittering potentate would go into an intolerably long oration of which I understood nothing. Prosperity, order and peace had returned until the next period of disorder.

In history, as in that play, the structure of Chinese society had held firm through recurring tumult. The institutions of China were rooted habit and attitude. They were not dependent on administrative efficiency or public order, they were not maintained through conformity but through an inward tradition, a resistant and individualistic set of loyalties, a concept of harmony.

It was in Peking that the conviction came to me that the solution to the social and personal inadequacy of the modern pattern would be found when it merged with ancient civilizations.

The restlessness and blind iconoclasm that the new Occident called progress needed a new interpretation by people deeply rooted. The ancient peoples could fulfill no mission now without what the Occident had accomplished in the miraculous five hundred years since the Renaissance. But without what they had and we lacked, we should never find our way home.

Our emphasis was on change. The increasingly frenetic rhythm of that incessant change had swept away the theme. Survival of the Chinese pattern of living and of the Chinese individualism that was not a separateness was one of the major lessons of universal history. Until we could win through to a pattern of changelessness within change we should have accomplished little.

The changelessness was in the need of men for one another and in the nature of that need. It was concerned with the organic group rather than with the organization. That was what had lived through the tumultuous ages of China's history and survived the liquidation of economic organization and political regimes. Call it the family clan or the village community or whatever an adequate analysis might show it to be.

That human creation, the community or group, living together in a closely related, face-to-face relationship to common ends, had come with us out of the milleniums and it would go with us to the end. It was both the stage and the drama of life. Its ethics and its pattern of emotion and behavior alone could give us meaning and fulfillment. It has been undermined and perilously weakened by the egocentrism of the Occidental pattern of progress.

It had nothing to do with conviviality and "nice guy-ism." Certainly it had little to do with the marital experimentation of the modern society where men and women sought restlessly for the right partner. It was not concerned in any important sense with people "liking" one another, that fetish of the modern man and expression of his aloneness.

The assumption that the great restlessness, the inward aloneness, the essential disorder of man in the modern environment was a natural state, was the Occidental heresy.

Man had learned the art of living and established the great societies in a geographic arc. That arc ran from Europe down over the Middle East through India and on up through China. In that vast arc lived the overwhelming majority of humanity. Where those societies were still intact there might emerge the synthesis of the modern and the unchanging that would close the epoch of the Renaissance.

There, not in the Russian steppes or overseas in the New World, man would seek the solution to his problem.

Such things ran through my mind as I sat on the lowest of the concentric circles of marble terraces of the most sacred spot in the old empire, the Temple of Heaven. There the emperors as delegates of the race had performed the high ceremonies symbolic of the permanence of this ageless and constantly revivified society.

In the Temple of Heaven I found that sense of proportion, that pagan completeness that is in the Parthenon and in the pyramids of Gizeh and at the Great Shrines of Ise.

There is a lot of almost open country within the thirty-mile circumference of the outer walls of Peking, and the Temple of Heaven lies far out, though within the walls. The walls of the inner Imperial City are some six and a half miles in extent and the Purple Wall, two miles in circumference, encloses the innermost Forbidden City. In this time of war most of the gates in the outer wall were locked. At night only a few heavily guarded gates were open, and all these gates, too, would be closed when there was a guerrilla alarm.

The memory of Peking that was to remain most vividly with me was of the sunlit mornings and afternoons within the Forbidden City. In those times the Forbidden City, which had been the residence of the imperial court, was wide open to certain strangers. You could go where you pleased and see what you pleased if you had, as I did at the moment, a kind of borrowed diplomatic status. There were almost no tourists. You were free to spend days on your own within that fairy city where the court and the princes of the Manchu dynasty had lived in imperial isolation.

Palace lay next to palace and hidden court opened into hidden court. Great halls, barbarically splendid, stood high on stone terraces, and there the emperors had received in state the ambassadors of subject peoples, dined ostentatiously or subjected themselves to elaborate ceremonial.

It became more intimate and alive one afternoon when a merchant came to the British embassy compound and spread out his wares, tribute silk from the storehouses of the Forbidden City and robes and silk coats of imperial officials and courtiers.

I bought a plum-colored coat of a court official with embroidered insignia of rank. It went as a gift to my father, who folded it away carefully and would take it out and look at it as a treasure, precious because I had thought of him and brought it from away off in Peking. My mother later sold it for a fancy price as I remember.

The Winter Palace, a series of gardens, pagodas and palaces on or near the shores of three lakes, lay near the Forbidden City. I crossed high-arched marble bridges from one unreality into another. Temples and convents clustered about what had been the seat of majesty and in their shaded interiors Buddha contemplated the folly of human ambition.

Peking is a great city without being a crowded city. People do not live on top of one another in the layer-cake fashion of the West. Behind drab walls along generally unseemly streets the inner compounds could be splendid and in any case there was room. There were even farms within the city walls.

If China had not been in one of those epochs of turmoil that last half a generation and fated to even greater turmoil later, Peking would seem to me close to what I was seeking as a resting place in the homelessness of my generation. Here, God granting, and by some absurd turn of fortune, one could have lived out one's life at peace. Nothing was actually repeated. It was the extreme opposite from "back there." There was an inexhaustible quality to Peking. In a lifetime you would penetrate only part way into the many-sidedness of its personality, rigid within ancient formulas unlimited in the variety of their expression.

Tomes have been written on the street scenes of Peking. The fertile Chinese imagination had brought forth the most improbable professions and tricks of trade in the ceaseless struggle to live. Perhaps because to live at all is such an accomplishment, the Chinese values the business of living itself and seems not to be tormented to the same extent with the Occidental necessity to give life extra meaning through things or careers.

The Japanese had settled into the city as if they meant to stay. Geisha houses and Japanese restaurants had appeared. Tokyo and Osaka were buying up property.

I dined one evening with a Japanese colonel in a pleasant Japanese restaurant in the usual private room. Everything was going along swimmingly. For a Japanese he was an exceptionally good talker. If you believed one quarter of what he told you, and that with a pinch of salt, he was satisfied. The business of beating the Chinese into taking a friendly attitude was a gory business, and the Japanese here in China did not expect you to accept the kind of rubbish that was handed out in Tokyo.

A messenger slipped into the room and whispered something to him. He looked stony for a moment and then beamed again. It was my first lesson in a Japanese attitude I had read about, the business of smiling out of courtesy because it is unmannerly to pass on your gloom.

He told me chattily what had happened. A brother officer whom he had known rather well had been dining at another Japanese restaurant three or four doors down the street. A Chinese cook had stepped into the room and driven a butcher knife through his back. He was stone dead.

I asked if we had better not conclude the evening as I presumed he would have duties to perform in connection with his friend's death. He said no. There was nothing he could do. The matter was in the hands of the intelligence branch and the military police. The Chinese cook had disappeared among the Chinese of Peking.

From then on, whenever someone entered the room to serve us, I instantly lifted my head so they could see quickly my nice, white, non-Japanese skin. He did not pay the slightest attention. His assignment that night was to entertain me and entertained I was going to be.

I began to understand why certain personal friends had told me in Tokyo that the Japanese were desperate. Guerrillas were all over the outskirts of Peking, a city supposed to be the great secure stronghold of Japan in China. You had to bribe a driver heavily to take you out to the suburbs in the western hills. One morning very early I sat having tea on a high terrace of the Summer Palace some eight miles out of Peking and watched Japanese planes bomb villages behind the western hills to drive the guerrillas out.

Japanese-occupied territory in China was a fiction. There were only Japanese-occupied cities, railways and occasional main roads.

China was not a government nor an administration. It was every village and every clan family. It was a society within society that had survived everything. The alien could ransack and torture it but could not conquer it until he himself became Chinese.

20

THE car out of Mukden, on the end of the train headed through Korea to Fusan and via overnight ferry to Shimonoseki in Japan, was half sleeping compartments and half observation lounge. At the Yalu River about dawn two Japanese generals and I got up. We had the car to ourselves and were not disturbed by other passengers the day long while we wound down through Korea to Fusan.

Served by a discreet steward, the car was immaculate. You had an uninterrupted view through the spotless windows. It was the most completely tourist experience that I have ever had. The Koreans in their white clothing, the rice paddies, the thatched roofs of villages, the tiled roofs of temples, the abrupt, rather theatrical mountains—all slid past like a picture post card folder opening out.

Those generals were the first frigid Japanese I had met. As the generals and I were alone in the car, I bowed my best Japanese bows with full indication of my respect for their rank. They gave no indication of being aware of me.

They sat stiffly in their chairs as if on horseback and gave the impression of being made of wood. Their gestures were like the movements of a mechanical toy and their faces were pinched up and frozen. You would have thought they were trying to act the stylized role of Samurai warriors in a traditional Kabuki drama. When lunch came they even ate like mechanical toys. At important stations delegations came into the car and presented flowers. This ceremony seemed ludicrous, but they responded with those same mechanical-toy gestures.

I tried to speak to them in English, French and German. They did not move a muscle nor look at me. It was only when we were leaving the car at Fusan that one of them, hours after I had last attempted to speak to them, turned and, with a withering expression of contempt, said in German, "Yes, we speak German."

He evidently wanted me to understand that it had been a piece of confounded insolence for a foreign civilian to try to talk to Japanese generals. I said something to the effect that I had merely wanted to inquire if they actually were Japanese as the Japanese were usually such courteous people. He turned toward me for a moment that pinched-up frozen mask of his and then climbed down out of the car.

I noticed later that when their War Minister, General Hideki Tojo, was speaking in parliament he had the same somewhat mechanical gestures and always seemed cold and angry, like an ill-tempered school principal calling down recalcitrant school-boys. Yet he too had a peculiar, not quite grown-up air about him. Pearl Harbor was the supreme expression of the adolescence of the Japanese. From the time Tojo's full militarist cabinet took over in October, only seven weeks passed until Pearl Harbor. Japan might conceivably have accomplished something for the peoples of the Far East with its Greater East Asia Co-Prosperity Sphere if it had not been for the blockhead-edness and narrow-mindedness of the professional military caste.

Yet part of the political power of the Japanese army was based on the people's faith in its officers. The ordinary man who had been in that army under those officers and under brutal discipline came away with great faith in the honesty and devotion of the Japanese officer.

I remember a talk given by the colonel in command of one of those schools the American army was so fond of putting you into during World War II. He had been a military attaché in Japan for some time. He said the Japanese officer was paid very little and lived most austerely. At night when other people were getting some rest, the Japanese officer would listen to the personal problems of the men under his command. If one of their families had difficulties, it was his duty to arrange to help the family. He would sit up until all hours of the night, writing to authorities or to his personal friends to straighten things out for one of his soldiers. There was nothing the soldiers did not have the right to ask and expect of him if it concerned their welfare.

It was the young officers who had protested against the political parties that were instruments of the great trusts, and against the corruption at top levels. Their outcry for the purification of the nation had been just and the people had recognized it.

In China the Japanese officer appeared to change. He was often corrupt to the point of betraying his country. It was generally known that a great deal of the strategic materials, arms and ammunition that went through to the interior got through because it was so easy to bribe the Japanese officer.

Oddly, corruption made them more human in a paradoxical sense: in China the Japanese officer was very often not the stiff martinet he had been in Japan, but he was capable of inexplicable atrocities.

On the Fusan-Shimonoseki ferry I lost track of my two generals and did not see them again when we arrived in the morning at Shimonoseki.

Moji and Shimonoseki, on opposite sides of the strait into the Inland Sea, are boatmen's towns. Everyone in Shimonoseki is always climbing into a boat for Moji as if that town had an irresistible attraction, and vice versa. Very Japanese, the cities had that additional attraction of vessels coming and going continually and the resulting awareness of the sea present in every household.

In Moji I saw a little old Japanese lady disgrace herself and embarrass everyone dreadfully. She and her husband, a couple getting gray and wearing the dark kimonos of old people, were with a large group of parents saying good-by to their sons who were sailing in a small transport for the war in China.

While the ship was lying at the quay and everyone was being tremendously gay, a hospital ship came in next to it. The mutilated and wounded were helped or carried in stretchers down the gangplanks to the waiting ambulances. Suddenly a group of staggering, war-crazed and shell-shocked men got loose from the ship and went swaying around the quay babbling sickeningly. Attendants rushed around to catch them, for they were upsetting the blind who stood, with bandaged eyes, huddled and humbled as the newly blind do, near the trucks that were to taken them away. The gaiety of the sailing ceremony at the other ship cooled down considerably, but the flags still fluttered and the crowd of parents kept smiling.

Suddenly the little old lady who had been waving her flag and beaming at her son broke down. She crept back into a shed on the quay and cried her heart out. I looked at her son on the transport. His face was grave and he moved a little as if to go toward the gangplank. Her husband went over and stood in front of her to shield her as much as possible from being seen.

The others there began to gaze around in every direction. The code had been broken. I knew enough by that time to know that it was a disgrace for the family. Her husband was so distressed he slunk away with her as if they had stolen something. She resisted a bit being led away, and then she made one last little effort and raised her face and smiled at her son, feebly waving her little flag. I suppose she wanted to stay and look at him as long as she could.

But she had to leave. It was her punishment for breaking the code.

I left Japan a few days later, but I might appropriately mention here another trip I made to the Far East in 1940, concerned mainly with a footnote to American history—the Philippines— and a footnote to French history—Indo-China. Both countries came to acquire a somewhat more than marginal significance, since it is conceivable that without them America and Britain might not have been drawn directly into the Far Eastern war.

The Philippines were our hostage within the area of Japan's effort to create a Greater East Asia Co-Prosperity Sphere. Japan's advance into Indo-China brought American-Japanese relations up to the breaking point.

The Japanese presumably did want the Philippines, in one form or another, in their sphere. Even without war the Philippines had every chance of becoming, economically, a Japanese province.

Japan was already selling things there like rubber shoes at twenty-five cents that cost six to eight times as much when imported from the United States. That item was quite important. Through the schools the barefoot Filipino had begun to learn about hookworm, and he wanted shoes.

The Philippines' tropical products were noncompetitive in the world market. The standard of living, and wages, had been raised just enough to accomplish that. Japan, however, could always take the Philippine output in turn for their own goods. Economically the Philippines made sense as part of a Greater East Asia Co-Prosperity Sphere, whether dominated by Japan or not. It was the perplexing side of the Filipinos' predicament.

The Philippines are located in the Orient but are not Oriental. Spain found them to be a little above the primitive level, having a feudal social structure. They became, in effect, an extension of the Spanish-American empire. During the early, decisive epochs of Spanish colonization the Philippines' trading fleet sailed customarily from Mexico.

By cultural osmosis the Filipino has become Caribbean and Central American and, above all, Catholic in the Spanish colonial tradition. As elsewhere, Spain had misruled herself into the hearts and souls of her rebellious subjects. She would remain with them forever. The Spanish civilization, linked intimately to the Spanish talent for bad government, appears to meet a profound human need.

American rule in this century had drawn the Philippines even

further away from the Orient. America had spent nothing on
the Philippines, but a schoolroom-and-gadgets type of Americanism, quite tenacious if not very profound, had been implanted.

By the time I visited there, the Philippine independence
legislation was already on the statute books in Washington and
the country was being prepared for full sovereignty.

America had squelched early Filipino *Americanistas* who
wanted their archipelago to set its sails toward becoming one
of the states of the United States. Ever since waging war on the
patriot revolutionaries we had ostensibly come to aid, we had
demonstrated an abundant lack of interest in the Philippines.

The Filipinos were in the same situation with America that
women are supposed to be with men. They could not get along
with us and they could not get along without us. Some formula
was wanted by which we would get out but not leave.

I remember talking to a Filipino politico at a dinner at the
Yacht Club. We were standing on the second-floor terrace,
looking down at the American squadron and the white presidential yacht where President Quezon lived most of the time.
I asked him what would happen if America just called the whole
thing off and that squadron sailed for home. He smiled and
said, "The yacht would sail right in its keel water."

He then explained that the Filipinos wanted complete self-
government, even if corrupt or incompetent, but at the same
time they had a mortal terror of being left "all alone out there
in the Orient." They were not Orientals, he said, and added
that what they would like most was to move the islands over off
the California coast.

As it turned out, the Philippine independence problem was
one of the few issues to be solved by the war: America did
succeed in getting out without leaving.

Rice and bananas, coconut-plantation and road-junction
towns without character, huts hidden among banana leaves—
this was Philippine life. There was an underlying tendency
to rebellion against landowners, lawyers and money-lenders.
But there was no evidence of a great and ancient civiliza-

tion, no central theme. The Filipinos were people without any definite tradition or aim. A Spanish-American republic with a Mohammedan dependency in the south and a good many plain primitives in the hills, it seemed rather an anomaly way out there in the Orient. It might prove more so as the Orient comes again of age.

From the Philippines I went to Indo-China on a cargo vessel which, years ago, had been chosen to cross the Pacific full of explosives because she was then so old that it did not matter if she exploded. No one had done much to her since except to unload the explosives. Her accommodations gave you a manly before-the-mast feeling. Soon after we left, her engines stopped dead. The crew hauled some cross-ties down off the deck and there was a tremendous pounding for hours. It seemed that the engine had slipped off its base. In the end she started again, making the most lugubrious clanking sounds, but she got to Haiphong.

It was a hot morning. The islands of the Bay of Along presented their famous mirage. I now realized that much of what had seemed to be fantasy in Chinese painting was merely photographic. The islands here were mirrored in the calm water looking, however, like reflections of their own distorted and ironic selves. They sat huddled in the sea like Chinese sages, winking at you. You felt that those islands were too fantastic to be real. Clearly they were imitating something painted on silk long ago by a Chinese master.

From Haiphong I went on up across the Red River delta to Hanoi.

In Hanoi you were brought from the station to the hotel in a *push push,* a bicycle turned rickshaw, with the passenger up front feeling like the groceries in the delivery boy's metal basket. The effect was heightened by the baggage that was stowed on top of you.

The hotel was old-fashioned French colonial with a terrace, plants and flowers. In each high-ceilinged, over-furnished room was a big bed with a great mosquito net, looking like a large tent set up in the middle of the room.

I was barely settled here when there was a knock at the door of the room. I opened the door to find an Indo-Chinese girl in the customary trousers and pretty silk jacket standing there. She said in halting French, *"Monsieur, je viens dormir avec vous."*

After I had composed myself I explained that it was a bit early in the day to go *dormir* at all and that I was going out. She reassembled her French words and explained with some difficulty that she did not expect me to *dormir* at that moment. It was that while I was there she would live with me. She was offering her services in the matter of *dormir avec.* I said no, that I thought I had better to sleep alone. She bowed slightly and trotted off like a bellboy who has brought ice water to the wrong room.

I gathered later that it was a routine matter. You could take or leave that special service. It was merely that, in those parts, the opinion prevailed that to sleep with yourself is no way to sleep.

Hanoi was the most exotic of French provincial towns. In the middle of tropical flowers and Indo-Chinese people, it lived its own, unrelenting French provincialism. At the time I was there Hanoi was politically an Oriental Vichy and it fitted the role nicely.

French Indo-Chinese colonies and protectorates had been established by treaty in 1887. The first French rulers had been admirals. Since then a mercantilism had flourished that smacked more of Louis XIV than of any modern epoch. Indo-China attracted the type of officer and career civil servant who had never made their peace with the Chambre de Députés and still talked about regicide. Above all it had been the refuge of that *fleur-de-lys* and *ancien-régime* type of Catholicism that accounts for much of the anticlericalism in France.

L'Administration française in Indo-China had a mentality like the Wang Keh-mins of China. They were French mandarins and considered themselves indispensable in their wisdom. They had worked for Paris and now they would work for Tokyo. The Indo-Chinese people, they were sure, would let themselves be governed only by *l'administration française*

As far as I could make out, the French in Hanoi were interested in just one thing: whether their various sinecures were secure. Indo-China was their career and they expected a pension back in France at a fairly early age. Many of them seemed to have accepted with equanimity the fall of France and were bitter against the British. It was the Vichy spirit.

French Indo-China had completely that feeling of being only a footnote in history, the history of both France and the Far East. France's empire was an African empire, not a far-flung maritime empire. There was no link of mutual need, such as a French market for Indo-China's agricultural and mineral products and an Indo-Chinese market for the surplus from France's export industry.

Indo-China was part of Far Eastern, not the then colonial south and southeastern Asia. Her neighbors, China and Siam, were sovereign states.

By the time I went there in 1940, Japan's effort to build up a system by which the Japanese tail would wag the entire Far Eastern dog was already turning out badly. However, to the extent that Japan was trying to annex Indo-China to the Far East, Japanese policy there made sense. If the Greater East Asia Co-Prosperity Sphere had been an association of equals based on friendship rather than violence, Indo-China would have belonged within it.

21

THE ship on which I left Yokohama for San Francisco in 1938 was a great old hulk of a vessel that the Japanese had secured in the division of German spoils after the First World War. Her tourist class was full of

American girls and some boys who had been to Japan on a cruise.

An English friend at the company's offices had, unknown to me, pulled a few strings. When I came on board, I was told that the berth I had reserved in the most modest portion of the first class was needed for someone else. Would I kindly change? There was some space on the ship they had been unable to dispose of and the passage price would be the same.

I was ushered into a great, tapestried room with tables, desks, furniture of all sorts and an immense bed, with an adjoining bath larger than a normal ship's cabin.

The Germans had installed some of those suites for people who were willing to pay for them in the spacious old days. It was true that the line could practically never dispose of them now.

Like a false prince in a fable, I made the whole crossing in the reflected glory of that suite. It reinforced my conviction that American young women are refreshingly uncomplicated. All the girls just adored the suite and anyone who could afford to travel in it.

I am afraid that to keep up a front I spent a little more than I should have in the bar and for snacks in the suite. But it was educational. It is almost impossible to arrange temporarily to be rich. Until you do, you have no idea what a thrilling, fascinating chap you are. Popularity is heady stuff and it was a grand trip.

Unnecessarily, I spoiled the very end of it. There are things you know the answer to but you still want to find out. The last day out of San Francisco I tried my experiment. Some of those girls just had to keep in touch with me, and I had invitations to visit people right away, shortly after we got ashore.

I told them the story of the suite and that I had been booked for cabin D somewhere in the bowels of the ship. It immediately ensued that they were going to be desperately busy for weeks after we landed. On the dock I went over to say good-by and all of them were distracted. It was nice having met me and maybe we would see each other some day.

The false prince was unceremoniously hustled back to the

stables. That experience proved nothing except that my country was inhabited by people much like those in other countries and much like myself, yet it succeeded in cooling whatever excessive emotion I might have felt on returning to it.

Actually I felt not so much a sense of return as of coming to a new land. People who come overland to San Francisco never have quite the experience of the Oriental, who comes from across the Pacific, passes the Pescadores and sees before him the Golden Gate. To the north of the sea amphitheater, with the gate in its center, the high hills of Marin County rise abruptly, and below steep pastures the Pacific swells break on desolate shores. Ahead lies the white façade of the Pacific front of the city, mounting slowly through the dunes to the hills. A barren ridge, half hidden in mist, sweeps away to the south.

Passing under the bridge, the most beautiful work of engineering in the world, we could hear the thunder of the morning traffic far up on the bridge roadway. Then the glistening waters of the bay opened out to reveal to the right the city on its hills, like the setting of an opera, and, far-flung along the mainland hills and lowlands, all the cities and towns of the coast. Mount Diablo stood etched against the morning sun. Like the "green fields of Eton," San Francisco is worth fighting for. America has nothing to equal it.

At that time San Francisco was still both gracious and rather bizarre. The crisis of the 1930's had halted the march of progress and conformity. People who call it 'Frisco had not yet arrived in droves as workers in the war plants. And only rarely did you hear the sonorous Spanish vowels turned into the flat bleat of the American short "a" when the name was pronounced by San Franciscans.

It was a city that was in certain places rowdy but not shoddy. It was young but not callow, friendly but not folksy. There was comradeship but not the glad hand.

How well it has since withstood the siege of the American mass communications industries and the attitude-forming sciences, I do not know. But, at the time that I was there, its flag was still flying.

San Francisco had an alchemy of its own. A city of immigrants to a large extent, it transformed them. I have even seen it take the gravel out of the voice and the personality of a full-blooded, raw native from the stone jungles of Manhattan.

My first day of work was spent, probably for reorientation's sake, in a peach orchard waiting at a telephone. I had a kindred feeling for the telephone hanging shamefacedly on a tree. We were both out of place. A woman had been kidnaped and deputy sheriffs in high-powered cars were rushing furiously in all directions. Eventually the woman walked into her home again by herself and the telephone and I went back to the city.

Shortly thereafter I settled down, under the title of foreign editor, to the job of trying to do daily approximately what a news magazine does weekly. It was not a bad try and the idea, which was not mine, was brilliant. The whole San Francisco *Chronicle* had become revolutionary and was reorganized to present the news in classifications; the promotion word was "streamlined." The theory behind it was presumably that news makes sense, an interesting hypothesis of dubious validity. For good measure, the San Franciscans and Northern Californians, like the Athenians, had an insatiable appetite for speeches and favored a maximum of public debate on everything under the sun. In the interests of promotion, I became a peripatetic speechmaker and learned from the audiences more than I had to tell them. It was a marvelous way to get acquainted.

I began to belong and it felt good. The world was suddenly full of people who stopped to talk. San Franciscans are incorrigible talkers. They are afraid of missing something. They are always bustling around and are, though much the opposite of lazy, so filled with curiosity that they are always willing to find time to satisfy it.

I know of no other city in the United States where it mattered so little what you earned or where your place was on the ladder of success. The normal pattern of relative status which is inseparable from the free competitive society existed, naturally; but San Francisco, because of that curiosity about things and people, had somehow altered the pattern.

Young as the city was after all, there was a great deal more tradition than conformity.

It was characteristic of that city with its lust for talk that clubs flourished. Although with a membership list, they were British coffee houses in the Johnsonian tradition, which is what a club should be instead of a catering establishment and a hotel or a marble mausoleum for the moribund rich.

The Press Club flourished with the rest. The newspaperman here was not a typewriter-and-news mechanic. He did not put in his hours and go home to his subordinate role in a matriarchal society. Slightly outside the law, he was still to a degree the disreputable town gossip that had been his traditional status in the former America.

Something of the isolation of the earlier California had remained as a state of mind. By California we meant the great central valley with its one outlet, the San Francisco Bay Region, and the coast range country. The other place, Southern California, was a misfortune borne with becoming equanimity.

Our California had the character of an allied republic of the American empire. Home was ourselves. In a slightly broader sense home was "the West." I am not quite sure just what "the West" means. But I do remember coming back from Europe only a little over a year after I had first come to live in San Francisco. I had been forced to stop over "back there," in the north central and eastern portion of the United States which was my native land, and it had thrown me into the customary depression.

When I woke in the morning a night beyond Omaha the train was running up toward the Great Divide. There was a welcome in that lifting of the land westward. When I saw the first sagebrush the burden of "back there" dropped from me and I knew that I was home again.

I owed a great deal of that sudden sense of belonging to California and the West to a man named Scott Newhall and to his wife, Ruth, who were old Californians. They knew of my ambition to become what we referred to as a "stuffed shirt," a moderately prominent citizen, which was a way of saying that I wanted to belong. They belonged by birthright, which was still possible in our California.

Scott edited the Sunday magazine of the San Francisco *Chronicle,* then called *This World*. He made his publication exciting.

The Sunday sections of a few, a very few, American newspapers are quite important in the life of various sections of America. They do what an elite portion of the European press did, and to some extent still does more nonchalantly, in daily leading articles and in the *feuilleton*. They present what is going on, which is a different matter from what happened yesterday.

The reaction to much of the straight news reporting in the daily newspaper is, "so what." Straight news reporting and presentation have been the particular fetish of the American press in response to a demand of the American public. The formula is based on an assumption that events are like cans on grocery shelves.

A desire to see parts as independent wholes is innate in us. We are a mechanically minded people and the organic nature of experience, in which the parts are meaningless except for the whole, annoys us. The laudatory newsroom term, "hard news," and the contemptuous one, "a think piece," are expressions of that mentality.

In the newspaper field the greatest accomplishment in presenting what is going on has been the Sunday magazine of the New York *Times*. It is unequaled in the world.

Lester Markel, who has made the New York *Times* Sunday sections what they are, has been probably the greatest single editor in contemporary American newspapers. He has been a perfectionist who even when he accepted the fifth rewritten version remained discontented. To him there is no such thing as a perfect article but only an approximation of some perfect way of presentation that could never really be achieved.

If there is an editor's heaven, a proposition which every reporter will vehemently deny, I hope it will not come equipped with perfect copy. Lester Markel would be miserable without his ideal of the unattainable perfect article. With the years he has become more mellow, though no less dogged. He has forgiven the human race for its incorrigible incapacity to say things quite right.

Scott Newhall did not have the resources of the New York *Times* but he did an exciting job at that time. His department was a kindergarten. They were all so young you expected the nurse to come around with the bottles at feeding time. But in the kindergarten they had a feeling for the art of saying it briefly without compressing it so it sounded crammed. The product was the most readable thing in west coast newspapers.

Whenever Scott worked late, which was often, we would go home together over the Bay Bridge to Berkeley.

The Newhalls were considerably younger than I but they took a protective attitude because they were pioneer California stock and felt that I could get hurt in my efforts to become a "stuffed shirt."

Those two people had not so much faith in life as a courage about life, which is quite a different thing from the conformist's machine-made optimism. Scott had lost a leg down in Mexico on an excursion into wild places and was still threatened with a poisoning that kept returning and might kill him one day. There was gravity behind their laughter. But he was mischievous and sniped at my tendency at that time to pontificate which came from the desire to be someone and establish myself as belonging to "the West."

Ruth Newhall, too, had worked in the kindergarten. She was outrageously brilliant and was kept track of by a psychologist at Leland Stanford like a guinea pig because of her ridiculously high IQ. I think she felt that having such an IQ was not ladylike, but that there was no way of getting rid of it.

There had been a certain amount of chatter to the effect that she was the brains in the Newhall organization. Scott's subsequent career has made that hypothesis irrelevant but, nevertheless, Ruth chose to get out of his office.

She had made a choice and it was a sound choice. I remember standing in the doorway of their house and looking in startled silence at their newborn twins. They were so small that I bent down to find out if one could hear the breathing of anything as tiny as that. Ruth was very matter-of-fact about them. Babies were part of the business of living as was the fact that she and Scott were so in love they did not even know it any more.

They lived high on a hillside across the bay. Their house was rough and ready at that time for they were building it little by little out of the theme of their lives and of that theme they were not yet quite certain.

You looked across the bay to the lights of the city far over on the other side, and then you went in to supper, feeling the strong response of being wanted, simply that, and it was enough.

Part Four

Europe Again

22

ALL the world that I had known since I had come out of the private realm of childhood into adolescence, at the end of the First World War, was now heading into the general bankruptcy of another war.

In the summer of 1939 I went back to Europe to write a series of articles entitled "Will War Come?" I stayed for the outbreak of the war and then went out once more to the Far East in the winter of 1940-41. Of that whole period a series of events and impressions have remained in my memory, reeling off a vivid, kaleidoscopic view of our age and of the people we are in our generation.

I came to Paris all pepped up again with clear, precise and concise ideas fresh out of the American bandbox. It was going to be hard for me to readjust to the fact that no matter how this came out, it was going to come out wrong. I had won back a considerable part of my compulsory American optimism, that is both a source of strength and an element of blindness.

Europe was at stake and Europe could not win. Europe, God help her, was at stake on both sides. Germany was her last great resource in the effort to maintain equality with the emerging and re-emerging huge societies of the Eurasian, Asiatic and overseas world. The total defeat of Germany could be an irreparable disaster. Vichy's policy later was impossible, but it was not a sheer perverted preference for treason. Europe was caught between the catastrophe that would result if Hitler did win and the catastrophe that might well result if he did not win.

Already in 1939 the French had a prophetic conviction that whatever came, the days of France as a power were over. France was querulous and disorganized but it was also adult and that is an incurable disease. The effort to maintain intact the Europe created at Versailles had been, you felt, the last serious effort of France as a major military and political force in Europe. Up on the higher level you could hear them say that they knew Versailles Europe was dead. France thought of the coming war in terms of a struggle to keep the Germans out of France. There was no evidence of interest, or of even the slightest faith, in the huddle of small nations in Eastern Europe on which France had based her bid to keep Germany in check and maintain a European balance of power.

All French policy had been stubbornly based on maintaining a European structure which, now that the test had come, no one took seriously. The Succession states in Eastern Europe had appeared out of the crucible of history and now they were going to disappear. France had given them up as a lost cause before the war ever started.

After a while the civil servants, political spokesmen and journalists began to annoy me. I had heard all they had to say so I decided to hire a streetwalker.

In a café I found one who was apparently vivacious, fairly good-looking and talkative. She understood that her job for the day was to get conversation going and move me in, accounting for my foreign accent and attitude and explaining that I was her boy friend who worked in Paris. We started off into the working-class *banlieu*. I wanted to find out how deep into the people that baffled pessimism went.

At that lower level you could cut the pessimism with a knife. They did not trust the British, whom they disliked, and who they were convinced would let them down. They had notions about Franco attacking France from the rear. Their faith, as far as they had any, was in the Maginot line. They expected to sit there and watch the Germans come and kill themselves trying to get through the Maginot Line.

For France this was the no-one-knew-which round and the

French were dog-tired. A too-powerful Germany would menace the security of France and Britain. So would a too-powerful Principality of Monaco for that matter. Europe had always ganged up to fight anyone who got too big for his breeches. These working-class French had a poignant sense of the staleness and sameness of it all.

My streetwalker handled me with the skill of a public-relations executive. A prostitute is not an outcast in Paris. She is employed in a traditional, if not necessarily respectable trade. She had read a lot of newspapers while sitting in the cafés waiting for clients and would have made a good reporter.

I recalled that my mother, who could be quite earthy on occasion, once told me that she had hoped if her child were a girl, it should not be a prostitute and if it were a boy, not a newspaper reporter. There is something to say for that viewpoint. A news story consists of facts presented in a form that will attract the reader and a certain degree of harlotry enters the process. All communication except for the purest art is a distortion. The mind seldom understands a reality that is not distorted by coherence, unity and emphasis. Human reality is neither coherent, unified nor, in general, especially emphatic.

All the conversations at café tables and "the zinc" were illustrated with that Latin vocabulary of gestures and shrugs, which is nearly as complete as the spoken one. My streetwalker would turn from the other men to me, half-smiling with a sort of Mona Lisa expression, and with a motion of the shoulders present a three-act drama compressed into a shrug.

When we had completed our joint investigation my girl showed disappointment because we were not going to continue the next day. She had enjoyed the change from her routine. She was a good little reporter and she had missed her calling— or had she?

Later that summer I returned to see France mobilizing. The men were hangdog, indifferent, even contemptuous. They were simply individuals sick of being kicked around by fate and the alliance system. You cannot turn that into an army and May 1940 was to prove it.

To the French, war meant bleeding to death in trenches. France had just a limited reserve of youth, the gift of the present to the future. Defeat would be less disastrous than such a bloodletting as the First World War. Out of a maternal sense, France knew that she must not undergo that again.

Switzerland was an island of sanity in the Europe of those days.

The Swiss were having a national exhibition that summer which might have given a distracted Europe a visual lesson in common sense if Europe had paid any attention. The entrance foyer to the pavilions on the shore of Lake Zurich set the note. There was nothing except one immense globe. On that globe was a tiny red spot and an arrow hung from the ceiling pointing to it. The spot looked ridiculously small. It was Switzerland.

Statistical tables and displays farther on drew your attention to the resources that Switzerland did not have. She is very poor in natural resources.

Then you came to maps and displays of her world-wide trade. She was a trade empire. You went past masses of machines built in her factories. Everything was there, from electric locomotives and huge diesels to precision apparatus.

Next to Britain and Belgium she has the highest world-employment rate in trade and industry but there are no really big cities. Sixty-three per cent of the people live in places with a population of ten thousand or less. Attention was called to the circumstance that she is a multinational federation speaking four principal languages and twenty-two dialects, and consisting of twenty-two separate states, each stubbornly conscious of their individual character and legally only loosely federated.

Each of those states, so small you can usually see the frontiers from any high place, is intimately home to its people. The almost tribal Swiss are notoriously placid. They are a little too industrious to have much time to be dynamic. Seven universities and I do not know how many technical and other higher schools flourish in the tiny country. The *Zürcher Zeitung,* stolidly opulent, demands of its readers a level of interest and intelligence that no other newspaper in the world would dare to pretend the reader had and it has no difficulty in maintaining its position as the leading paper in the country. The press as a whole is one of the most informative in the world.

The Swiss are living proof that the great restlessness, the homelessness and anonymity of our industrial society, is not so much a necessity imposed by the machine as a willful surrender to the machine. They have no totalitarian apparatus. They practice a form of initiative and referendum democracy that would drive the top-heavy bureaucracies of the great democracies frantic, and they seem to feel no need of the histrionic devices and the publicized personality cult of mass party politics.

Swiss are rather grave people. They do not have the firm handclasp, the ready smile and the confident personality. Many Americans and, for that matter, most moderns find them rather stodgy. In his heart the modern disapproves of contentment, perhaps because it is an undynamic attitude.

From Switzerland, I went down into Germany—a Germany now filled with soldiers and with factories running furiously on three shifts. Everyone was in a hurry. Germany was "dynamic." I have wondered since, with some satisfaction, whether one or the other of those Great Reich Germans felt so infernally dynamic while coughing his life out in a Russian ditch. There were others, however, who would not die trapped but whose lives were a flight from the mediocrity of life into the final adventure of death.

In Danzig I was sitting in a hotel lobby when a group from the Condor Legion, ace flyers of the German Air Corps, came through. Their planes were parked near by in East Prussia, ready for the opening of the campaign. They had already fought in Spain. Their presence at that moment in the Danzig Free State was a mocking of the Poles.

As a civilian in a rumpled suit, you felt a certain inferiority. They were superb. Their walk was feline, graceful. They were trained and ready to the breaking point.

Like arrogant beasts of prey, they walked past me with a light shining in their eyes—all blue-eyed for the lot of them were high Nordic. I knew what they had been trained to and what must be in their minds. They did not expect to live. Somewhere out in the vast empty sky, on some unknown morning, they would go down in battle having fulfilled themselves. I doubt if they cared too much what they died for. There is a courage for the sake of courage and a conquest of self that asks for no ethical justification such as a cause for which to die. Living that way made one perhaps more complete within oneself and less dependent on others and the world.

The burghers of Danzig were not made of such stern stuff. Hanseatic, brick Gothic Danzig was a slightly tipsy, though seldom drunken, town of solid people who had preserved the bluff hearty commercialism of the old trading ports and developed an inordinate capacity for alcohol, copious meals and a querulous attitude, that was largely artificial, toward their customer, Poland. A tight organization of Nazi party hacks had rounded up ambitious or maladjusted youngsters into an organization and harried the town into a bulwark-of-Germanism attitude and a belligerence that was not genuine.

Both the Hohenzollern Reich and the Third Reich had always had a little trouble with the Hansa towns which had a city-state mentality of their own and a resentment against being pushed around by people who did not have the feel of salt water to them. I had German Reich currency with me and experimented with offering it in stores with the cheerful remark in my best German that they would soon be part of the Reich. Enthusiasm was nil. The whole idea had no appeal. I thought to myself that propaganda is a wonderful thing. For years I had been going around thinking that Danzig was a burning center of National Socialism and wanted union with the Reich.

Warsaw at that time was in an uproar of preparation. Troops were pouring through to take up their positions in one of the most idiotic displays of bad generalship in the history of modern warfare.

German officers expected the Polish soldier to fight to the last but they had a complete contempt for the Polish general staff. That contempt unhappily turned out to be fully justified. Poland was led by men who were brave, as a bull in a bull ring is brave.

A great deal more could have been done with a people as fanatically courageous as the Poles. After the war had begun the Germans raged because civilians fought them almost barehandedly. A sincerely outraged German officer once told me that an old grandmother had sneaked up in a barnyard and stabbed one of his soldiers through the back with a pitchfork. He took it as an example of what barbarians the Poles were.

The Poles themselves at that moment rather liked the word barbarian. They told you that they were not like the Czechs. The recent collapse of Czechoslovakia without a shot fired had disgusted them. They granted proudly that they were more primitive than the Czechs.

The Poles did not seem to have illusions. They did not expect to last through more than the winter, but they hoped that by that time France and Britain would attack Germany in force. They did not know that France and Britain had no such intention and were quite incapable of attacking Germany in force. On the other hand they seemed oddly relieved that there appeared no chance of Russia's marching to their aid.

Later, in America, I met a highly placed Pole whom I had known in Warsaw. He told me of how, when the Polish forces in the west were cut to pieces, he had fled eastward in order to set up resistance there. He had not been too well informed on what was happening elsewhere. When from a great distance he saw a gray military column on the march toward the west, he was delighted. When he reached it he found they were Russians. By that time he was anxious for any help and was still delighted. He said it took a while to get it through his head, but when he finally understood that these Russians had come to occupy eastern Poland, he gave up his country for lost and turned south to emigrate as fast as he could.

Down in Cracow, in southern Poland, I came across a bedraggled collection of Czechoslovakian refugees. They lived by the aid of the British Quakers who were desperately trying to get them out before the Germans marched. To be caught by the Germans would mean sure death for most of them.

Consular officials and foreign offices saw no urgency and the

Quakers, with little money and no time, began to boil with a most un-Quakerlike anger. They had a full catalogue of brutalities being committed by the Germans in Czechoslovakia. At the last moment many of those refugees, especially those who were labor-union people, found refuge with the Russians. After the war they had a chance to repay their debt of gratitude: many of them came back as members of the Communist cadres that prepared the Communist coup in Czechoslovakia.

From southern Poland I went through German Silesia, which was bulging at the frontiers with massed German troops, down into the new state of Slovakia. Adolf Hitler, after occupying Prague and the Czech portion of Czechoslovakia in the spring of 1939, had cut off Slovakia and recognized it as an independent state. The capital of this puppet state was Bratislava, on the Danube.

The morning after I arrived I went around to the building that housed most of the ministries. No one was there but a couple of clerks who were not doing anything and showed no signs of intending to. It must have been after eleven when a young man came in. He was blond, rather gaudily dressed and looked at me as if I were funny.

In response to his query as to my business, I said that I wanted to see Monsignor Tiso, head of the state, and a couple of ministers. I added that I was in a furious hurry as someone was starting a war and I had several countries still to visit. He said people might be available after lunch. Around noon a few officials arrived. I began to wonder what sort of administration this was. He suggested we go to lunch.

Over lunch, which was excellent, I asked him about the total absence of activity. He said there was not much to do in the morning. I asked why. Giggling and choking on his beer, he explained that around noon Seyss-Inquart's people called up from over in Vienna. Seyss-Inquart was the German governor in Austria.

I asked what that had to do with people coming to the office. He giggled again and said that that was when the government of Slovakia was told what to do. I asked if the government of

Slovakia did not have anything to do of its own. He giggled once more and said no, nothing that he had heard of.

Monsignor Tiso turned out to be pompous, noble in his gestures and completely tiresome. The ministers might have gotten by as notary publics. After I had seen them, the young man asked me if I now felt better informed. I said not particularly. He giggled. He was in a way the most informative public-relations man I have ever had to deal with. That giggle actually said about all there was to say about the Slovak State.

My memories of the hectic period after that are confused. The coming war hung over everything like a thundercloud and everyone was distractedly trying to get done what he had to get done before it burst.

In a restaurant across the street from the hotel where I was staying in Rome, a brawl broke out between Italian and German flyers. Italians respond sharply to people and they did not like the number of Nazi functionaries and officers around Rome; it appeared they just could not take that arrogance any more.

They were angered also by the anti-Semitic literature which was, under German urging, put on the newsstands. Italians were not anti-Semitic and they did not like the doctrine of the Nordic supermen. They knew that they were classified by the Nazis as lesser peoples.

However, they felt about the British the way they felt about the Germans. The British, too, were arrogant. The Italian reaction to the rest of Europe had a querulous tone to it. They had a put-upon feeling. They never would grant that one of their main problems was just that there are always more Italian babies than there is Italy.

But you cannot blame them for the babies. One night in San Francisco I had been ordered by an Italian mamma to take the small *figlia* up on the flat roof of a house on Telegraph Hill before supper. You could see all the bay, the lights on the great bridges and on the hills along the western shore. Her small majesty sat wrapped in her blanket on my arm and looked at all that. She said "lights" with a slight lifting and outward reaching of that warm small body.

Then she turned those great black eyes on me. I said, *"Ti voglio bene,"* which can be a passionate declaration you would make to a signorita and not to a small creature sitting on your arm. But, I could not believe that splendor. The beauty of that night and the beauty of a thousand nights in the far land of Italy was mirrored in the splendor of the baby's eyes.

In London Hugh Baillie, United Press president, borrowed me from Paul Smith to go to Berlin. I had finished my series of articles. The title, "Will War Come?" had begun to sound ludicrous.

A clerk assigned to routine duty at the British Embassy in Berlin rode with me on the train to Germany. Four days later he rode another train back to where he came from, together with the entire staff of the British embassy. His assignment had come up in normal rotation and that is why he had traveled in with us just when war broke out. In His Britannic Majesty's Foreign Office they apparently did not read the newspapers. I thought of the Czechoslovaks trapped down in Cracow by consular routine.

23

At dawn on Friday, September 1, the *Reichswehr,* which was to show itself to be the greatest land force of modern times, crossed the Polish frontier.

You could not have lived in Berlin and made friends and acquaintances for nearly eight years and not know what they felt. Their despondency was complete. Foreign Minister Joachim von Ribbentrop and his clique alone considered this another brilliant coup. Hitler had won again and invaded Poland without bringing Britain into the war. To them it was another Munich without the nonsense of a conference. They were shocked when the joint British and French declarations of war came on the morning of Sunday, September 3.

The ordinary Germans had expected those declarations of war. They had the surer instinct. And on that Friday the whole calamitous business was suddenly clear to them. For one moment they saw clearly the fantastic band who ruled them and the hysterical figure of the man called *Der Fuehrer*. They repeated like a litany the same expression—"twice in one generation." They could not believe that it could have happened to them once again within the period of a lifetime.

Before my eyes they went back to the little-man-what-now Germans of the dreary crisis period before the Hitler miracle. You saw them shrivel. But as they weakened under that shock, they became people. It was a strange moment for me. I could reach them again. I had known them well and I had thought that they were gone for good into that dynamic mesmerized state.

It was an unlikely moment to feel happiness but I was glad to find them again. I had missed them.

Now old acquaintances smiled at me sadly, as if they were trying to remember me clearly. I was no longer a foreigner as I had been so completely at the end of my long residence in Germany. We were all huddled together in the wretchedness of "twice in one generation" and for a time San Francisco and the rest faded.

I had just been through a great part of Europe. I knew that we there in Berlin were not alone in that wretchedness. The humanity of many nations and many tongues was in mourning. Europe was going down, trapped and betrayed, into the abyss.

Josef Goebbels' propaganda machine spun out of gear for the first time in six years.

That dark Friday after Hitler had returned from making his war announcement to the rubber-stamp Reichstag, a small crowd gathered on the square in front of the Reich Chancellery,

Hitler's office and residence. Uniformed SA and SS men lined up around the square. In the Propaganda Ministry at one side of the square, officials hurried out onto the terrace roof to look over the crowd. The public address systems began to function, playing martial music. For a moment Goebbels himself appeared to survey the situation.

More people, curious as to what was happening, were drifting into the square and the crowd was swelling.

Goebbels apparently felt that a demonstration was called for. Discreetly, the glass door leading onto the Fuehrer's balcony from which he traditionally acknowledged the plaudits of the multitude was opened. The uniformed troops got their orders. They started chanting: *"Wir wollen unseren Fuehrer sehen.* We want to see our Fuehrer."

It was the familiar signal for what I had seen and heard I do not know how many times. The crowd would get caught up immediately into the enthusiasm of the thing and would all shout at the top of their lungs that they wanted to see their Fuehrer. After it had been kept up for a proper period the Fuehrer would appear briefly or less briefly, according to the occasion, to accept the tribute of his grateful people.

On this day it went sour. The uniformed duly chanted but the crowd remained stone silent. People hurried out onto the roof above the Propaganda Ministry entrance and hurried inside again. The broadcasting horns struck up a great martial clangor. That, it was apparently felt, would do it. The whole thing was tried again. Once more came the chant. The Propaganda Ministry and all its cohorts wanted to see the Fuehrer. Stony silence from the crowd. They clearly felt no longing whatsoever to see their Fuehrer.

After a while, the glass door onto the Fuehrer's balcony was discreetly closed again. The Fuehrer had been snubbed.

It was only much later in the day, when organized formations had been marched onto the square and into the Wilhelmstrasse, that the door opened once more and the "people" let a waiting world know that they wanted to see their Fuehrer.

What had happened? You found the answer easily enough

in conversation with those Germans. Adolf Hitler had acquired the reputation of a magician. He could do all those dangerous and thrilling things that were giving the German back his confidence and his country its place in the sun, without getting into war. When he did get into war, he was just another stumble bum. He was now no smarter than Wilhelm II, who was still regarded as pretty much of an unmitigated ass.

Even those influential Germans who had long been close to Hitler lost their illusions now. After I returned to San Francisco I met the German consul general, Fritz Wiedemann. I went to see him one day in his office. At that time the Germans were battering at the gates of Egypt and there was talk of their moving down through Turkey into the other side of the Middle East. Hitler was doing great things. While listening to my recital of the familiar news facts, Wiedemann took a rubber band. He stretched it very slowly and looked at it steadily. Finally it broke. Then he looked up and smiled. He was German consul general and loyal, but we were friends and he had given me an answer. He knew Adolf Hitler.

In the days following September 3, determined to force the gears to mesh again, the Propaganda Ministry unleashed a barrage of propaganda, first about the atrocities allegedly committed by the Poles against *Volksdeutsche,* the Germans living in Poland. That had some effect. Then came the victories in Poland and the radio announced them with a great blaring of martial sounds. It helped a little. Nevertheless, the atmosphere of despondency never quite disappeared while I was there all through the first month of the war.

The victories in Poland caused us some embarrassment. Certain "neutral" military attachés helped to keep the press informed on what was going on. But there were regular German briefings as well. We had the impression that the German briefings were overly optimistic. For instance, we wrote, what about that Polish strategic reserve lying in wait in the northeast of Poland?

The German major in charge of press briefings looked amused. He told us that our informant, Lieutenant Colonel

So-and-So, a foreign military attaché, was a better military strategist than the Poles, but as a result our dispatches were inaccurate. It would have been very sound of the Poles, said the major, to hide an army where the lieutenant colonel said they were hiding one, and they would be even better off if said lieutenant colonel were commanding their forces. Alas, the Polish high command did not have so much sense as the lieutenant colonel. That strategic reserve did not exist.

The Polish forces, the major went on to say, had been strung out in a long line on the frontiers, like a small boy's tin soldiers. The Germans had cut through them with armored columns and were in the process of surrounding them and knocking them out. The Germans had even sent a column down a single road leading from East Prussia to Warsaw, with no defending flanking forces. It was an unorthodox and dangerous thing to do, but they could risk it. The Polish high command had no one to attack that column. Now, the lieutenant colonel would have thought about that particular flank movement from East Prussia, but not the Polish high command. The major smiled and bade us adieu, asking us to convey his best regards and compliments to the lieutenant colonel.

In the west the guns remained silent. After the short Polish war was over, there followed the period of the west-front "phony war."

On my way out of Germany, in Holland, I met a man who had come up from Switzerland on the regular express. The train had run along the Rhine with the German forces on one side and the French on the other. He said you felt rather under strain, there being no legal reason why the heavy guns on either side should not blow train and tracks to bits at any moment. The train personnel, however, were completely unmoved. They had got used to it and come to the conclusion that there never would be a shooting war in the west.

24

AFTER Pearl Harbor I rejoined the New York *Times,* then put on an army uniform like a lot of other people, neither helped nor hindered the progress of war, and in due time became once more a civilian.

The war had passed over for me, as it did for so many, as time out from the narrative of one's lifetime. The society's necessity to survive erases the personal factor. War, for the individual, becomes a state of obedience.

The postwar months found me trapped in New York. New York, as I have experienced it, is a labyrinth of hedgehog defenses against the mob, a honeycomb of innumerable walled-off compartments each containing an individual or a small group. New York is not a city, it is Man seeking refuge from the Behemoth that has devoured him. It is a heaped-up mass of masonry and men. For me there is no other environment in the world that so blatantly blasphemes against the aspirations of the human spirit.

I have not encountered elsewhere in America or in the world the New York phenomenon of discourtesy raised to the status of an ideology. It is the expression of hedgehog living. Everyone in New York seems the one man too many, always in someone's way.

New York is a beachhead of immigrants who failed to push on to the new home in America they had come to seek. They substituted an insular New York nationality that is a negation and rejection of Europe and a self-imposed distortion of America.

I remember sharply an early experience in the New York slums. As I was passing through New York on the way home from school, I decided to spend a day there between trains. In the exuberance of the collegiate age I had acquired, by economizing, a striped coat in the colors of my college. Besides my blazer, which was at the time clean, new and rather dramatic, I had on ultracollegiate tweed knickerbockers. It was quite a getup.

Down in the tenement district a few boys were standing on a high stoop in front of an old building as I came by obviously sightseeing. The boys froze, looked at me balefully and one suddenly spat on my blazer. Then they cursed, erupting into the obscenities which are the routine running comment on life and the passing scene of much of New York's population.

One of the boys hissed, "Damned American."

An actual foreigner would never have thought of spitting on my blazer or calling me a damned American. He might have found a bird of such brilliant plumage highly amusing but he would not have been offended.

I am quite sure this boy had no objection to my formal citizenship, which also was his own, presumably. He was a bit of a cultural anthropologist and philosopher. I was an alien there and I was being obnoxious about displaying my tribal regalia. The blazer was an affront.

This boy was merely in the process of acquiring that special, negative, belligerently egocentric nationality, the New York nationality, which is characterized by the sharp elbows, the tough mien, the contempt and boredom, the gravel voice. The term for the other nationality, that of the continental Americans, is "out-of-towners." In the fully naturalized New Yorkers there is a latent hostility toward this other breed.

New York nationality lacks a sense of cohesion. New York is a state of competition, not a state of belonging together. It has been suggested that if New York were to acquire a national flag it should be a pair of elbows on cloth-of-gold. Streams of overseas immigrants and immigrants from the rest of the American continent still enter the life of a city that has already developed its definitive human type. Both are subject now to the process of becoming nationalized New Yorkers. Both develop the sharp elbows for getting ahead in a mob and a hybrid mentality that is neither European nor continental American. The net result is a society, or rather the heaped-together absence of a society, that is like a basket of crabs.

To me, New York was the extreme expression, the symbol, of "back there." Here was the ultimate exaggeration of what the returned peasant emigrant in Poland had spoken of in that springtime so long ago: that absence of the future. This was a lifelong mass pilgrimage into nowhere. A sort of despair took hold of me. I felt on the one hand nostalgia for San Francisco and on the other the urge to return overseas to continue my search for the secret that escaped me.

The office, oddly, was the one oasis that I had. There had been in Adolf Ochs a patriarchical kindness, a Judaic desire to render justice, that had established a tradition in that office. The one element of actual strength that I have found in New York is where some portion of the Hebrew tradition is a living reality.

About two days before Christmas an executive came over to me, smiling widely. I was, he said, going east to Central Europe.

Things became hectic. Planes were not flying because of winter storms. I was told there was no berth available on a ship for weeks. I had to be there quickly or lose the chance.

After finally getting my passport and military permit from Washington to go to occupied territory, I still had no way of getting there. It looked grim when I stopped by the Cunard offices the morning of December 31.

Inquiry had been made there before and they had no berths. The clerk said, however, that a ship was sailing New Year's night. I asked if they had any free berths. He said they had about a couple of thousand. The ship was the *Queen Mary*.

She had not been listed for passengers because she was still a military transport and you had to have a permit. I got, by luck and by running fast before the office closed, a permit.

The ship was silent as I have never known a ship to be. Her

few passengers went early to their cabins and to bed before she
sailed. Her dock was empty. Almost imperceptibly, she slid
out into the North River and moved noiselessly down toward
the sea.

I stood out in the winter night on her deserted afterdeck and
watched the lights of New York fade slowly. Never have I
known a happiness so intense. The faith given me by my father
before he died was blurred and weak but I kneeled in the darkness and tried to give thanks for my escape from that city.

Years before there had been a play called *Outward Bound*,
the scene of which was a liner bearing a group of men and
women newly released from life and going to the other shore.
They only discovered in the course of the voyage that they were
dead, because except for themselves there was no one else on
the ship.

I was reminded of that play now. The huge public halls of
the *Queen Mary* had been put in order again but you seldom
saw anyone there. There was a ghostly quality to that quiet
winter voyage across the gray Atlantic. Only the monotonous
sound of the sea broke the calm.

I imagine that it was because my father was gone now to
what he had so firmly believed was the haven of eternity, that I
felt on that voyage a sense of weariness with all this living. The
world had just come through a period of great issues. Hitler
and Mussolini had given their people no peace, preaching that
life was struggle, nothing but struggle. Back there where we
had sailed from, men also proudly insisted that life was struggle,
action, competition. They were so sure of themselves, it seemed,
and yet we were all outward bound and whether we were homeward bound we did not know. All desire left me except for
silence and the sea.

It was toward the end of the trip that the humorous aspect of
that crossing came to my attention. There was an Army ships
unit on board. They were rough and tough soldiers, most of
them regulars. They were accompanying the small group of
wives and children who were being shipped over in the operation intended to calm down the American officer overseas by
putting him back in his customary habitat, the great American

matriarchy. Discipline was slipping, if not gone, and a baffled War Department was throwing in the American wife. She turned out to be a formidable weapon and actually worked a miracle at that time.

But although the American matriarchy is an admirable disciplinary institution, it is nerve-wracking.

The noncoms on the ship were in misery. They had become nursemaids. Orders for bottles, diapers and what not descended on them in showers. They ran around with a harassed look and jumped nervously every time a sweet or strident feminine voice sang out.

I recall going around a corner and colliding with a war-scarred master sergeant. He clutched to his breast the bottle complete with nipple that had nearly slipped from his hands and he seemed very alarmed.

When I laughed, he looked very bitter. He would have liked to do something about it but he was handicapped by the bottle in his hands. After a pause, he said in an aggrieved tone, "Look, sir, this is a hell of a life for a soldier."

I felt ashamed of myself but got out of there before some matriarch thought of sending me for fresh diapers.

Europe was like an injection of a powerful, strengthening drug. The heaviness and despondency dropped from me as I rode the army transport plane that was bucking the winter winds across Europe. Except for Belgium, where smoke poured out of factory chimneys and trains shuttled about, Europe appeared from the air lifeless. Roads were empty. There was little movement in towns. Germany and Austria could do little more during that first postwar winter than try to live through it.

There is still an organization known as the "Survivors of the Vienna Press Camp." The USFA press camp was quartered in an old hotel that had once had a discreet entry from the theater next door and equally discreet private dining facilities. It had long since become respectable but had a depressed look, as if respectability did not agree with it.

The food was bad and the rooms were worse. The plumbing was erratic and the heating equally temperamental. When the wind blew, the place creaked like a sea-weary freighter. There was nothing to say for the press camp except that we were happy in it.

After my loneliness in New York, it was what I needed. We lived in a huddle, like rabbits in a burrow. Some aspects of living here reminded one slightly of *Alice in Wonderland*. My neighbor on the other side of a paper-thin partition was an Irishman. His companion, so he alleged, was a leprechaun with a long brown beard. You had to be very careful not to sit on the leprechaun at breakfast. Unfortunately, leprechauns are invisible to all but west country Irishmen. The commanding colonel, like the Red Queen, was constantly in an advanced state of irritation. He favored cutting off everyone's head but fought valiantly for the privileges of his protégés.

Vienna itself was amiably daft. Having little or nothing to eat, the Viennese, sensible people that they are, opened the concert halls almost before the guns ceased firing. Since there was no heat, audiences sat bundled up in shawls and overcoats and the performers looked overweight because they were obviously wearing all the underclothes they owned. It was contended that in that freezing atmosphere the music was clearer and purer in tone, a thought that would occur only to a Viennese.

For anyone a little obsessed with what is meant by home, January of 1946 was not a bad time to arrive in Austria.

For twenty years, from the end of the First World War to the Hitler *Anschluss*, a substantial majority of the Austrians had refused to regard their little state as home. Up until Hitler came to power in Germany, the Austrian Social Democratic Party had an official policy of wanting unification with Germany. Strong burgher elements had the same policy. Later, Austrian National Socialism came into the picture.

Others regarded the country only as the widow of the Hapsburg empire, a republic in mourning. Self-pity became the Austrian trademark. Mass unemployment entered the economic picture. Everyone gave the same excuse for it. Austria had lost her vital markets with the collapse of the empire. Alack and alas.

But mourning for the Hapsburgs went out of style during the period when there was so little to eat in Vienna that people would lie down half the day in order to have strength enough to get around during the rest of it.

Austria had presented the spectacle of a man searching everywhere for what he already had. The miracle of postwar Austria was that the Austrians finally settled down to live with themselves in their land and found out that they were quite well off.

Much of the credit could be given to Hitler. The Austrians crawled out from under the debris of the *Anschluss* with their ardor for union with the Reich cooled to the freezing point. But, the Germans had built a war economy and produced a great many things in Austria which the Austrians had assumed could not be produced there. The Germans had not had time to cart the plants and equipment away with them.

Then America moved in with her Marshall Plan contribution. She did as effective a job of economic planning as our not-always-too-efficient planners have done anywhere. Also, with four occupation forces sitting in the country, the Austrian internecine quarrel of the classes and castes became rather pointless.

As Europe got back on its feet and trade was resumed, it turned out that Austria had a rather well-balanced economy. Austria's agriculture meets a great part of the country's basic needs. Its industry is varied and includes a fairly firm base of heavy industrial productive capacity. Mineral resources are more adequate than most Austrians had believed. Water power is abundant. The labor force is intelligent and, again partially due to the Germans' efforts, skilled. The country is not particularly heavily populated and tourism has become a lucrative business.

Even at the time that I was there the Austrians were beginning to take a long look at Switzerland. It had dawned on them that Austria is a better Switzerland, having three or four times the natural resources per capita that the Swiss have. Yet the general standard of living in Switzerland has long been substantially superior to the Austrian.

Continental Europe could stand another Switzerland. In the

black days when I saw it, Austria was starting to become for the first time a nation, and possibly a nation with a mission.

Stefan Zweig, whose love affair with Europe had been one of the epics of modern literature, named his home on that fabulous hill in Salzburg, *House in Europa.* There are few more splendid mansions in the world than the great valleys and Alpine majesty of that land at the crossroads of Europe. Few cities hold the heart with a nostalgia equal to that of Vienna.

Out of the tumult of the centuries the Austrian may have at last turned homeward, leaving the glories and the tragedies of the past to rest in the shadows of that historic crypt where the emperors and princes of the House of Hapsburg await the Judgment Day.

25

MY CLOSEST friends in Vienna were Gustav Herzog and his wife. They lived over in the Soviet sector in a street behind the Belvedere Palace gardens.

They had, of course, no heat in the place and their supply of food was meager, as it was with all Viennese. Gustav was having a rough time earning a living, writing features and scrabbling around wherever he could get a few schillings. He was skin and bones, nervous and at first hard put to it to keep going.

In that household the two of them lived like the Buddhist monk who sweeps his robe before him as he walks so as not to tread upon the lowliest living creature and thereby do evil. You spoke with kindness of others or you held your tongue. Suffering had taught them that.

Gustav's wife awed me a little for she was radiant. She lived in hourly awareness of what had happened to them, as before a high altar.

Their furniture was old and worn but the kind you sink into and stretch out on with a sigh. She had shaded the lamps so that there were shadows all about, kindly shadows that were resting too. She would come and sit near Gustav and then there was a great peace. You fell into reverie, caught up in the presence of her radiance.

There was a reason for all that.

It was not long after Hitler seized Austria in the spring of 1938 that they had taken Gustav away for the crime of being half Jewish. His wife, who was Jewish, went about hiding here and there with friends after she learned they were looking for her too. Then she had covered the entrance to a closet and fashioned an entry through a false bottom of a closet above. At night she would lower herself into her refuge and sleep there curled up and hidden as an animal hides from its enemies.

During the day she kept on the move, living as best she could. That went on all during the war years. She was a "submarine," there all the time among them and in front of them, but they never caught sight of her. There were a fair number of such people playing a desperate game of tag with death. It took quick wits and self-control.

Gustav meanwhile was taken from one concentration camp to another and finally to the great death camp at Auschwitz in southern Poland. The number who died at Auschwitz is estimated at four million. Gustav slept in the stench of the tiers of bunks in the concentration camp barracks built so close on top of one another that you could barely raise your head. It was as if you were already in your coffin. He became accustomed to barbed wire and the knowledge that a guard might come at any moment and call him away to die.

The business on hand there was to use up the last forces of those who were destined to die. Men worked driven by the fear of death and the blows of the guards, and hungered and grew weak. When they reached a certain degree of weakness, they were sent to the gas. A few tried to live longer by buying food from others in exchange for a little tobacco. The craving for tobacco, for something that was pleasure where there was only suffering, became an obsession with those whose nerves were gone. They would sell for tobacco the food that was strength and their only chance to stay out of the gas.

It happened that in the night those who tried to live by buying another's strength were killed. That was the secret law. You should go into the gas in your proper time and order. The code was simple for there was nothing in life but the issue of weakness and the fact of the gas.

When the Russian armies were rolling toward southwestern Poland and Auschwitz, Gustav was driven west in a column of starving men. The Gestapo held to their slaves and to the end sought to satiate their appetite for slaughter. Gustav was not released until he fell into American hands in western Germany.

By one mischance and another he could not get east again to Vienna. The Soviets had occupied the eastern zone. Germany was in chaos. Though the war was over, no mail got through. His family and friends accepted the obvious. They had heard nothing in years. He had been in Auschwitz. The facts were clear.

Her friends worried about his wife, however. The years of hiding had left their mark and she was not well. She accepted no fact. She wanted him and he would come back to her. In those times and after those years, she may have been at the breaking point. I do not know. But, for her there was no fact. He would come back to her.

One day she was on her knees scrubbing the floor of their wrecked apartment. She was haggard and dirty and weary. Her insistence on preparing the apartment for Gustav was one of the things that troubled her friends. She later talked with me about it. It seems she was herself a little aware that she might be getting near that border line where the tired mind seeks refuge in the other side of reason.

At least she wondered if it had not at last all become too much to bear when she found herself on that afternoon hearing a little tune. It was a little tune that he used to whistle when he came home late at night from work. It was a signal and had something to do with there being no porter at the street level door to let him in. He would stand down in the street and whistle it softly.

Sitting there on the floor with the scrub brush in her hand she knew the familiar signal must be only in her mind. But she was a woman and had been waiting all that time, so she went and opened the door.

I know that she was dirty and disheveled and that he must have been a skeleton and a scarecrow of a man. But I know too that the bare apartment and the broken windows and shabby furniture faded away. Where they were in those hours they do not quite know except that they were clasped in each other's arms.

They have tried to tell me for I was close to them and they were dear to me. But I can only surmise what it may have been like. I have never been in that strange and wondrous land. When the three of us sat together in the quiet of their shadowed room I would seek to consider calmly the nature of that radiant joy that enveloped her. But I did not understand for I have never been beyond the bounds of space and time.

Gustav and I were constantly in contact with the stream of Jewish refugees pouring into Vienna and then westward or southward. They came out of all the east of Europe.

Many had been in Russia, having fled eastward before Hitler's armies. Others had been in concentration camps to the end or were released and caught up in the maelstrom of the Soviet armies driving westward.

At first they had gone back to what had been their homes in towns and villages from the Baltic to the Adriatic seeking for their families, their houses, for what had been theirs in life. They went back alone to those places and found that nothing awaited them and no one wanted them. No one pitied them and called them friend. Their fathers, mothers, children, all kinfolk were dead or thought dead.

That homecoming of the crucified was one of the terrible pages in the human record. It was terrible because the hardening of hearts against them was spontaneous, individual, part of no imposed fanatical system. It was terrible because by that time the extent of their tragedy was fully known to those who again persecuted them or received them with contempt.

Where they had expected to find pity and help, they found resentment—as if it was an insolence to have survived.

It was then that they broke and fled south and west, seeking the ports of the Mediterranean. They came crying "Palestine." They had had enough.

The Rothschild Hospiz, a great old barracks of a hospital building with a wall around it, was the transit center in Vienna. You did not know what gauntness was until you had seen these refugees. They had been famished for years. They were all tendons and stringy muscles, looking like anatomical exhibits. Their foreheads bulged because their eye sockets were so hollow. Only Goya, in the war paintings that hang in the Prado, had ever given full expression to that gauntness. The Hospiz stank. The rancid sweat of fatigue so saturated their clothing that they could not get rid of it.

They were hostile even toward those Gentiles who tried to understand and meant to help. What they had just experienced in the places that were once their homes had put its brand on them. Because pity had been refused them, they had fled to one another. You noted that they were never apart, but went always in pairs or groups. One of them, his eyes fever-hot, told me, "I am going to Palestine and I never want to see again a face that is not a Jewish face."

At that time there were some seven thousand actual Austrian Jews who were regular residents of Vienna. Of these, six thousand seven hundred were jobless. Most of the three hundred who had jobs worked for the occupation forces or the Jewish agencies. The Viennese were taking care, where they could, of those whom they regarded as their own, but they did not easily forgive the Viennese Jews the sin of being sinned against. In the National Socialist period Vienna had had a bad record in "Aryanization" of Jewish property, betrayal of Jews in hiding and extortion wherever the opportunity occurred.

The postwar Austrian government tried to wash its hand of the whole affair. The Minister of Property Security blandly announced in parliament that Jews would receive only such property as was actually there and in its actual state (often bombed and burned) and that for further restitution they would have to look to Germany. The mention of Jewish restitution automatically set the Austrian to grieving for his poor conquered country, victim of National Socialist imperialism.

One day in March a riot broke out at a football match between the Jewish sports club, Hakoah, and the Police Sports Club. The crowd was not actively anti-Jewish or they would not have been there and the authorities were blameless except, perhaps, for the matter of the leopard's spots. The riot started when a Jew objected to an anti-Semitic catcall. Furious, the crowd began to chant, "Into the gas with them." I knew Hitler's *Mein Kampf* from cover to cover and I recalled that he had acquired his hatred of the Jew in Vienna and from the Viennese.

In summer Jews started thronging in from Poland with stories of a wave of violence. Out of the Balkans came reports of pogroms.

The issue was always the same—restitution. Reappearance of an owner who had presumably been disposed of in the gas chambers seemed to fill people with fury. Where there was work, it was not for Jews. Half the Jews in Rumania could find no employment. Only eleven per cent in Hungary had a livelihood.

To the credit of the Communist or semi-Communist popular front regimes, everyone who arrived with a new story of violence nevertheless granted that the governments fought anti-Semitism. The Communist regimes employed substantial numbers of Jews but it boomeranged. One of the Nazi propaganda lines had been that if the Germans did not win the war the Jews would rule. Right-wing opposition movements down in the Balkans, shot through with fascism, claimed the Germans' prophecy had come true.

Slovakia had distinguished itself the year before with an outbreak of pogroms. Under the Tiso regime during the war, Slovaks had been the direct beneficiaries of Aryanization. Patriotism now came to their aid. There was a general move to classify Jews as Hungarians or Germans because those had been the languages of the schools in Hapsburg times and Jews had gone to school. It was a pretty clever device for silencing importunate claims for restitution. The Jew who found himself put more or less on the footing of a Nazi or a Magyar Arrow Cross fascist presumably felt somewhat confused.

In Bohemia the Czechs had restitution bound up in bales of red tape. I met a Jew there who was seeking restitution for what he had lost under somewhat peculiar circumstances. He and his brother had owned a large business in a Czech city. His father, who had been the founder of the firm, was too old and feeble to flee when the Germans were invading Bohemia. The son had to flee and called in the principal Czech employees in the management. He made them a present, namely the business. They rose in an hour to opulence.

There was one condition to the gift. They must promise to get food regularly to his old father. The grateful employees swore with tears of gratitude in their eyes that the old man would never know want. The father was so old and feeble that even the Nazis did not bother him. He stayed helpless in a corner of the apartment where he had lived many years. And he starved to death.

The Communists' generally good record in the treatment of Jews broke down too as soon as the issue of restitution touched the Soviet's interests. Russia's solid hold in Austria was the collection of industrial establishments and other properties classified as German assets and which had been given to them at Potsdam, or so they claimed. When a law went through the Austrian parliament concerning restitution of certain Jewish property which had become German assets, the Soviet opposed it strenuously in the Allied Council.

No matter who the people concerned were, or what their attitudes otherwise, restitution raised a storm. The struggle against it went on for years. It remained the central issue of the hostility which the Jew encountered in eastern and central Europe through the years after the fall of Hitler.

The Zionism of those homeless people became fanatical.

They longed and they hungered for the Promised Land. Animosity toward the British, who were trying to keep their promise in Palestine to both the Jews and the Arabs, grew steadily.

Major General Harry Collins, commander of the American Zone in Austria, got into the middle of it at one point by issuing an order barring British visitors from Bad Gastein, the biggest Austrian mountain resort. This move enraged the Austrian authorities and did not exactly improve British-American relations either. The problem was that eight hotels in Bad Gastein were occupied by Jewish refugees. They were bitterly anti-British for they were determined to get to Palestine whether the British liked it or not. Bad Gastein was not a safe place for the subjects of His Britannic Majesty. But Austria, with almost no functioning sources of foreign exchange, was slowly building up the tourist trade again and the British were traditionally Bad Gastein's best customers. A demand came from the Austrian side that the Gastein Jews be ousted from the hotels and put in camps. The American opinion was that they had spent enough time in camps, including concentration camps.

What I remember out of all that is the desperate longing of men wanting to come to the end of their wandering. That desperate desire finally to have done with it all and go home to their own meager land was a devouring passion. There was no arguing with them and no compromise.

I remember the visit of an investigating committee to the Rothschild Hospiz. The big building was bursting with tired, bitter, determined people. Some had left in midwinter and climbed secretly over the Alps because the Italian border was closed to them. They had been willing to face death in the winter nights because of a desperate determination to reach the Mediterranean and, by some means, Palestine.

Everywhere the committee had been asking the same question and got the same answer. This time again the entire gaunt throng stood up and cried in unison, "Palestine, Palestine." Many of them were too broken to live but a few years more and they were weary of living but they, whose forebears had not seen Palestine since the days of Rome or Byzantium, were going home to die. They were about to finish the journey that had lasted for centuries and I envied them for they knew at last what they meant by home.

It was only in later years, after I had left Vienna and Europe and had become acquainted with the Middle East, that I began to wonder if the Jew turning homeward out of the West would ever truly be home again until he became once more a Semite among the Semites of the Middle East.

I cannot remember the Jews in Vienna heading homeward without remembering also the Kurdish Jews on their homeward journey who had turned up in Teheran and established a temporary camp in a large cemetery there. They had come because the Kurds in the isolated mountain country near the Iraq and Turkish frontiers had begun to persecute them after the Palestine war. The Kurdish Jews, several thousand strong, were almost entirely unknown to the world. All sorts of stories were going around about them since they had come down from the mountains. One story was that they spoke ancient Hebrew.

The rabbi whom I encountered among them, a venerable and vigorous man, explained that they did not speak Hebrew. Possibly they had once thought it was Hebrew, but it was a dialect probably of ancient Assyrian. After leaving Babylon, they had lived for a long time among the Assyrians. The wanderings of the Kurdish Jews, the rabbi said sternly, were God's punishment for their having stayed in Babylon when Cyrus had let the Jews go home.

He talked about it the way you say that your father decided to stay in Chicago. And you felt that he regarded the matter of picking up Assyrian as something equivalent to acquiring a southern accent the moment you move to Atlanta.

I asked hesitantly if he meant Cyrus, the Persian, who had overthrown the Babylonian Empire. He nodded. They made the mistake of staying on in Babylon, he explained, because they were blinded by the prosperity of the Persian Empire. They greatly benefited by it.

It took an effort to keep in mind that he was talking about the Persian Empire of 2,500 years ago. You expected him to add that all this trouble about the Anglo-Iranian oil had not yet started then.

Now, he said with obvious relief, they were at last going back to Palestine where they belonged. I was glad they were all straightened out again but that little matter of the 2,500 years bothered me. What had they been doing with themselves?

The rabbi said that they had stayed in Babylon where they were so prosperous. Then, as he put it, there had been trouble in Babylon and they had moved north. I remembered from a look at the remnants of old Babylon near the Euphrates that there must have indeed been a bit of trouble at some point.

Well, and then, he said, they had moved up into the Kurdish mountains, presumably to seek security from some invader. I wanted to get the date straight on that, but he was not very clear whether it was a thousand or two thousand years ago. It was clear that he considered that only a detail now that they were all being flown back, planeload by planeload, to where they should have gone in the first place except that there had been that boom on in Babylon.

The Kurdish Jews were poor, simple people, dressed and looking like Kurdish mountaineers. Many of them had been farmers and others were tradesmen and peddlers.

The wonder had happened to them in their generation—the Jews of Babylon were now going from the mountains of Kurdistan home to Zion after two and a half milleniums. The sin of their forefathers had at last been forgiven. They were overcome with the marvel of it.

They looked eagerly at you in your business suit. It was people from the unknown West in business suits who were concerned with their going home. I had seen this eagerness before among the survivors of the concentration camps in Europe.

But there was an element in the homeward pilgrimage of the Kurdish Jews that made it different from that of the people I saw in the Rothschild Hospiz in Vienna. The Kurdish Jews, as other peoples in the Middle East, were something apart and yet they were bound as all the others with a bond that was no part of our Occidental life. Only after I had lived in the Middle East, and had seen and felt that the intimate kinship of the tribe and the religious community is something far stronger and more permanent than the mere conformity of national citizenship, did I begin to understand the Jew and Zionism. Tribe, clan, kin and faith were something older, sterner, more deeply rooted in the passionate stuff of life than the modern idea of citizenship and nationality.

The Jew's notorious clannishness, his holding together and his ability to build and rebuild his Jewish community under the most ferociously adverse circumstances, is evidence of a deeply rooted human need for human kinship and intimate belonging which is present in the Occident only as a vague nostalgia. The Jew, I came to understand, would never have retained these things that set him apart if there had not remained alive in him the loyalties and compulsions out of the environment of an older world. He is what he is because he has come out of the Middle East.

Modern territorial sense of nationality, the nation-state, is of recent vintage. Presumably it is a passing phase in the history of political organization. It does not compare with a thing as ancient as Zionism. The Hebrews' longing for the land of their fathers is on another level of experience than patriotism.

The justice of its own, imperious necessity is for the Zionist cause. Justice in terms with which modern man is familiar is on the side of the Arab. But the justice of the Zionist cause and the justice of the Arab cause is the question of how many potatoes are equal to how many oranges.

The injustice in the terms of our day is that the Zionists did come to set up a community of their own, employing their own language, in Arab-inhabited Palestine. The Arabs were never asked whether they wanted to share their small and meagerly endowed homeland with another people. They were prevented from resisting effectively by the armed forces of the British mandatory power.

The Arab refugees from Palestine were bitter; they brooded on the injustice that had been done to them until they were sick people. In the Arab refugee camps and the slum areas of towns in the Levant where they were housed, the atmosphere was pestilential with that incessant thinking. You recognized a refugee not because he was badly clothed, as many others were, but because of that brooding, inward-turned look. The struggle in Palestine had gone on so long. A whole generation had known little else; boys had grown to manhood in it and adults come to old age. It had ended in defeat and exile.

All efforts to help them ran into bitterness and suspicion. To forget it, to find a new life and get well again meant to them to accept the defeat and justify the injustice. They did not want to be well. There was a compulsion in them to display their misery as one might display the scars of a whipping.

The same rancid stench hung to their clothing that was the smell of the Jews in Central Europe waiting to reach Palestine and deliverance from their intolerable life. Arab refugee camps came to look more and more like Jewish refugee camps in Europe as barracks and sheds took the place of tents.

My memories of Christmas at Bethlehem are of the exiled Arabs and their wretchedness. It was a cold afternoon up on the ridge where the drab little town stands. Most of them lived in caves or hovels somewhere in the countryside, and some in tents. They had come wandering up into the town.

Children in patched, ragged little robes like nightshirts huddled in the sunny spots with their thin arms wrapped around their legs. They wanted to be warm. They had pinched, wrinkled-looking faces and were tired. I think they were always tired. They and their people were homeless.

It was not the Christmas I had been brought up to, the Santa Claus festival of pagan Germanic origin, the department stores and the glitter. Perhaps the scene here brought one a little closer to the Child in the straw, to the Man who prayed alone at Gethsemane and to the naked, tortured body hung on the Cross at Golgotha.

I went out a way and stood and looked across at the distant walls and towers of Jerusalem on that high hill.

The concept of Zion and the return to Zion is so ancient, so clothed in legend and mystery, so deeply rooted in a religion of paramount significance that its legitimacy is hard to deny. But, I asked myself if the Jew in Israel was not still in the Diaspora.

Would he ever be home again until he is a Semite among the Semites, an Arab among the Arabs, as was Abraham of old, a family-clan patriarch who came up as a wandering Semitic tribesman from the land of the Chaldees?

I remember a scene outside an oasis, in the arid hills between the desert and the sown land, that was symbolic to me of my experience with the people in Vienna who were so determined to return at last home to Palestine. The hills stood empty under the hot sun. Back during the autumn rains the far-traveling camel tribes, the people of the deep desert, had gone out from the borders of the sown land on their long journey into the desert, from sparse pasture to sparse pasture. Summer had come and now they were returning.

The long lines of their camels came plodding slowly up out of the desert and the horizon. There was a patience in those people, a patience as old as their age-old nomad life.

The arid hills filled now with their black tents. The desert wanderers were come home again and all the land was filled with rumor of their coming. This homecoming of the men of the desert, of those who lived the great part of their lives out in that unchanging emptiness, always awed the noisy Arab townsman a little.

The return of the ancient tribe of the people of Jehovah after the milleniums, home to that harsh and lovely land, is the fulfillment of a prophecy that is known to all the desert East. They came once before, after forty years' wandering, with the pillar of cloud by day and the pillar of flame by night, out of the land of Egypt.

We and, in part, they choose to interpret their return in our terms of a modern and passing nationalism. But they are there once more, and have borne with them the Ark of their Covenant, their unsevered link to ancient days and the symbol of their deep need for a righteous and fruitful life.

However, fate had placed the Israeli in the wretched position of, in effect, driving the Palestinian Arab out of his homeland. A way must be found to right the wrong. The Hebrew must convince the Arab by acts and by words that the return of the Jews is a homecoming to peoples with the same inner convictions as his own, and that his intent is to strengthen, not weaken, the Arab community.

The State of Israel is placed squarely at the crossroads of the Arab community. If Israel insists on acting independently of the Arab community and its essential policies, there is only one rational policy for the Arabs to follow: they must try in one way or another to get rid of Israel, and to keep on trying.

The practical necessities of a solution to the Palestine problem and the emotional necessities of the Israeli people are the same. A little Occidental republic under the Zionist flag, cut off from a hostile world around it, will remain a mere appendage of the Occident. It will be in effect a protected state, dependent in one form or another, be it military, political or financial, on charity. Emotionally it will represent no fulfillment, no true homecoming for the children of Israel.

Today, south of the Taurus mountains and west of Persia, the various nationalities and citizenships are all contained within the vague unity called the Arab world. In some fashion Israel must find its place in that conglomerate.

But this has been a long digression ahead of the story. I had not yet reached the Middle East but was still working out of Vienna.

26

FOR ME, the whole issue of the political fate of South Tyrol became a matter of cutlets versus no cutlets.

In the spring of 1946 the Austrian government transported a press party down to Innsbruck, capital of the North Tyrol, on behalf of the issue of South Tyrol.

Although Austria, occupied by four powers, was anything but sovereign, the government had decided that it stood a chance of getting from Italy the South Tyrol, which had been part of the Austro-Hungarian Empire until World War I.

This was the Tyrolean country I had first seen back in my youth standing on the Zugspitze to watch the dawn wash over the far peaks of the Dolomites. It had been spring then as it was spring now, but I would never again experience a spring so wonderful as that one long ago.

In Innsbruck the Tyrol did itself proud. There was a grand parade. It was no stiff, brown-shirt, outthrust chin, master-race parade. First came red-coated boys in full Tyrolese costume bearing bound volumes containing 123,000 signatures signed to petitions asking that South Tyrol be returned to Austria. They were followed by the mountain village bands and the people of the villages marching in full regalia.

A former deputy in the Italian parliament, now professor of international law at the University of Innsbruck, made a fine speech while formally presenting the petitions to the Chancellor. He said, "Carry these documents to the victorious powers and ask them whether it is compatible with the principles of the Atlantic Charter to separate a people from its brethren after so clear a pronouncement against Italy."

It was all the finer speech as everybody in his right mind knew that said victorious powers had not the slightest intention of trying to change that frontier. The State Department and Downing Street had troubles enough without driving the Italians stark mad.

The next day a party of us in cars was escorted over the Brenner and down into Italy. The idea was that we should secretly visit the German-speaking element in the South Tyrol.

They had stirred up matters pretty thoroughly. Slogans were painted on rocks along the way and it was evident the people were agitated and ready for change.

We came from 1946 Austria. Most stores in Vienna were boarded up, whole streets were choked with rubble and a good part of the city was in ruins. The doled-out ration was just enough to get a case of the rickets. In Innsbruck food was not to be had in public establishments, and the proprietors of the shops that were open, having nothing at all to sell, must have been only practicing. There were only seventy transient beds in the town which had once been a tourist and traffic center. There was a roaring bear market in the future of Austria as a state and as an economy.

Now, in South Tyrol, we were taken to a large mountain farm home where delegations had gathered from all around to tell us what a hard life they had with the Italians. I have never forgotten the sight of a servant girl almost staggering as she carried in an immense platter with a mountain of cutlets on it. Those cutlets changed my whole outlook. The possibility that anyone would exchange anything as deeply moving as that magnificent spectacle for the Austrian diet as it was then, was beyond my powers of perception.

The South Tyrol was booming. Shops were filled with goods and though prices were high so were the peasants' earnings. The two provinces of Upper Adige (South Tyrol) and neighboring Trentino were among the most prosperous places in Europe at the time.

I kept asking in South Tyrolese for an answer to my obvious question. The answers were all much the same as that of a citizen of the town of Brunneck who said, "You can get used to poverty but you cannot get used to Italians."

The point seemed to be, as I carefully noted down, that Italians were not liked.

The next day we went down through Bolzano, the provincial capital, a pleasant old town but partially modernized in the Fascists' little-Johnny-plays-with-blocks style of architecture. There were fifty Italians working in the prefecture and only seven Germans. The Germans called the Italians Fascists and the Italians called the Germans Nazis—a matter of pots calling kettles black.

Spring was well advanced there south of the Alps. Indigo and white flowers tranquilly contemplated the white clouds and the blue, winter-washed skies. Orchards starting to bloom covered the hills up to the mountain walls, and the customary crop of puppies, calves and other young things fell over their awkward legs in barnyards. Alpine streams ran full and strong, tossing spray into the air at rocky barriers and chuckling and talking to themselves in the fashion of mountain waters. Old men tended with skillful fingers the vines turning green in vineyards on slopes facing south to Italy and the sun.

As evening glowed like a volcanic fire among the rose and red rocks of the Dolomites, we drove south in a broad, high-walled valley toward the frontier of Trentino province. Night had come well before we turned off into a steep, narrow side road and went climbing up toward the mountains. The road passed through a huddled stone village and twisted upward again, and we found ourselves before the massive closed gate of a castle. We heard people scurrying about before the big doors opened.

It was a castle such as a castle should be. The host was a Tyrolese nobleman, his wife an Italian princess. Liveried retainers waited at the marble staircase. We dined in a great high hall with paneled walls. The experience would have delighted the little boy that I was long ago, and even now I was looking partly through his eyes.

We did not really know where that castle was, for we had come secretly in the night. The Italians were not supposed to know that we were there. However, on the way back toward Austria the lot of us were captured at Bolzano by an ogre named State Counsellor Innocente. He was the prefect of the Upper Adige.

We had halted at Bolzano and left the cars in a courtyard. When we returned, we found that the cars had been seized by the police, and we were requested rather firmly to come to the prefecture. We were in a pickle. Our presence in Italy was illegal, and the Italian authorities presumably held that we had been conspiring.

Ready to assert vigorously our rights, if any, and our importance as members of the Fourth Estate, we arrived at the prefecture and were greeted most courteously by Signor Innocente. He said that he had regretted—was there a tone of irony?—that we had not done him the honor to call on him.

Signor Innocente was a Florentine, a slender, witty rapier of a man. He explained cordially that his police had known where we were and what we were doing all the time.

He hoped we would forgive him, but he had made the little gesture of seeming to impound our cars in order to have the pleasure of meeting us. Of course we could have our cars whenever we wanted them, but he had prepared a small tea and would appreciate it if we could find time to accept his invitation.

The small tea, laid out in the next room of the prefecture, was on the order of an afternoon banquet. Among the guests were two or three principal spokesmen for the German-speaking element, the people we had come to talk to secretly.

Signor Innocente felt it was only fair that they should be there so that we would hear both sides. While he defended the Italian side with agility and firmness, he did not deny that the signatures to the petitions represented the opinion of the majority of the German-speaking residents of South Tyrol. But, he reminded us, the whole matter would be decided by the Great Powers. We had known that before we ever began, and we knew also that the Great Powers were not going to change the frontier.

On that note we took our leave. The prefect assured us that his police had been instructed to show us every courtesy so that we might complete our secret mission satisfactorily. I kept looking at his hands as he gestured. They were the hands of a Florentine gentleman such as you saw in Renaissance paintings hanging in the galleries at Florence. Apparently the breed had not died out in this city on the Arno.

I returned to Vienna just in time to take off with another tour for Tito's Yugoslavia. It was my first experience in a Communist-governed country, and at the time the Tito regime was orthodox Communist.

We had actually come down to see what UNRRA had been doing for Yugoslavia. The country was possibly more de-

pendent on UNRRA aid than any other in Europe, for it had
come out of the war prostrate and has few natural resources.

It was hard to get my mind off the regime itself, however.
The mass demonstrations, the ever-present men in uniform, the
way people looked around furtively when they conversed—all
had something very familiar about it. Only slowly did it come
back to me that I had lived in this atmosphere for six and a half
years under Adolf Hitler.

Serbs and Croatians are generous and freedom-loving, if not
downright anarchistic, people; they are passionate, disorderly
and violent. But democracy does not flourish in disorder and
violence. Democracy is a plodding, not passionate, approach
to living.

As far as the Yugoslav regime and the Communist-controlled
UNRRA mission was concerned, I got off on the wrong foot in
my reporting from the start. People were still influenced by the
memory of the magnificent heroism of Tito's guerrillas in the
war, but I was doubtful and suspicious.

I found that non-Communists down the line in the UNRRA
mission wanted to know why on earth all that UNRRA gasoline—of which there was a drastic shortage in the country—was
being used for military movements. And when I reported that
UNRRA trucks had been used to move military equipment and
that an UNRRA employee had been arrested for taking the
numbers of UNRRA trucks moving such equipment, the lid was
off. The UNRRA people with us became angry. The purpose
of the trip was propaganda and I was not playing the game.

The great name Tito was painted on the walls everywhere. I
was weary of it all. I had gone through years of it in Germany,
years of the arrogant self-righteousness, the swaggering importance, the whole rancid atmosphere of Fascism and Communism.

However, it was to be only the beginning. Back in central
Europe the Communists were preparing for their seizures of
power.

27

M<small>Y</small> <small>DISTANT</small> Scottish ancestors would have most certainly turned over in their graves had
they seen one of their descendants throwing money into the
gutter. Winnowing out the dead money from fistfuls of bills
and tossing it away became a chore. The streets were strewn
with money.

The great postwar inflation was battering Budapest and
Hungary in the spring of 1946. Distracted and uncomprehending people were tossed about like small boats in a storm on a sea
of increasingly worthless paper.

The hundred trillion notes at that stage were not worth
much, but enough of them would buy one cigarette. Billion
trillion notes had a certain value. You felt angry with yourself
when you found notes for one trillion and similar trivial sums
in your pockets. They were worth nothing and should have
been invested in a quick beer a week or more ago.

At the end of May the pengö rate against the dollar had been
a mere fifty or sixty billion. Those had been simple figures. A
trillion was twenty dollars roughly. After that the thing began
to get out of hand.

Total bank-note circulation at the end of May had been only
65,588,000,000,000,000 pengös. Toward the end of June it
was 78,424,250,000,000,000,000, and in my opinion this was
a clumsy, difficult figure to deal with. Prices by late June were
126 trillion times what they had been at the beginning of the
inflation.

Hungary had established a record. The great Hungarian inflation had since May left the figures of the German inflation of the early 1920's in its dust and climbed beyond any previously imagined figures.

Plagued bank clerks proposed the establishment of a new system based on light years. For a time bank notes had been reckoned not in pengös but the milepengö or 1,000,000 pengös. The number of 1,000,000 pengös became so absurd in any transaction that the basic unit was raised to 1,000,000,000 pengös. The only people who knew what they were talking about any more were the astronomers who were called in on the off-chance that they could get it straight.

The Hungarian currency was reborn every morning at new figures that baffled everyone, and it died shortly after lunch when the banks closed. After two o'clock you did not know what money was worth because you did not know what it would be worth in the morning. Workers were paid daily. Housewives were frantic because they got their husbands' pay after that day's money was dead. A decree was issued to compel storekeepers to stay open after the banks closed, but no way could be found to compel the storekeeper to accept national currency after two o'clock. Neither he nor anyone else knew what it was worth except that the later in the day it got, the less the currency was worth, and this did not help you in trying to calculate the price of an egg.

Storekeepers were likely to demand payment in terms of the restricted index pengö, called more commonly the tax pengö, payable the following day. You needed a degree in economics and sound mathematical training to understand that spinning top of the inflation, the tax pengö. It was actually only a mathematical abstraction and changed its value in currency constantly, but it at least remained more stable than anything else.

Daily existence got to be a game of "Tag, you're It." Everyone who was given money for anything hurried to get rid of it. In the streets there was a jerky movement, as in an early movie, of people stopping and suddenly rushing on and just as suddenly stopping again. Those who were rushing had just received money and were hurrying to get rid of it because the longer you had it the poorer you got.

The government launched a planned one-day economy; prices of necessities would be announced at six in the morning and would remain the same all day. Anyone charging more than the announced price would be guilty of a black-market operation. All Budapest laughed. The police laughed and the judges laughed.

Wages were then attached to the tax pengö which acquired a new value every morning. Every morning each worker was to get an automatic raise of so many sextillion or some other incomprehensible sum. Upping wages every day burst the last dam.

New issues of currency in multiples of trillions were coming out like special editions of newspapers. Currency had to pass from hand to hand as fast as people could get from one office or store to another because the value of the total currency circulating in the country was only $400,000 to $1,000,000. Financial experts, who talk in terms of volume and velocity, were like little boys at the circus. All the things that in monetary theory could happen but never would, were happening. Velocity was terrific. The flying pieces of blue, brown and yellow paper were maintaining whatever momentary value they had by the pure velocity of their circulation—or was it the other way around?

The meager supply of foreign currencies in Hungary had fifteen times the real value of the national currency circulation. Including gold coins and American money, the country was operating on less than $7,000,000.

About fourteen per cent of government expenditures was covered by current income; the rest was obtained through the printing press. Those were the government estimates. Private estimates indicated that only five per cent of the government's expenditures was being covered by taxes.

By sheer velocity of price increases, every wage earner in Budapest had been reduced to destitution. Workers' weekly wages were worth a few cents, and directors of corporations were getting monthly earnings that ran to eight or ten dollars.

Office staffs, factory workers and store clerks often literally worked for nothing except where the establishment could secure something that was not money and pass it out to employees.

By mid-June thirty-five per cent of the population was on municipal relief. As large or a larger proportion of Budapest's population was living on private and church charities, or country cousins.

Seeing this demonstration of the hopeless dependence of people on an abstraction—money—ate like an acid into your courage. People had worked. They had saved. They had led decent lives and kept their affairs in order, but they found they had accomplished nothing because the society's mechanism for facilitating and recording the exchange of goods and services had gone sour. Government's bad management had made their lives useless and senseless.

I felt an agonized fury against the fact of human interdependence in its modern version. It had you by the throat all your life—not face to face where you could deal with it but as a fate that followed you and would not let you rest, or even work to an end, with any security.

I did not want to do it, but I had to get out and talk to them and find out what it felt like to be ruined through no fault of one's own. The older people made you sick all over.

A woman out in the suburbs, gray-haired and still gracious with the manner of the years when she and her husband had been confident and at home in the world, ended up weeping hysterically.

All through their married life they had saved regularly. They had done their job in life. He had to retire toward the end of the war. Prices were high then, and they had not had what they had hoped for when it became time to rest. Then came the inflation. The husband was now too old to work very effectively. There was at the time no work to be had anyway. Now they ate only a little bread and vegetables twice a day and could not pay the rent. They were staying in their small apartment only because of a government regulation which forbade expulsions under the circumstances. Later they would lose the apartment and, living on the municipal dole, would have to take a single room somewhere in the poorest section of the city. They were trying to screw up courage to kill themselves. It would be better that way.

I did not offer my good-for-nothing consolation. The free "you must not talk that way" advice would have sounded idiotic. From any viewpoint concerned strictly with this life and not with their religion—which was their own business—they were right. It *would* be better that way.

Working people had their hunger. It was about all they did have. They talked about nothing but food or the absence of it.

A young woman in a textile factory received as a week's wages one-tenth of a liter of oil, two pounds of meal and cash enough to buy a little less than two pounds of bread. For that she worked seven and a half hours a day for six days.

Another textile worker had eleven people in his family. He received for a week's work enough to buy two pounds of meal and nothing else. The family of a worker in a metalworks had nothing but soup, without meat in it, at all three meals. A municipal gardener did not get enough to buy the small bread ration, and his family lived entirely on potatoes. They did not know what they would eat when the potatoes ran out, and so they ate as few as they could.

But you ran into the feeling of status and success even at that level. A house painter boasted that he was doing well compared to the neighbors. Status is so much a matter of being able to see people down below you. His week's wages were five pounds of lard. You could do a lot with five pounds of lard on the black market. They had also sold clothing and bought a chicken to eat Sunday. That they had bought a chicken was the sensation of the neighborhood. They kept the chicken, a big one, in a crate on the back stoop and watched over it carefully. Children came and looked at it as if it were made of diamonds.

From the workers' suburbs, I went into more prosperous districts.

I talked to women and got heartily sick of myself for plaguing them. Old women are so attached to things. They would cry. It was something new to me. I had never cared about the possession of things.

One widow told me about a cabinet that her husband had given her on their first anniversary. It was the loveliest thing she had ever possessed. She said that she had wanted it to be near her when she was dying because it would have comforted her. Now she had sold it for food. When she went and stood next to where it had been, she seemed to be trying to put her hand on it. It was as if she could not quite accept the fact that it was gone.

The rector of one of Hungary's four universities received as his month's salary slightly less than the sum needed to pay his gas bill. His wife, who was well along in life, had gone to work as a hand in a textile mill so as to have the food from the factory.

Stores in the inner city were loaded with second-hand "directors' coats," long black overcoats with tremendous fur collars. They had been the uniform of the managerial caste.

Hungary's inflation was the result of the government's refusal to intervene in the economic process. I talked by the hour to bankers and economists who had acquired almost unequaled experience during this disease of inflation.

They emphasized that Hungary had removed price controls immediately after her liberation from the Germans. As soon as price controls had been removed, wages rose rapidly. The politically powerful workers' parties saw to that. Extensive credits were granted to keep industries producing or to finance reconstruction.

In addition the reparations payments had entered into the reckoning, but at the time Hungary was paying only one-sixth of the annual reparations debt.

The bankers made comparisons principally with Austria. The Austrian schilling had strengthened on the black market from 150 to the dollar to about 65 in the same six months that had seen the pengö shoot up into the billions and trillions, although the shortage of food and consumer goods calculated to force prices up and the value of money down was probably as great or even greater in Austria. After all, Hungary was normally one of the granaries of Europe.

But Austria had rigidly controlled both wages and prices. Funds had been frozen in blocked accounts, and credit had been rigidly restricted. Austria had had the additional advantage that it had no reparations to pay. But my banking acquaintances felt that the primary explanation was that government had intervened and placed the economy in a strait jacket.

During the delirium of the Hungarian inflation, we few Americans were cast in the role of clown. America and Britain had military missions in Budapest, and Hungary was officially under the control of an Allied Control Commission of the three powers. But the Commission had a permanent Soviet chairman, and the real authority was vested in the Red Army of occupation.

The American and the British generals on the Commission could just as well have stayed home in bed. Their presence served no particular purpose except to undermine their two countries' prestige. They were being continually slapped down by the indifferent Russian chairman.

Nevertheless, the Americans succeeded in being the most conspicuous people in town. They had a street blocked off in the heart of Budapest for a parking lot. American cars and jeeps were always rushing about on no apparent business at all. I have often noted, in other places, this American genius for making ourselves conspicuous.

At one point the mission became, unofficially, a trading post for the purchase of diamonds, other jewelry and cameras from the natives. A night club for enlisted men, cynically called the Pengö Club, had been established in the basement of one of the few hotels left intact. A rococo casino of the Hungarian magnates, definitely on the gorgeous side, had been taken over by the American and British officers. Champagne was the customary soft drink, and you went on from there to alcoholic beverages. Floor shows were the order of the day, on one occasion complete with an elephant painted pink.

Where there were dollars there were women, tribes of women,

until the enlisted man from the mission began to regard them as a nuisance. It is the only time I have ever heard soldiers complaining of too many women.

In contrast, Russian officers generally kept sedately out of sight. You would hardly have known their all-powerful mission existed. The same was not always true of the ordinary Russian soldier. Budapest was his leave town and he would on occasion paint the town red—in the nonpolitical sense.

One night a friend of mine, an American civilian, went into a crowded bar not noted for the elegance of its clientele. Two Russian soldiers, walking arsenals, sat down, one on either side of my friend. They were set on drinking dry that place and any other one they could think of. They wanted company. The American played coy at first but decided it was better to be drunk than dead.

Both Russians made it clear to him that when they offered drinks they wanted them drunk up Russian style. They adopted him as a brother, which, with a couple of well-armed Russians, can become a delicate relationship.

As the three of them were going out to find a better drinking place, two Hungarian gendarmes came in with carbines strapped on their backs. One of them, swinging around at the crowded bar, batted the American in the face with his weapon. It was not intentional.

Brotherhood welled up, however, in the two Russians. They would not tolerate such an insult to their comrade. Calmly, they picked up the gendarme, swung him back and forth a couple of times to get up momentum and let him fly headfirst to the other end of the long bar, where he landed with what the Russians obviously considered a very satisfactory crash.

But there were also quiet places where the gypsies played. A gypsy with a violin is an opium smoker's drugged dream set to music. It is memory music, a casting back into distorted yesterdays and a conviction of regret coupled with a sordid element difficult to define. The regret, the indefinable sordid element, the drugged lament of gypsy music was the voice of Budapest.

I remember the city best as it was later during the winter,

when there was snow in the streets, and the mood of the city was the mood of that drugged sadness.

Budapest at that time was a confusing city. The vast flamboyance of the Hapsburgs' massive palace on the hill above the Danube and of the aristocratic old town beside it had been reduced to rubble. Elsewhere ruins were only in spots here and there. The city lived with a sick, fevered vigor of its own. It was intolerably restless as if blindly seeking for itself.

It had always been a histrionic city. The wealthy Hungarian overlords of vast estates out on the plain; the cultured, overly elegant bourgeoisie; the opinionated, fiery journalists; the literary cafés; the incessant conversation and rapid gestures—all had seemed to be part of a play or, better, an operetta.

The play was over but the actors kept on gesturing. Half Mongol and half Slav, a man of hot passions, disturbed imagination and quixotic courage, the Magyar had reached a point where nothing was left but confusion and regret.

In the villages the race had maintained the barbaric vitality of the horde that once stormed across Russia and over the Carpathians into the great fertile plain. But there had been too many wars. Violent and arrogant Magyar princes had through the ages raised up enemies against the Hungarian in all the Slavic lands. The threads of Hungarian life had become completely twisted in the endless conflict to preserve the supremacy of St. Stephen's crown, the supremacy of a nation that after all the centuries still remained alien.

In the gypsy music, in the lament of a nomad folk without a home, there was a sickness that was akin to the Magyar's sickness. The blazing, neurotic pride and abundant energy of one of Europe's most colorful peoples had encountered total frustration.

In winter you ordered a carafe of heated Hungarian wine with a towel around it to hold in the warmth. That stuff was a soporific. The gypsy band leader by tradition went to each pair at the tables and the girl sang with him one or the other of those passionate laments for no one knew quite what.

The sensuality of it was unhealthy, it scratched at your

nerves. It was better to let the hot wine and the gypsy's lament and the sensual moaning of those love songs alone. The gypsy and the Magyar may understand each other, but it was not for those of my breed.

28

THE INFLATION in Hungary ended in August when the pengö currency was abandoned and the new forint set up in its place. Before the end the pengö had reached the point where no one would accept pengö notes of any denomination. The old currency had died of inflation.

After August it looked as if Hungary were going to settle down to work things out. But it only looked that way because we did not understand.

Hungary's laissez-faire price policy, which let the inflationary forces run rampant, had been introduced by the Communists in the coalition government who primarily controlled economic decisions. That the Communists of all people should have backed a policy of letting the businessman and the peasant charge what he wished, had been downright weird. It looked like, and almost certainly was, a matter of letting the opponents of Communism hang themselves by their own rope.

After the war Hungary, like neighboring Czechoslovakia, had sought to find a middle way between the communist East and the capitalist West. That effort was to be destroyed first in Hungary and later in Czechoslovakia. The failure of this attempt to escape the horns of the dilemma of two exaggerations—individualist, competitive capitalism and state-dominated totalitarianism—cannot be debited to the account of the capitalist West. The West neither sought to undermine it nor had the opportunity to do so. On the contrary, America demonstrated its readiness to help both Hungary and Czechoslovakia make a success of the experiment, and gave material aid.

The responsibility for the failure to achieve economic stability rests squarely on the Communists and Soviet imperialism in eastern Europe. However, in the case of Hungary some responsibility rests on the middle-of-the-way Smallholders' Party, who had a majority. These vacillating men had made a vital blunder right at the start. They put a Communist in command of the police power by permitting him to become minister of the interior. The majority leaders had the excuse that the Communists' demand for that key ministry was obviously backed by the man who was Soviet commander of the Russian occupying force and chairman of the Allied Control Council, Marshal Klementi Voroshilov. Presumably, he would not have accepted a government representing purely the majority party, the Smallholders.

No government with the faintest claim to legality could have been formed without the Smallholders, however. Even though the Soviet chairman ignored the other members' opinions, Great Britain and the United States were, after all, equal members with Soviet Russia on the Control Commission. At this early date Russia was showing a respect for legal form that indicated she did not yet feel strong enough to install her own uncamouflaged dictatorships, a move that would have amounted to outright annexation and would raise a fundamental issue with the West in opposition to her. For this reason, too, Russia allowed free elections. The Smallholders were in a position to refuse to permit a government to be formed with a Communist minister of the interior.

The Smallholders were Europeans. They knew that in European continental states the ministry of the interior is the real power. It is the coercive instrument of any government in continental Europe, and the state exists and functions only by virtue of its power to coerce.

You cannot turn the police power over to a revolutionary party and not expect the revolution to happen.

At first the pattern in Hungary was not quite clear. The offices of local Smallholder officials were stormed by mobs. Some were forced out of their administrative jobs while the police stood by. The country was kept in continual disorder. The leftist press clamored incessantly about various "reactionaries." Then the left went into a purge hypnosis. Steady demands were made that certain Smallholder deputies leave the Smallholder party and resign from parliament. The Smallholder leaders yielded and again yielded, fearing the Communists' threat to leave the coalition government, the only type of government which, it was believed, the Russian occupant would permit.

I began to keep lists of the purged, the suspected and those still untouched. It was a daily bookkeeping job shifting names from the suspected to the purged lists and from the untouched list to the suspected list.

Revolution by purge is one of the most boring forms of the revolutionary technique. You start out on the right wing with people who are tainted. From these you keep discovering blemishes on others. It is a chain reaction. Someone had contact with a man who is already suspect because he was a friend of someone who has been charged.

The new Communist minister of the interior, Laszlo Rajk, was in a state of constant indignation that such things could exist as he disclosed, but you could never tie down exactly what he was disclosing. It was always that someone had contact with someone.

When a deputy of the extreme right Liberty Party, Janos Nagyivan, said that what Hungary needed at that moment was not a three-year economic plan but rain, the public prosecutor immediately requested parliament to raise his immunity so that he could be brought before the courts.

The left-bloc press announced that the shortage of goods was due to a conspiracy. Hungary's industries were half in ruins and all Europe was short of goods, but apparently that had nothing to do with it.

The atmosphere was exactly that of the first years I had gone through under the National Socialist regime. That same intolerable self-righteousness was there. Once again refusal to believe arrant nonsense was considered sinful and perverse.

This had become the age of the sacrosanct lie. To believe in the conscious lies of one's own propagandist had become the touchstone of totalitarian loyalty. The National Socialist propagandists had known they were lying, and yet their indignation had really been sincere when you expressed doubt about their lie. Doubt showed that you were perverse. These people had the same baffling sincerity about the sacrosanct character of a lie once the lie had become an instrument of the cause.

My mind would drift back to the days before the Reichstag fire in Berlin. In Hungary all the stuff about treason, conspiracies, plots was customarily told to me in German, and all I needed to do was close my eyes and feel it again. The words were the same. The tone of alarmed indignation and manly repudiation was the same. There had to be a Reichstag fire.

I felt in my bones that something big was coming.

It came when the Communists, working through the so-called Political Squad of the small Hungarian Army, discovered a "conspiracy." That was around Christmas. Some fifty-five men were arrested.

From the Communists' standpoint, there was one perfect thing about many members of the Hungarian Unity, the secret right-wing political society that had been unearthed. They knew so many people and were constantly approaching members of the government and deputies.

Shortly those Communist model confessions began to come out. As the ministry of the interior's police wrung confessions out of the arrested men, everyone they had approached became involved.

The suspects had also drawn up the handiest documents and left them all over the place for the police to find. A member of the conspirators' supposed central committee of seven had drawn up the sort of thing which Russians, caught in the great Moscow purge before the war, had confessed to. The document said that "reconstruction and the tempo of production must be sabotaged to prevent the strengthening of the democratic republic." An economic specialist of the Peasant Union confessed, so it was announced, that he had asked the peasants to halt delivery of produce to the cities in order to prevent monetary stabilization.

Accused young Smallholder deputies surrendered their parliamentary immunity rather than have the majority party forced to lift it because of the Communist clamor and fear of the Soviet occupation command. They went into the cells of the political police and began to confess. The confession mills rolled steadily.

The Communists completely controlled the whole swollen investigation. They permitted no supervision of the means by which confessions were secured, and no one was allowed to check the accuracy of the signed confessions. The non-Communists only saw the signed confessions or later heard them repeated in court by strangely mesmerized and completely transformed accused persons who seemed to seek their own destruction.

One of the supposed chiefs of the "conspiracy," Valentine Arany, did suddenly declare in court that his confession had not been made voluntarily and that he had not signed it himself. The court promptly recessed and sent him back to the cells. He was transferred to the prison of the Soviet NKVD. When he was brought back to court a few days later, he was a changed man. He confessed in full, giving details in the best Soviet trial fashion.

Number 60 Andrassy Street, the headquarters of the political police, became the focal point of a city-wide nightmare. When the terror is running, you feel it like a physical presence. It drives men into isolation, each within his own fear. Budapest cafés became increasingly quieter. No one wanted to talk. People looked up nervously when anyone entered and buried their heads again in their newspapers. The phrase "terror stalks the streets" is not a literary expression. It must have come from people who have experienced it. The thing becomes so palpable that you almost expect to see some immense haggard figure appear that is the terror.

The United States and Great Britain suddenly awakened out of their lethargy and sent sharp notes. The American note said flatly that the Communists were trying to seize power in Hungary by force. It was too late for that sort of thing. The Soviet rejected the notes.

I left Hungary in the spring and was in Vienna when the leader of the Smallholder Party, Premier Ferenc Nagy, came through Austria on his way to vacation in Switzerland. As he had left his small son in Budapest and later bargained his resignation against the boy's return to him, there can be no question about his running away. He expected to return. You can only judge that he was very stupid to leave at such a moment.

Soon after Nagy reached Switzerland the thing went off like an alarm clock. Probably no one was surprised except Ferenc Nagy. Bela Kovac, Secretary General of the Smallholders' Party, a notoriously strong and stubborn man, had been arrested by the Russians on a vague charge of being involved in espionage. A confession signed by Kovac implicated the premier in the "conspiracy."

It was essential to return from Vienna to Budapest immediately. But I had no permit for readmittance to Hungary and was unlikely to get any within a reasonable time.

Then an American came through Vienna in a badly battered Volkswagen. That car had a notorious reputation because of its disposition to stall. The American and I took off together for Budapest. He had proper documents and I had some crazy idea of talking my way over the frontier.

We halted briefly at the Austrian frontier post and then got back into the Volkswagen. After responding to the starter with a few tired buzzing sounds, the car lapsed into a determined silence.

I got out and pushed it about an eighth of a mile over to Hungary. All ideas of what to say at the Hungarian frontier had left my head. I just stood there, dripping and puffing, leaning against the back of the machine.

My friend went in, showed his documents, and then came out and got in the car. The motor—me—started pushing. The frontier guards viewed the operation with detached interest. It apparently just never occurred to them that I was not part of the mechanism but actually human and should, accordingly, have documents. When we got to a hill, the Volkswagen spluttered, and away we went to Budapest.

Louis Dinnyes, a crypto-Communist but officially a Smallholder, became premier. It did not matter who was premier. The country was being run by the Communists' leader, Matthias Rakosi, and the politbureau of the Hungarian Communist Party under Soviet guidance.

We journalists who were on hand worked our heads off, for we knew that there was not going to be much more reporting out of Hungary. Everyone was resigning, fleeing, trying to get away from offices and positions that had once been the ambitions of their lives. In their haste to be forgotten, people had little time for you.

The only serene person I ran into in that harassed and depressed city was a former Hungarian magnate. A couple of years before he had owned many thousands of acres and ruled over his far-spread villages from his ancestral home and his big house in Budapest.

Still a fairly young man, he had found a job as barman in a baroque, elegant little bar that was a hide-out for people who could not take the grimness of the streets any more. He was a very elegant and suave barman, and he said that he enjoyed it. Rather proud of himself, he confessed that he had not known that he could earn his own living. Claiming he had never done any work before, he was so amazed to find that he could live on his own efforts that he was quite indifferent to revolutions.

You understood why people sat all evening at his bar in the dim warm light. In his movement, his quiet speech, an occasional witticism was memory. I had never known Budapest at its height but I had known it before the war and the memory could be warm and comforting—the elegance, the music, the women who were not like other women but like the tawny strength of old Tokay. Except for that little bar, all Budapest was gone.

Early in July I was back in Vienna and Paul Vajda, a Hun-

garian who had been Associated Press correspondent in Budapest for years, arrived in a box. The American military mission
was smuggling them out that way in military trucks.

29

In the spring, before the final
Communist triumph in Hungary, I had gone to Bratislava
where the sad, fat priest, Monsignor Joseph Tiso, who had been
Hitler's puppet chief of state in Slovakia, was being tried for his
life.

He was tried before the Slovak National Court on charges of
high treason for his participation in Adolf Hitler's disruption of
the Czechoslovak state and his close collaboration with the
Germans during the war.

Monsignor Tiso was a pathetic, stupid, pudgy man in a black
cassock. All his defense was futile. Through the tired hours of
testimony you learned how he had been dragged in deeper and
deeper until his own indolent dullness overwhelmed him, and
he let his name be used to cover anything the Germans chose
to do.

There had been a rebellion against the Germans in Slovakia
toward the end of the war, and his name had been used when
that was crushed. He showed his fear when this was brought up
in court. You have to pay, and that dull man's resentment and
his querulous effort to stave off paying were a painful thing to
watch.

He sat there alone, and you knew that he did not want to die this way for something that did not exist any more and that had always been rather a farce. The court and the prosecution were heavy-witted and dreary like the accused, but they plodded on through the weeks while we sat there and stared at Tiso, knowing that he was going to die.

We ate well in Bratislava. There was also a good strong wine from the local vineyards, served in little tankards. An old man played the violin crudely and we talked politics with friends into the night and went over to a café for late coffee because the music was better over there.

High on the hill to the west the ponderous ruins of the castle rose above the comfortable square in the center of the town, dimly but pleasantly lighted.

It was good to be alive, better than to have been a rather ridiculous chief of state, sitting on your bunk in a cell at night, waiting and thinking about the hour that was coming when they would take your life away from you.

I was not there for the execution. But, if you had sat in court watching, you knew that he must have been both horribly afraid and tortured by hate when the officials of the law were killing him. Most Slovaks were sullen about the whole thing. As they saw it, he had merely separated them from Bohemia when it fell.

To the Slovaks the nation of Czechoslovakia had always been only a necessity, like earning a living doing what you do not like to do. They detested Czechs and especially President Beneš. He had, in the winter after the war, warned that another split in the Czech republic would bring to Slovakia not independence but Russian rule. The Slovaks understood this as a threat to turn them over to the Russians as he had turned over Ruthenia, which had been ceded to the Russians shortly before.

Except for one period in the ninth century, the Czechs and Slovaks had not been together until 1919. Through most of its history, Slovakia had been part of Hungary.

Bohemia, the land of the Czechs, had been one of the principal kingdoms of the medieval German empire, and later it was part of the Austrian, more western European portion of the Austro-Hungarian Empire. Bohemia was one of the striking realities of Europe, and golden Prague had been one of the glories of the continent.

Slovakia was merely a peasant's dialect, a linguistic area. In the first Czechoslovak republic, Slovakia became the tail of the Czech dog. Previously the Slovak had been a Slavic-speaking, lesser sort of Hungarian. Now he had become a lesser sort of Czech. This was not something which had been done to the Slovaks; they enjoyed constitutional rights and all that went with it. The unimportance of being Slovak was a joke that fate had played on them. One Slovak whom I met later in Prague expressed it rather brutally. The Communists then having taken over Czechoslovakia, I twitted him a little on the point that now Slovakia was, for practical purposes, part of the Soviet Union. My Slovak thought a bit, shrugged and said, "Why be a Slovak all your life long?"

Slovak national feeling was like so much of eastern European nationality: passionate but pointless. A Viennese, talking about Bulgaria, expressed it. He said the only thing you could really say about Bulgaria was—why?

The main trouble with Czechoslovakia, however, was that it straddled the mysterious line between western Europe and eastern Europe. Slovakia lies east of that line running from the Baltic to the Adriatic that divides the east from the west. There is an eastern Europe, a mentality and a reality.

The Slovaks are not European in the western sense. The Europe that has changed humanity, the great ringing name, has been the Europe of the Latin and Germanic peoples. Only one Slavic people was wedded to it and part of it; the Czechs are not of the east. They are Slavs but have next to nothing of the Slavic spirit.

Stand in the morning on the Belvedere opposite the Hradcany above Prague. Watch the mist from the Vltava clear away from the baroque and Gothic panorama in the valley beneath and on the hills around. Try to deny that all this is of the true Europe, the great heritage that is the Occident.

Slovakia under the Košice agreement, which set up the second Czechoslovak Republic after World War II, was close to self-

governing, with its own cabinet—called a Board of Trustees—
and parliament, but was also represented in the national parliament and government in Prague.

The Slovak elections in late 1946 had given a sixty-two per
cent majority to the Slovak Democratic Party. It was a party
like the Smallholders' Party in Hungary which had received
fifty-seven per cent of the vote in the Hungarian elections. It
not only controlled the Slovak semiautonomous regime but was
the second largest party next to the Communist Party in the
parliament in Prague.

Saturated at the time with the Hungarian experience, I
pricked up my ears when the official Czechoslovak Communist
Party paper, *Rude Pravo,* declared in April of 1947 that the
Slovak Democratic Party must either "get rid of its subversive
elements" or "cease to be regarded as a party serving the positive aims of the republic."

It was practically word for word the central theme of almost
every major policy editorial in the Hungarian Communist paper.

As it turned out, the Communist discovery of a "conspiracy"
in Slovakia and the campaign against the Slovak Democratic
Party followed very closely the pattern with which I had become
familiar in Hungary. It was to be part of the complicated story
of the fall of the postwar Czechoslovak Republic.

30

It was cold on the St. Wen-
ceslas Square in Prague those winter nights at the beginning of
1948. Six nights a week I went down the long square in the
heart of the city feeling the nipping cold. It was quiet at that

late hour. I always stopped at the booth of the man who sold me toasting hot sausage roasted over the coals. We exchanged greetings in terms of my few words of Czech. He was a bear of a man, red-faced from standing in the cold. The sausage was a nightly ceremony, and we were very polite to each other.

Across the square, in bright lights, stood the words *Svobodne Slovo—Free Word.* My late pilgrimage in the crystal winter nights was to *Free Word,* the newspaper of the second largest Czech political organization, the Czech National Socialist Party. Once the party of Beneš, it was possibly the most typically Czech democrat of the five Czechoslovak parties.

That big shining sign—*Free Word*—was a cheerful sight. It is a good thing, freedom. There is something about it that says: Lift up your heart and go seeking. Life is perhaps less of a burden without it, but the word holds open the door of tomorrow.

I went to the paper to get the latest edition off the press and pick up any late news from the staff. Since I went there so regularly, I began to think of that sign as a friend. *Svobodne Slovo* were brave warm words; they were among the first Czech words that I had learned, and I was childishly proud of my small vocabulary. There was both a strength and a melancholy minor tone in the sound of the hoarse Slavic consonants.

On the night of Tuesday, February 23, 1948, my sign went out. A jubilant Communist voice spoke from the broadcasting horns on the square. In literal translation, it said, "Colleagues of the *Free Word,* your light has gone out forever."

The brilliantly executed operation by which Communism overthrew the free Czechoslovak Republic was drawing to a close that night. The words, *Svobodne Slovo,* faded away.

I remembered a night almost exactly fifteen years before, when the brown-shirted cohorts of National Socialism, bearing torches, had marched past the Reich Chancellery in Berlin to salute the new Chancellor, Adolf Hitler. They too had been jubilant. You asked yourself why. What was it about freedom that men could be found to fight against it? Freedom was a good thing, but there seemed to be some fault in it. Why should its enemies repeatedly be able to mobilize such forces against it?

The Communist coup had now been running for four days. I was tired, and that question about freedom stayed in my mind.

Friday night, the night before the Communists had started the coup that overthrew the Republic, I had sat up nearly all night, most of it in the office of the *Svobodne Slovo*. We had waited there, believing that President Eduard Beneš would call on the army to maintain order and the republic. Only this last chance to preserve freedom remained. It involved risk—civil war, dead people in the streets, the usual heartbreak and suffering. He might not have won out in the gamble, but it was the only way.

That night of waiting for one man to save a people is another of those times for which I am perversely grateful. The cage of self, that crushing, restraining thing, fell away. I was an American and safe within the walls of my little function as news gatherer. But all at once my identity did not matter. Freedom is a greater thing than nationality. Nations come and go but the human drama does not change. At that moment the Czechs were all the rest of us.

We have made the word freedom hackneyed. Like money passed too often from hand to hand, words become soiled things; they are used too often, and the freshness goes out of them. But during that long agony of waiting for one man to act, you knew what freedom was—that tired word. It was dying, and you wanted desperately for it to live, live in the lowland villages and along the high ridges of the country on the plateau there in the heart of Europe. This was not the place your passport came from, but did that matter?

You wanted to go out in the morning, after that night of waiting, and see the troops standing guard over the right of men to live their own lives and dream their own poor dreams. There was no living without freedom. It was not an empty sound but a thing, precious and intimate, and terribly menaced. It was alone and lost in that night when the word that could save it did not come from the somber castle above the Vltava because a man there could think only in formulas. Then, and later, he had sought to preserve the form of parliamentary democracy. It was his terrible weakness that he always mistook the form for the reality.

The Czechs, in the sudden volcanic fury which in February overwhelmed their effort to find a resting place between two worlds, were pathetic. Thousands on endless thousands were brought out to march in demonstration during the five days of the Communist clamor surrounding the overthrow of the republic and the setting up of the dictatorship. The wretched thing about it was that a great part of those throngs were not Communists at all. On the contrary, they had had a warm, domestic pride in the small republic, and they had their memory of the wise, fatherly figure of Thomas Masaryk.

They did not want this thing that was happening to them, but they marched, demonstrating against their own republic and their hearts' desire. They feared for their jobs.

In the state-owned enterprises, the Communists threatened and bullied. Whoever did not march would be out in the street with a black mark on his employment record. Managers and office workers were told to go and march, and they marched. The Czech is orderly and industrious and needs his status, his desk to sit behind. He is, like so many of the rest of us, not something in himself but dependent on his status, on the little something he has achieved which gives him his place in the human hierarchy.

When that was threatened he got up and went out to march. Knowing fairly well what he was doing, he demonstrated for the overthrow of his own freedom. He knew by that time what life would be. He knew of the terror and the constant suspicions of the Communist. The good, somewhat kindly, free life where you were your own man among other men would end, and life would become a hangdog sort of thing through to the end. But he marched.

I stood on St. Wenceslas Square in the midst of that and watched an immense throng of Czechs, with the inevitable brief cases tucked under their arms, march. They looked frightened and they were ashamed. Many did not look anyone in the face. They had no right to, not while they did what they were doing.

Here and there I saw the tears. How many still remember now the day they marched, demonstrating against their republic, their freedom, their right to manhood? Perhaps those who could not keep the tears back as they trotted along clinging to their brief cases will remember longest and carry with them to the end the stigma of that shame. There had been no violence, only the threat that if the Communists won and they did not march, they might lose their jobs, their status.

Something about it made me crawl. I was afraid. Did I know what I would do? There was much about this betrayal that came too close. I wondered if I would not have marched too. We are expendable in this generation which is in transition to a different life which we shall never know, expendable down to the last shred, even, of our poor treasure of self-respect.

The Czechoslovak Republic had been the victim of a number of circumstances, but first and foremost of the aberration that the totalitarian, the antidemocrat, has a right to participate in the democratic process. There had been a strong pro-Soviet movement following the liberation of most of the country by Soviet Russian troops in the spring of 1945. In May 1946, after the Russians had left, the Czechs had voted heavily for the Communists. Sitting in parliament as the largest party, though not a majority party, the Communists had received the premiership and the ministry of the interior with its control of the police power.

But the government had been a true coalition of all parties and not a façade for Communist rule.

There had followed one of the most interesting experiments of contemporary history—the Czechoslovak middle way. All basic and large industry had come into public ownership. By 1947 between seventy and eighty per cent of Czechoslovak industry was government-owned. Small industry, employing in a few categories up to five hundred persons, and commerce remained the field of private enterprise. Banking and large-scale finance became a government monopoly. Peasants retained their holdings and land reform increased the number of peasants working their own land. The all-embracing Confederation of Labor and its member unions had been given a status close to that of a special estate within the realm. The over-all economy was a planned economy working within a system of government programing.

Possibly there was something to say for the middle-way effort to get definite control of the new artificial environment we must live with in the industrialized world. It was concerned with man's effort to have the new forces be concerned with him and not with abstractions like the operation of economic law or the maximum profit on risk investment.

There had not been time to demonstrate the actual value of the experiment. Certainly the Czechs showed a definite pride in it. They wanted to be a bridge between East and West, a proof that both sides are, in different ways, seeking the same thing. They had the idea that both the communist and the capitalist have a contribution to make, and perhaps they both do.

It had seemed to me that earlier even the Czech Communists, as opposed to the pure Muscovites, had felt a certain pride in the Czechoslovak middle way. Possibly they were for a time what the Communists call deviationists—heretics.

I do not know just when the Czechoslovak Communists changed and took the road to dictatorship. It seems to me that it may have been at the moment when a Czechoslovak delegation headed by the Communist premier, Klement Gottwald, visited Stalin in July 1947 after the Czechoslovak cabinet had accepted participation in the Marshall Aid Plan. Immediately after Gottwald had talked with Stalin, a hurried long-distance telephone call to Prague canceled Czechoslovak participation. At about the same time the Communists probably began to feel that they were going to lose votes in the elections scheduled for the spring of 1948. I rather think that the latter consideration was of equal weight with Stalin's wrath over too much compromising with the West. The acid test of a democrat is his willingness to step down. Communists are after all not democrats and do not claim to be in terms of any definition of the word but their own.

In any case, the conspiracy charges against the Slovak Democratic Party leadership blossomed into a full-scale purge campaign like the one in Hungary. The other parties began to report that witnesses were being prepared against their leaders. Minister of the Interior Nosek, the Communist, was transforming the whole police force into a Communist police organization.

A full crisis arose over Gottwald's effort to install a Communist-controlled regime in Slovakia after the predominantly Slovak Democrat Board of Trustees had been forced out by a Communist maneuver. The leaders of the other parties got a rude shock when Gottwald, during the Slovak affair, which ended in a momentary stalemate, tried to force a ruling that mass organizations should participate in the decisions of the government coalition. What he called mass organizations were the Communist front organizations.

On all fronts, economic and political, the compromise on which Czechoslovakia was based—the middle way—started breaking up as the Communists drove ahead.

I had absolutely no right, professional or otherwise, to say my two cents' worth. Just the same, I did. My professional pride in reporters' neutrality suddenly seemed trivial and cowardly. People have to stay free, and there are no neutrals when freedom is actually at stake.

There were few people in Prague who had gone through the Hungarian Communist coup. I knew a lot of deputies, newspaper editors, members of party secretariats and the like. My notes on all I had seen and heard in Hungary were in my bag. I memorized as many details as possible and started my own small propaganda campaign where I could and as I could. All of those political people were still talking in constitutional terms instead of armed force. I wanted to help convince them that only the army, the one non-Communist armed force, mattered now and must be used quickly. It was not a particularly sound business for a foreigner to be engaged in and was even quite immodest.

Everything that had been developing came to a head when the democratic parties' ministers in the cabinet demanded that Minister of the Interior Nosek reverse his sudden appointment of eight Communist police commanders in Prague, thus replacing non-Communists. By that time it had become hopelessly clear what the Communists were preparing for. Because Nosek refused, twelve ministers resigned. In effect the coalition had collapsed.

What the democratic parties had really done was turn to President Eduard Beneš for succor. There was no way left but a trusteeship cabinet of neutral, civilian functionaries and army rule under presidential authority, with rapid elections. Elections were scheduled for late spring anyway. The people would have to decide whether they did or did not want what the Communists were preparing.

On the day after the resignations, however, Beneš received a delegation of Communist workers.

He told them, "When the crisis began there was a rumor that a government of officials would be formed. As soon as I heard of this from Premier Gottwald, I stated categorically that a government of officials does not exist for me and that I would never name a government of officials. We have a parliamentary regime."

At the moment he spoke, Czechoslovakia no longer had a parliamentary regime. The Communist action committees or local soviets, set up quietly months before for the Communist coup, were going into operation. Ministries, party headquarters, public and private establishments were occupied by force. A Central Action Committee was forming to direct the coup and in effect govern extra-legally. What Czechoslovakia had was a civil war but the democratic side could not fight. Democracy had not been organized in advance for civil war. It did not control the police power of the state as the Communists did. It had no armed worker battalions. The army, the great majority of whose officers and men were loyal to the republic, stood by and received no word from Beneš, its commander in chief.

On Wednesday President Beneš accepted Gottwald's new cabinet. It really did not matter any more. The Communist revolutionary regime already ruled.

While the Communists acted, President Beneš sought the proper constitutional formula to end the "cabinet crisis."

All through his political life he had always had one paper formula or another. He had been the perfect League of Nations statesman, idol of the more learned editorial writers and well-intentioned political scientists. He had mastered every dispute as long as it was a matter of words. The only things he could not deal with were the passionate realities of history, for he was dry as the paper on which his formulas were written.

Munich had taught him nothing. The postwar experience of all eastern Europe could teach him nothing. He was a wonderfully consistent man.

There is a way to be what Eduard Beneš really was that is more human and more amusing. *The Good Soldier, Schweik,* a superficially stupid and amiably clever Czech soldier who always dodged front line service, was a literary figure that fascinated the Czechs.

They knew why he fascinated them. The Czech, after the battle of the White Mountain and the defeat of the Hussites, had submitted to a religious Counter Reformation and a reimposition of Hapsburg rule and custom. He had made his compromise with life on the basis of defeat.

There were portions of Europe where the Counter Reformation was a noble resurgence of the great historic faith revivified under the preachers and teachers of a penitent and profound Catholicism. In Bohemia the Counter Reformation had become a lip service that grew into a tenacious but crippled faith rooted in conformism. Hapsburg Catholicism was a political and social regime more than a spiritual conviction.

The Czech had been mortally wounded in that struggle in a fashion from which there is perhaps no recovery. In the long years of the Counter Reformation and the slow acceptance of the Catholic formalism of the Hapsburgs, he had lost too much. The Czechs would produce occasional brave men and groups, but essentially the Czech, God help him, is but seldom fully master of his own soul.

Neat, erudite, arid and cosmopolitan, Eduard Beneš was another Good Soldier Schweik, always absent when there was nothing left to do but fight, win or lose.

Of Eduard Beneš it has been said that he was an excellent secretary to Thomas Masaryk, and he remained a secretary to the end of his life. Papers, documents and formulas were the realities of his life. Freedom is a living, desperately human and hard-to-hold thing; it is not a formula, something to be duly documented and attested and put away in the files.

The Czech nation had not fought for its freedom, but it took the occasion in the spring of Jan Masaryk's death, through suicide or murder, and in the autumn of Beneš' death to pity itself. Both occasions were moving spectacles. To bewail the loss of what you were unwilling to fight for is so very human.

Jan Masaryk lay in state in the Czernin Palace, the massive baroque monument to the pride of the once great house of Czernin which had sought to rival in splendor the imperial house of Hapsburg. It stood back on the Hradcany hill beyond the great square and served as Foreign Ministry. Masaryk at the time of his death had been foreign minister.

Some two hundred thousand people stood in line hour after hour. Many of the women and children held in their hands little nosegays of white flowers that wilted as the hours of waiting went by.

That line of common people standing four to six abreast stretched in loops within loops for a distance of about two miles.

This multitude who waited had known and loved Jan Masaryk best as the voice from London during German rule. "London calling" warmed them during the dark epoch of the war. That dramatic phrase, which told them not to despair, had rung out a few days before on the square before the castle. The response to the students who had come chanting "London calling" in a last effort to reach Beneš, had been a police charge and the crack of rifles.

It was here, where the throng waited, that those few youngsters who had dared to oppose in the streets the new regime had been dispersed with blows and violence and been, when captured, dragged away to waiting police trucks.

They had been what was left of a nation's honor.

This castle hill, where the people stood today, had been the home of Bohemian kings from ancient days. Fleeing Bohemian nobles and soldiery had swept down through here in 1620 after the battle of the White Mountain that had overthrown Czech independence for three hundred years. The waiting throngs would be added to the memories of that place of memories.

When you talked to those waiting, you found that they were there to say farewell to both father and son. Thomas Masaryk had come home just before Christmas in 1918 to be president of a free republic of free men. That had been only thirty years before.

At the funeral ceremonies the next day you wondered again what kind of man Eduard Beneš was. He was still president. He sat silent while Klement Gottwald delivered a funeral oration that was one unbroken piece of insolence. Sad-faced and unctuous, Gottwald installed Thomas Masaryk's son as a saint in the Communist heaven and, turning toward the coffin, concluded in a low, emotional voice, "Dear Honza, we shall always be with the people and go forward with the people. This I promise you." "Honza" was an affectionate diminutive for "Jan."

Eduard Beneš had sat impassive through that and through the opening ceremony, when trombones softly played "Ye Who Are Warriors of God," an old Hussite melody. He seemed nothing but the dry paper man who had solved the "cabinet crisis" by placing his country in the hands of a despotism.

But, something at last got through to that gray, tired-looking little man. At Thomas Masaryk's funeral back in the days of the free republic, a folk song had been sung, "Plow Your Land, My Son," a song of an earth-bound, peasant people. A children's chorus now sang it again, warm and clear. The dry man, whose formulas could not master the passionate stuff of life, broke and wept. It was good that he wept. It was easier to forgive him.

A few months later he had the decency to refuse to sign the new constitution and resigned the presidency. Gottwald took his place.

On the third of September in the early evening, Eduard Beneš died.

This time there was an element of desperation evident in the reaction of the people. The Czechs had been under Communist police rule for six months.

The Ministry of the Interior and the Central Action Committee issued ugly statements warning "reactionaries" against using the occasion for "anti-state provocative acts." Buses were halted coming into the city. Pressure was put on to keep delegations from outside from attending.

Prague began to fill up with police and armed worker defense guards. Police reinforcements armed with rifles appeared at the Central Post Office and certain other strategic points.

The throng waiting to pass the bier in the Memorial Hall on Zizkov Hill formed on Monday morning, and it kept moving past all through Monday night and up to Tuesday midnight. On the second day the line was about three and a half miles long.

When the doors of the hall were closed Tuesday at midnight, the people rioted. There was neurotic shame and fury in the way they showed the need to see the dead body of that man whose defeat was their own defeat.

The throng cried out, "We want to see our President!" Their president was actually the alcoholic Klement Gottwald up at the Hradcany, presumably snoring in his customary half-drunken daze. But the people obviously did not mean him.

Police formed a cordon across the entrance to Zizkov Hall. The people promptly broke through it. The police formed a wedge and moved in to break up the crowds near the door. They were driven back. One section of the doors was closed. The throng promptly broke the door open again.

It took an hour's struggle for the police to force the crowd far enough down the hill to get the doors closed and the situation under control. Ambulances came for the injured and police trucks for the most recalcitrant.

Next day the funeral procession was a military demonstration of Communist power.

Eduard Beneš' dead body was borne through the streets, a captive of those who had conquered and shamed him. Armed troops marched ahead of the cortege and behind in massive array. Armed worker guards and police lined the streets on both sides facing the people, ready. Double rows of armed men surrounded the gun carriage bearing the body and the long line of ministers and high officials who marched behind it. They watched steadily the windows of buildings along the way.

The massed onlookers were sullen. Nothing happened. It was too late for anything to happen, far too late.

It would be too late for any people from the moment they permitted Communists to occupy actual posts of power in any democratic government. A Communist had no more place within a democratic regime than a democrat within a Communist one. That was the lesson of Czechoslovakia and a lesson not to forget.

I left not long after Beneš' funeral.

The fertile plateau of Bohemia is a maternal land with its villages and people nestled firmly against its fecund old body.

It was a ridiculous moment to feel envy, but the people here were rooted. They had bowed to alien rule before but they were tenacious and utterly European. More than Communism would be needed to uproot them.

The winter snows on the plains and the winter wind crying along the ridges, the spring rains and the summer and the autumn harvest were one with them. Their cities were not sprawling metropolises but merged into the land, and you were soon out of them and among village people.

It had been the peasant song, "Plow Your Land, My Son," sung by children, that broke the futile, brittle self-control of Eduard Beneš. I had not understood why they still were fond of him after he had failed them so completely. But then I had never been at home as they were at home on the wide plateau there in the heart of Europe. He was one of their own. They forgave.

Now that I was leaving, I understood a little better why what had happened in Czechoslovakia had been so personal to me. Most of these people too were not fitted to deal quickly and determinedly with crises. They too sought peace and work, the quiet productive years. History would not let them alone and they were weary as I was weary of its bawling, strident voice, crying out slogans.

They were people of the middle way.

It is little consolation to those of the middle way that in the end theirs will probably prove to be the right way.

Part Five

Middle East

31

I spent Christmas Eve, 1948, on a train traveling from Vienna to Italy, sharing a compartment with two American girls from the United States High Commissioner's Office in Vienna. They had sandwiches, a cake and a small artificial Christmas tree with lights which we set up on a table. This was our Christmas celebration.

We noticed a Russian guard, a big, rather clumsy young man, standing out in the corridor, looking quite lonely. When one of the girls offered him a piece of cake, the effect was electric. He galloped away, and then returned carrying oranges and vodka. These he presented bashfully and then remained standing in the doorway looking at the tree with the closest attention as if expecting it to disappear if he did not keep staring at it.

He became happier by the minute. He was so glad to be with people on Christmas Eve that it hurt, and with his broken German he tried very hard to join in the conversation. When the train reached the frontier of the British zone he had to get off. He looked again almost worshipfully at the tree and shook hands all around several times before he hurried out.

Christmas Day in Venice was overcast and very quiet. The massed tapers on the altars of St. Mark's set up a flickering glow along the gold mosaics. Incense filled the Byzantine vaults, the aromatic odor drifting among the pillars, here stronger, there fainter.

It was cold, but there was a warmth in the movement of light and shadow, the Latin cadence of the office and the embroi-

241

dered wealth of the vestments. San Marco di Venezia could only have been built by a people long in communion with the Orient. It seemed to me a symbol of the fruitful marriage of the Middle East and the Europe that I now knew so well.

I cherished Europe. I had come very close to a feeling of belonging there, for I had worked, traveled and lived there until I was saturated with Europe. But in this Europe that had evolved out of National Socialism's absurd adventure in dynamic futility and war, I could not find my place and I had no conviction of belonging there.

All of this Occident—my beloved and baffling Europe, and America which I had never understood—was rooted in the past of the Near Orient. The faith of the Occident, the arts, the sciences and the thought processes had come out of the crescent of lands at the eastern end of the Mediterranean. The names of those nations and peoples—Egypt, Israel, Persia—were like clarions calling out of the shadows of time.

I was now going down into Egypt and the Middle East, and I was glad to stand quite still, watching the light engaged in some nonchalant business of its own among the altars and marble columns and mosaic stones of St. Mark's in Venice. Here one became aware of the wholeness of things.

I had never been in Venice when Venice was alone. There were no visitors that cold Christmas Day. People kept indoors. The waters of the canals were steel gray.

In that hush I walked quietly over the little bridges and through the narrow lanes between the houses and palaces and drank a boiling espresso in one little bar and then another in another little bar and walked on. The winter morning turned to afternoon, and then took refuge in the mantle of night.

I kept on walking. In a stone-vaulted restaurant with cheerful checked tablecloths, the soup was hot and comforting, and red wine thawed me out. I must have come to the same palazzos over and over again, for Venice is confusing even if you know it fairly well.

They seemed friendly, the palazzos, and vain from looking at themselves in the water—or was it the red wine I had been drinking that made me think so? Only very occasionally a boat or, much more rarely, a gondola slipped through a canal.

I was seeing a Venice I had never known before, a Venice alone with its memories, somnolently listening to the sounds of the winter night.

In Alexandria I got my things stowed away in the hotel room and went down to the lobby to find the Greek porter and his assistant pushing people away from the carpet that stretched from the main doors to the elevators. The revolving doors had been made stationary and open. The porter, having a flair for the dramatic, was enjoying himself as he shouted, "Make way! Make way for the Prince of Arabia!"

The prince and his retinue were all that a newcomer could demand. As I noted later in other Middle Eastern cities where they appeared, the sons of King Abdul Aziz ibn Saud always lived up to expectations. Wherever they went, they brought the desert with them. No other national dress I have seen equals in dignity the flying robes of the aristocracy of the desert. Even the guards were splendid with their crossed cartridge belts and the sheathed daggers hanging at their sides.

The desert Arab is small, lean, lithe and dark. Only in his robes is he himself.

Later in Levant I encountered a young man who had only recently become paramount sheik of a famous northern desert tribe. Wearing a French-tailored suit, he looked rather a fop. Few men look like much in a French-tailored suit so it was not necessarily his fault. But even in manner he was rather mincing and perhaps embarrassed, giving more than anything else an impression of silliness. I felt that if he was a sheik, the tribes of the desert must be going to wrack and ruin.

I met him again in Damascus, but did not at first recognize him when he greeted me. In his robes he had no resemblance to the other, silly young man. He had put on his personality with his robes. He was grave and self-confident. Everyone in the room was aware that the leader of a restless desert horde was present.

I was somewhat astonished to see that the hotel in Alexandria was quite wrought up over its "Prince of Arabia." Apparently, for Alexandria a Bedouin prince is as exciting as he would be for New York—assuming the humanity of New York capable of excitement without the mechanical aid of a loudspeaker voice to tell it to be excited.

Geographically, Alexandria tends to be a cross between a small-scale Chicago and a Miami Beach. Like Miami Beach, it is all a façade along the water front, but the façade, like that of Chicago, bulges inland at one point to form a business district not unlike the Loop. Four or five miles of what seem like tall buildings stand facing the Mediterranean. The rest of the flat expanse of sand—actually an island—is covered with villas and gardens in the residential district, and a huddle of slums everywhere else.

The city functions as a resort because of a theory that in Alexandria you can escape the heat of the Egyptian summers. As theory, the idea has its points; there is a refreshing night breeze.

There are a lot of garishly lighted cafés, and on the sea front certain restaurants close to or hanging over the water serve a most satisfactory roast fish. At the western end of the city is a massive display of brick and concrete warehouses and factories on the vast expanse of water within the cement breakwaters which form the harbor.

All of that should not say much one way or another. The trick to Alexandria is that the streets appear to run right into the Mediterranean, and there is the sky and something luminous.

Alexandria's people, a mixture of Greeks, various Levantines, Italians and Egyptians have, in a way, untroubled minds. Those better off never think about anything except how to make money, which simplifies things. The others are generally thinking about where their next meal, if any, is coming from.

One day at the Union Club a rather grumpy Englishman told me that most Alexandrians were too poor to have any morals and that the idea had never occurred to the others.

The royal palace of Ras et-Tin, its large dome making it look more imposing than it was, stood right on the harbor, facing the sea. No one ever explained to me what the palace was doing down there on the harbor. It turned out, however, to be a very handy arrangement when King Farouk began his exile on a yacht.

At the other end of Alexandria was another palace, Munta-zah, with a park. There was also a neat royal villa on the break-water that was supposed to be the coolest place in the city at night. The kings of Egypt never like to be cramped for lack of a palace.

In summer the court, the government and the cotton pashas came down to Alexandria. Big cars with immaculately uni-formed chauffeurs rolled about in all directions.

Night clubs flourished and dance bands played. The rich were really rich and the poor were really poor. Everything seemed so uncomplicated, there being, apparently, nothing at stake but the price of cotton and the terms of trade.

Among the sights of the harbor that summer was His Egyp-tian Majesty shooting around in a high-speed mahogany motor boat while wearing nothing but a pair of bathing trunks and an old canvas hat. He was built like a Japanese wrestler, and the imposing muscles of his arms and thighs were much admired by good royalists.

One day when I was going over to Beirut on an evening boat I had occasion to study at leisure the total royal torso. He was in his speedboat, alongside our steamer, saying good-by at great length and at the top of his voice to a French singer who had spent the winter and spring in Egypt. She was the darling of the cabarets—and not only of the cabarets.

At the quay, on an Italian luxury liner preparing to sail for Italy, a substantial portion of Cairo society hung over the rail watching the King and the singer. At one point he dashed away at top speed toward the palace landing and halfway over struck some cement obstruction in the water.

An accompanying speedboat swept him up, and in a quarter of an hour he was back in another glistening mahogany speedboat, the same model as the first one which was now ignored as it lay waterlogged in the harbor.

When we sailed, the King of Egypt trailed us down the harbor and at the entrance waved a buoyant farewell. Our captain blew his whistle in response and the speedboat rushed away through the dusk toward the palace.

Significantly, Alexandria lay with its back turned to Egypt, isolated on its island. You could have towed it away and set it down in front of some other country and it would probably immediately start doing business with an equal indifference to the country concerned. In that, it was rather like New York.

Alexandria is the physical and obvious symbol of the alien European façade that has been built up in front of the actual Egypt. The façade is found again in modern Cairo.

The Egypt of today, and it was even more true a few years ago, is not unlike the Graeco-Roman and Byzantine Egypt in which a foreign civilization flourished in the Hellenic towns and created a Hellenized caste of Egyptians. That period lasted for close to a thousand years. The most potent civilizations of late antiquity raised a façade in front of Egypt. Yet they have left almost no heritage.

During the time that I was in the Middle East, the royal dynasty was overthrown by the first wholly indigenous Egyptian regime to come to power since the conquest of Egypt by Alexander the Great. The royal dynasty had been founded by the Albanian adventurer and statesman, Mohammed Aly, a century and a half before and the family had remained more Turkish than Egyptian. Until the end, many members of the royal family were averse to the use of colloquial Egyptian Arabic, the actual language of their country.

Commerce had been largely in the hands of the Greeks, Levantines, Italians and a few western Europeans. To a degree, politics had been torn between European and indigenous compulsions.

Xenophobia had been the central theme of Egyptian political history since late in the last century. The constant agitation which had shaken Egypt had often been blind and senseless. It was, however, a process which had painfully pushed indigenous Egypt to the fore.

Cairo was the center of the conflict, expressing in its own European and Oriental split personality the whole issue.

On New Year's Eve I arrived at Shepheards Hotel in Cairo just as a lady who can only be properly described as a fat wench started doing a rather unclothed midnight dance. She symbolized the coming of the Occidental New Year.

Shepheards had been, in its whiskey-and-soda fashion, a temple to alien gods for four generations. While I was in the Middle East, the mob burned it down. Although the mob presumably did not indulge in historical or philosophical speculation, the burning of Shepheards was in its way symbolical.

Having admired the leaps and bounds of the scantily clad New Year, I went to bed and was awakened, for the first time since I had visited Fez in the years long before the war, by the muezzin, crying out into the dawn that there is but one God.

32

EGYPT IS a womb, incestuously breeding within itself a superfluity of human life.

The valley of the Egyptian Nile is a human environment unique and complete, fertilized and irrigated by the yearly flood, isolated in the sands, warmed and made fruitful by the brooding heat of its long summers. There men seek to force out of the soil the maximum of its capacity to produce crops and appear to prize above all else their own procreative powers.

The compulsion which possesses the Egyptian fellah is expressed in his belief that the life-giving waters and sediments of the Nile transmit their fertile potency not only to vegetable growth but to men and animals.

Where the procreation of life is so compelling a force, death becomes an urgent obligation. In the narrow confines of the valley of the Nile, where so many must live from so visibly little, death becomes evidently a necessity. Birth rate and death rate in Egypt compete with the few highest in the world.

I recall passing through a portion of the delta of the Nile when I first arrived in Egypt. There was some sort of fair or festival going on. The fields and the roads were filled with fellahin. By the time I went through there the third time I realized that this was no fair or festival. There were simply so many people that the countryside was as well populated as are the streets of a town.

Herodotus said that Egypt is the gift of the Nile. Everyone since has parroted him and with good reason. Egypt is silt from the Ethiopian plateau brought down the Blue Nile in the annual flood and deposited. One hundred and ten million tons of silt annually pass Wadi Halfa where the Nile enters Egypt. That red-brown silt is saturated with natural mineral fertilizers.

Before the Pharaohs, the flood rose over the land, deposited its silt and drained away. The Egyptians improved on that. They built mud-walled basins, let the flood in to deposit a layer of silt and let the water flow out again afterward. They were soil conservationists. One crop a year was grown. Constantly renewed, the soils of Egypt stayed young for six thousand years.

Through the milleniums the partnership of the Ethiopian mud and the Egyptian cultivator continued. Neither the soil nor the man changed. The fellah of today was the Egyptian of yesterday. He maintained himself through all invasions and the resemblance of the modern Egyptian to the ancient statues is one of the fascinations of Egypt. There is a familiar story of the archeologists who unearthed a statue that was the absolute likeness of the headman of the neighboring village.

Since the early Egyptian first planted in that Ethiopian mud, peoples and civilizations by the dozens have appeared and disappeared. One after another they have succumbed as the basis of their economic existence crumbled.

Egypt is still there, awesomely and perhaps shockingly the Egypt of the Pharaonic countryside, and the Egyptian is still there because the soil stayed young.

The Egyptian stayed true to his mud and his mud stayed true to him.

Then came modern man. He constructed dams to introduce perennial irrigation. He brought chemical fertilizers. Progress entered the picture.

Egypt had always been a one-crop country. Now it became a two- and, in spots, three-crop country. The whole equation of Egyptian life changed. Production doubled and tripled.

The age-long plague of Egyptian poverty seemed to have been overcome if only to the degree of a promise of modest comfort. However, a certain amount of medical care, a minimum of modern hygiene and more orderly administration undid the good that had been done. The infant death rate eased a little and the population rose from six million to ten million by 1900 and then to twenty-two million by the middle of the century.

At the same time, after the milleniums of constant rejuvenation, the soils of the Nile are at last growing tired. The greater part of Egypt now depends on artificial fertilizers as the soils steadily deteriorate.

Only one-twentieth the amount of silt is deposited on the perennially irrigated lands fed from dams as is deposited on the still existing basin-irrigated lands above the dams in Upper Egypt. The Ethiopian mud now drops to the river bottom behind the dams, is deposited in canals or carried down to the sea. Constant irrigation threatens the soil with salinity despite elaborate soil drainage.

Population has swollen to the point where there are now three and a half times as many desperately poor human beings as there were before. A constantly greater burden is being placed on Egypt's only real resource.

Elaborate projects have been started, planned to roughly

250

double the annual volume of irrigation water. When that day comes, at the present rate of population growth, agricultural production per head will be just what it is now. Egypt must keep running to stay where it is.

To speak of a nation going bankrupt commonly refers only to the finances of a given government. Egypt is one nation that can go totally bankrupt. When it has drawn its last check against the depleted reserves of the Egyptian soil it will be literally and hopelessly finished.

Egypt is an example of the dynamic modern drive blindly at work. What has been done to Egypt was profitable for planters, business, government and the British cotton industry. Therefore, it was common sense as the free competitive society understood common sense. The basis of an age-old economy of extraordinary durability was torn to shreds. Progress came to that ancient land and it surged forward into a dead end.

On a night in February I was having one of those very black coffees in a very small cup at a neon-lighted bar open to the street in the center of modern Cairo. As usual you could not without shouting make yourself heard above the steady battle cry of the automobile horns.

The streets of Cairo were running rivers of sound. That mechanical outcry mingled into a single pulsing wave that from a distance had a melody reminiscent of childhood's steam calliope on circus days, heard from way uptown when the parade was downtown.

Down in the center of it you had a sense of drowning. Sound washed up the sides of buildings and fell back heavily as if it were water.

Arab drivers simply drive with one hand solidly on the horn button. Speculation as to the reason for this was one way to while away the time when you could not sleep during the siesta. The subject was full of psychological and sociological possibilities. A fair number of articles had been written about it in Cairo newspapers.

British people had a habit of putting it down to the Arab's alleged inferiority complex. The British attributed nearly everything in the Middle East except the low annual rainfall to the natives' inferiority complex, and they did it publicly. It is one of the reasons why the British are out of so many Middle Eastern places they used to be in.

The coffee bar was full of people bellowing at one another tête-à-tête. An Egyptian acquaintance came up and took my arm and yelled at me. I took a deep breath and roared back that I was feeling good but tired and thought that I would go off to my hotel.

He yelled that I should not go to my room but stay in the center of town because of an assassination. I asked rather urgently who had been assassinated. He shouted back that no one had been assassinated yet. I should stay because somebody probably was going to be assassinated. I wanted to know how he knew. He replied at the top of his lungs it was just a thing that had got around.

It had got around town that Sheik Hassan el Banna, the head of the Moslem Brotherhood, had left his house. The ceremonies for Premier Mahmoud Fahmy Nokrashi Pasha, customary forty days after death, had just taken place. Forty days before, Premier Nokrashi had been assassinated by Abdul Meguid Ahmed Hassan, a member of the Moslem Brotherhood, in revenge for the premier's order suppressing the Brotherhood.

The situation called for the assassination of Sheik Hassan el Banna by one of Nokrashi's young men among the Saadists, his political party. The Sheik had sensibly retired to his house and stayed there surrounded by certain well-armed followers. However, he had picked up the idea that after the traditional forty days he could circulate again. The idea was not shared by Nokrashi's young men and apparently everyone in Cairo knew it but the Sheik.

About half an hour after my acquaintance had suggested that I had better stay around, Sheik Hassan el Banna was shot. He died shortly afterward in a hospital.

Sheik Hassan el Banna was to a degree typical of a long line of reformers that had appeared since the early days of Islam. Inherent in the nature of Islam is a protestant desire for return to simplicity, to the austerity of the desert and to the Koranic environment, similar to the Christian protestant compulsion to return to the Biblical simplicity.

The Moslem Brotherhood was the vehicle of such a rebellion against the noisome, bureaucratic corruption of modern Egypt. With time the Moslem Brotherhood had gone terrorist. The phenomenon was also familiar in the history of such Islamic orders. The presumed purpose of the terror was to intimidate the police and the courts in preparation for a seizure of power.

Cairo took on the appearance of occupied guerrilla territory after the murder of the Sheik. Police with carbines were everywhere.

I went one day to some medical congress which Premier Abdul Hadi was to visit.

Groups were standing around in the entrance hall when squads of police erupted into the building. We were abruptly ordered to stand with our faces to the wall and our arms stretched out, the palms of the hands held open in the direction of the police. The premier went through surrounded by a squad of police with drawn weapons.

With the insight characteristic of the born journalist, I decided that something must be all awry in the Kingdom of Egypt.

33

MY ASSIGNMENT was called the Middle East. There is some argument among the learned as to what constitutes the Middle East. Probably my assignment, which included all the Arab states, Iran, Libya and the

Sudan, roughly covered the area which all authorities agree is the Middle East, irrespective of what else they believe should be added.

Rambling around in that wide area was a good life. There was no point in setting yourself up in an office. Telephone communications were either nonexistent or might as well have been. Telegrams arrived the day after they were sent, if they arrived at all.

The only way to find out what was happening anywhere was to go there, preferably just before it happened.

You hopped about in the second-hand airplanes that some local air line had purchased. The air view of the Middle East is instructive. It goes to the root of the thing.

You look down on an island archipelago. Scattered islands of fertility are surrounded by desert, steppe or bare mountain land. The population lives in such islands. And the nomads can best be thought of as the equivalent of fishermen who go out to sea from island ports.

The desert is the great geographic fact in that whole area; it makes the scattered, inhabited islands insignificant. Except in the Lebanon and parts of Iran, the desert is a constant presence, summoning you away as the sea summons you away to another place over the horizon.

One of the princes of the desert, Abdullah, king of the small Kingdom of Hashemite Jordan, had been shot and I was there when they took him to his grave.

Trembling, stepping delicately, a nervous little Arab stallion, saddled and bridled and draped in black, followed behind the coffin on the gun caisson.

On the dead king's breast lay the holy Koran open at the confession of faith, man's desperate effort to reach out for the compassion of the infinite expressed in the harsh harmony of Arabic speech.

The regents of the two Hashemite kingdoms, Prince Abdul Illah of Irak and Abdullah's son, the Prince Naif, walked behind along the road through the hillside grove. Behind them came the other representatives of the two royal Hashemite houses, the delegates of the Arab states and the diplomatic corps.

Officers and men of the rugged Bedouin household regiment, drawn up along the road with reversed arms, wept and sobbed openly. The delicate Arab animal grew restive and his eyes wild. He had to be calmed with soft words for he had known no others, that companion of an Arab's life and soul.

Black mourning flags flew from every house and the women of the Bedouin had torn their clothing. They had stood for hours at a time striking their bodies in rhythm and chanting an old sorrowful chant of the desert people. The tiny man with the black beard had been a descendant of the Prophet Mohammed and an emir of the Meccan house of the Hashemites, a great and ancient clan in the annals of Islam.

Before the grave, Sheik Hamzah Arabi, Supreme Judge of the Islamic Courts, cried out "Oh, Abdullah," and the title he had intrigued and struggled for fell from him. He was left a man like others, a suppliant for the mercy of Allah.

The assassin's bullet had ripped Abdullah's life out of his body the Friday before in the Mosque of Omar in Jerusalem.

Jerusalem was a tarantula's nest twisting about in its own poisons. Murder had become a trade there during the long secret struggle between Arab and Zionist. The walled city was the political fief of the Husseinis, patricians grown desperate and violent, mortal antagonists of Abdullah.

The half-literate, insignificant Mustafa Ashu, the assassin, had been shot down by the King's guards at the door of the mosque. Mussa Husseini, a big, bluff, fingers-all-thumbs man, was found guilty as chief agent in Jerusalem of the conspiracy and hanged.

Abdullah's creation, the Kingdom of Hashemite Jordan, consisted of the big crumbling gully through which the meager Jordan flowed to the Dead Sea, a few arable spots on the barren hills of Judea and Samaria and, to the east of the Jordan, strips of grazing or arable land and the desert. It is doubtful whether Abdullah himself had seen much future to it. He had referred to it only the year before as part of the heritage of his grand-nephew Feisal, the boy king of Irak, though without arousing any enthusiasm either in Jordan or Irak.

A week before, there had been another assassination. I sat in a second-floor café in Beirut, pounding out my dispatches. The café was in the same building as the French Lebanese wireless service, and I had good reason to be there but did not feel overly secure.

Outside, a mob was smashing and raving through the streets. The news had come through of the assassination in Jordan of Riad es Sohl, former premier of the Lebanon. He had been trapped by the killers on his way home from a visit to Abdullah.

The bazaar had not closed quickly enough in sign of mourning, and the Moslem roustabouts of the docks and their like had risen in protest. They felt that the Christian merchants were displaying indifference to what had befallen a Moslem leader.

Two men were killed in the riot, the windows of three hundred shops smashed and cars left wrecked all over the streets. Finally tanks came up to support the struggling police and quelled the riot. I was glad to see those tanks. The two policemen at the doors downstairs had not looked like men who were going to halt that mob if it decided to come in.

The killing of Riad es Sohl went back to something that had happened during my first weeks in the small Republic of the Lebanon just north of Palestine. Clearly infected with Germanic racialism, a certain Antoine Saadeh had come up with something called the Syrian race. His followers greeted one another with "Hail, Leader."

His political sect, called the Syrian Popular Party or the Syrian National Socialist Party, had its principal following in the Lebanon but there were cells in Syria and Jordan and even among the Lebanese in Brazil and the United States. The Lebanese government, finding the party fascist and seditious, prohibited it.

Saadeh was deeply offended. He allegedly made some deal with Husni Zaym, short-lived dictator of Syria, and got weapons. A few hundred armed followers were sent into the Lebanon from Syria. Saadeh had a plan for raising a revolt among the Dandash and the Druze tribes.

The trouble was, however, that there was not much point in raising a revolt among the Dandash. Up in that part of the country the situation was considered normal when the Dandash were in revolt, and the police grew worried when they were not because it was assumed they were planning some new deviltry. Lebanese, with the exception of those who lived near them, spoke rather affectionately of the Dandash. They were a national institution.

The Druze were another matter. They had killed many thousand Maronites the last time they had revolted—back in Ottoman times—under the impression that the world was coming to an end. The Druze consider it their function to act as the advance guard of the Angel of Wrath whenever the world comes to an end.

There was obviously no reason for them to be interested in Antoine Saadeh, a Christian infidel.

While the "Fuehrer" of Syrian racialism stayed in Damascus, his forces in the Lebanon made a series of small attacks on *gendarmerie* posts, culminating in three sharp encounters with Lebanese troops supported by gendarmes. A *gendarmerie* commander was killed and a number of police were wounded.

Riad es Sohl, then Lebanese premier, who controlled Syria's sea traffic through Lebanese ports and had the Arab states behind him, laid down the law to Syrian dictator Husni Zaym, whose police promptly arrested Antoine Saadeh and turned him over at the Lebanese frontier. Within a few hours Saadeh was tried by a military tribunal and shot the following morning.

From then on Antoine Saadeh's people kept on trying to kill Riad es Sohl. A year after the execution of Saadeh, a Syrian National Socialist fired at the premier point blank in the street in Beirut and missed. It took another year before they caught him momentarily unguarded en route from Abdullah's palace to the airport at Amman.

I had some pleasant afternoons in jail in connection with the whole affair.

One of my friends was Ghassan el Tueni, editor of a newspaper founded by his father. He lived in a big block of a house up in a quarter of the town that managed to look like Beacon Hill, Boston, with palm trees and bougainvillea.

Ghassan el Tueni had been to Princeton as well as the American University in Beirut. Being young, with a newspaper of his own, he was constantly in trouble with the Lebanese regime.

Ghassan had nearly landed in jail before, but he went and stayed with the head of the Greek Orthodox hierarchy. He was of a distinguished Greek family which had nothing to do with being Greek but with being Greek Orthodox. It meant that the other Greek Orthodox protected you because that was your religious nationality.

However, there were certain things concerning which you could take sanctuary with the head of the Greek church and certain things concerning which you could not. You had to be a Lebanese to know.

On this occasion Ghassan had written an editorial castigating the government of Riad es Sohl for sentencing Saadeh within a few hours after the latter was turned over.

Ghassan was no fascist but he had picked up ideas about due process of law, and he was promptly put in jail for libeling the government. As he was going to run for parliament, he was not particularly cast down. Getting tossed into jail was a somewhat routine aspect of a political career.

On visiting days the courtyard in the center of the jail, complete with flower beds, was jammed with people. The jail was, in its way, a social center, and there was a great scurrying about with black coffee. All the prosperous prisoners had hired the others as servants, and their principal business was making black coffee. I enjoyed that jail. Everyone seemed so relaxed and friendly, and it was a great center of political discussion.

The Lebanon regime was corrupt; it was forever engaged in maintaining such an intricate balance of Lebanon family clans in participation and representation that only a genealogist could grasp the personnel policy applied to the Civil Service. Ghassan wanted a modern state and society. He deplored the fact that everything in the Lebanon had to be explained in terms of your uncle's first cousins-in-law. He and all the reform crowd complained bitterly to me, naturally taking it for granted that I was for progress. Americans were always for progress.

I knew that I should approve and tried to cover up the fact that I was falling in love with the Lebanon, just as it was, corruption and all.

Ghassan would not have understood. He did not know that home is neither good nor evil but a heritage that I and mine had nearly lost. In the house of the Lebanon everything was left strewn over the floor and father stole from the family cashbox, but it was home.

In the Lebanon, men belonged in every way that men can belong. There was your family clan and your village and your religious community which seemed to amount to a special sort of nationality. Then there was your region or *pays* in French. Besides, there were only 1,300,000 people in a country not quite four-fifths the size of Connecticut.

You can get desperately fond of something that small. It is hard to be in love with half a continent.

There was only a coastal plain, rather narrow, and "the mountain," which meant the mountain range sprinkled with villages and the green, interior valley of the Bekaa. I think that I could have stayed there forever and drawn it around me as you draw a quilt around you in bed when it is cold at night. When the people there talked to me about the great nations, and my great nation, and looked at me as if I myself contained all that power, I wanted to ask one of them how he would like to be number one-hundred-sixty-two-million.

The Lebanon was full of minorities. In fact there was no majority. It was heartening, this absence of a majority. You felt more at your ease, less arithmetical.

One night I was taking off my pants and started to think. An inspiration came to me. In college I had a housemate, later head of the mathematics department in a New England college, who could never think with his pants on and took them off to study.

I put the pants back on and walked the two blocks to Ghassan's office to tell him my idea—he was out of jail—but he had gone.

The thought, however, stayed with me. In the Lebanon there was no way to be just like everyone else because there was no everyone else to be like. There was no average man.

It was the average man back where I came from who had in a fashion become the symbol of our anonymity and homelessness. The average man and his little wife-and-children family was drowned in the void of his own vast numbers.

There was a secret to the Lebanon that explains all those minorities. The lower mountain slopes are steep, quite often cliffs, and the high mountain country up above is fertile. There is a geological explanation which I had studied and of which I did not understand a word.

Up there all the minorities were safe from whoever was thundering about conquering the Middle East.

The first who discovered that refuge from conformity, and from whoever was being dynamic at the moment, were the present Maronite Christians who, back in the sixth century, were in trouble with Byzantium. The others, Christians and Moslems of minority persuasions, drifted in. The Maronites eventually entered into communion with Rome, but their priests wear astonishingly long beards and rear large and completely legitimate families. They are still nonconformists.

America, I remembered, had been like that at the beginning when it was a refuge for the nonconformists of Europe, before the new epoch of the common man. There had been a time in America too when you could not be like everyone else because there was no everyone else to be like. But that America, I had noted, was dead and gone to the history class. My father had still been part of it. I thought to myself, maybe that is what is the matter with me, maybe I am too American and therefore don't belong there any more.

By the time I arrived in my Lebanon, they had built well-paved, atrociously dangerous roads up into the mountains. You went to the square in Beirut, paid a quarter or so and any number of you piled into a taxi and you tore up into the mountain around the curves. Coming down was ghastly. Climbing the mountains used up a lot of gasoline, and the taxi men made up for it on the way down. They didn't use any gasoline and they didn't use any brakes.

But once you were up there, the feeling came of being hidden from the world in a hermit kingdom built into the sky. Far below was the Mediterranean.

Every village in the mountain had a few small hotels. I knew such a hotel in a grove of cedars. There were few cedars in the Lebanon but it had some. The hotel or inn had been built of fieldstone, presumably to stand off a siege. There was a big dusky hall down the middle lined with old furniture, and a living room with lace curtains.

From the window of the bedroom you saw the lights of the villages. I would sit there looking at the lights and remembering the small *figlia* who sat on my arm in San Francisco and reached out for light.

The great wind moved and went still and slumbered. While the mountain sought to find where the wind slept, I lay on the white bedspread and drew the night darkness close around me, safe from the cities of the plain and the future and the brazen voice of the years.

Above the gorges and the falling away to the sea, the land was terraced. Other generations had brought the stone on their backs in wicker hampers and tucked in soil that was bread. More rocks were brought every year in wicker baskets, for as long as the soil stayed on the mountain, man was safe in that high refuge from the heat and the dust of the plain.

If you looked into the gorges where the rivers came out from the feet of the mountains, you saw the banana plantations. It was hot and humid in the gorges. One was grateful for the bubbling coolness of the water in the narrow irrigation canals. The clustered bananas were small and sweet. Three or four houses would hide together down there among the banana leaves as if pretending they really weren't there at all.

From afar you heard the sharp, hard Arabic cry of a child, sounding like the voice of a pagan god.

Here and there on the outskirts of a village were the houses of wealthy Lebanese Brazilians. In Brazil, the Lebanese from that mountain were known as Turcos; there were many of them and many who were wealthy. They flew in from Rio de Janeiro and occupied their houses for only a few weeks a year.

The village in the mountain held them. They came and sat in the crude coffee house by the road and listened to the shrill Arabic moaning on the radio. There was not much to such a village. But it held them hard to its stubborn breast.

Some came home to the mountain from trading posts in West Africa, some from New York and many other places. Where there was money there were Lebanese. They were great emigrants.

The Lebanon was called, and it was only half in jest, the empire of the cousins. Cousins kept sending telegrams and letters from all over the world. Old men got up from smoking their water pipes in the backs of shops in the Beirut bazaar, went out to the corner, formed a syndicate and bought silver in Hongkong and gold in Macao, anything and anywhere. I recall a Beirut syndicate that one day bought a warehouseful of pipe from a plumbing house in Italy threatened with bankruptcy, and sold it the following week at something like 150 per cent profit to another Italian plumbing house down the street.

The merchants of Beirut, like the Alexandrians, thought a great deal and they thought about making money.

One old man with a dusty office piled with account books and other odds and ends did business with a large, spic-and-span outfit in New York. He did a good deal of business in ways that were not always clear to his American associates. One day two young men in the junior executive class arrived. They were respectful and friendly, for the old man was a millionaire. They stayed for quite a time. After they had gone, an American from the consular or the commercial attaché's office went to call. The old gentleman sucked thoughtfully on his water pipe and soon the two of them got through the coffee and compliments stage.

Then the American asked him how he had liked "our New York friends."

The old man was ecstatic. They were so "what you call dynamic," he said, and so "what you call in American clean-cut," and they were so energetic and systematic, always busy. He gestured vaguely at the rubbish piled in his office. He was not systematic and clean-cut. In fact, he concluded, he had felt ashamed of himself.

He had only one small criticism to make. Slightly raising his shoulders and gesturing with his hands, he said apologetically, "I noticed only one small thing that I did not understand. They did not seem to have any time for thinking about making money."

That Lebanese observation greatly appealed to me. I know of no freedom within the framework of our age that is not rooted in property or savings. So few in our great shining civilization of the high living standard had enough of their own not to need the boss, and freedom is not to need the boss.

Money, however, was not merely a personal affair to the Lebanese. It poured back from overseas to families in the villages. Emigrant receipts were a fat, formal statistical figure in the balance of trade.

People were always loaning money and getting money back and finding jobs for someone in the clan. There was a constant conferring about the family clan, about who was hard up in the clan and what to do about it.

Rich or poor, they were bound to the clan which was their own security against the anonymous sadism of the greater society, the empty thing which is the system and the mass of men. They were not soft, not even generous with the generosity of the modern which is so largely a matter of collective pressure and a certain fear that his own luck might turn. But they recognized the family and clan and its holding together as a necessity, a law of survival.

They had none of the flabby fatalism of the common man in our great society. They were not the spendthrift, consumer mass, the slogan-haunted cattle in the stockyards of modern merchandising and engineered consent. There was little in these people of the fatuous herd at the sales counter. The

Lebanese were grasping and money-minded because money is the right to say no.

My Lebanon, which I drew at times so close around me, was a cloak of many colors. Beirut was Levantine to the heart, astute, multilingual, many-minded and with an element of sheer bawdy wickedness. Tripoli up north beyond the great headland that came out from the mountain and plunged to the sea, was Sunni, fanatic, austere. Tyre and Sidon slept in the sand by the sea. The people of the plain were not the people of the mountain a mile away. The Maronite was no Druze who had in common with the strange Nusairiya only the element of a secret faith restricted to the inner circle of the elders. You passed from one nation to another while going around a bend in the road.

Life was lived in depth. The state was almost a nation but not quite. Maronite, Sunni, Shia, Orthodox, Druze were sovereign powers but not quite. Beirut could be a man's whole life and affair, but he would go suddenly to his village and be content there. The village alone was home but gave way to the family clan.

There is no need in such a society for individualism and there is no place for the average man.

Much in that society is very old and is the answer to life given long ago. Halfway up the north coast from Beirut there is the village of Jbeil, once called Byblos—hence Bible or book—because it traded in papyrus. Cedar wood went down from Byblos to Pharaonic Egypt. It is most probably the oldest seaport in the world and may be the oldest continuously inhabited place on the face of the earth.

In Byblos I found the remains of a temple built 1800 years before Christ, tombs of kings who quarreled with the Pharaohs, and a crusader fortress.

Butterflies fluttered among the banana leaves and the noonday heat was oppressive and sensual. I sat against the fortress wall on the seaside. Phoenician craft had ridden there in the amethyst water, loading cedar to house the mummied dead of Egypt.

A naked child came wading through the water and squatted not far away, regarding me gravely. You knew that there must have been another naked child squatting there gazing at a visiting Egyptian long ago.

From the moaning passionate embrace of the naked generations through the milleniums in that place, the ignominy and the aspiration that is life had ever renewed itself. Man, fearing death, has ever sought to leave a living heritage.

I thought of my own immigrant, nomad country where the dead have no part in tomorrow.

34

AT ONE POINT during my stay in Lebanon I started going over the mountain to the Syrian *coup d'état* which was in three acts, all with the same plot.

After World War II, following the long struggle with the French mandatory power, Syria had settled down briefly as a sovereign state. It quickly became the rather private preserve of an oligarchy of large landowners with President Shukry Kuwatly at the head.

The oligarchy got in trouble because the Syrian army had made a bad showing in the Palestine war, which was drawing to an end just as I arrived in the Middle East. Faced with the choice of being angry at itself or angry at the president, the Syrian army chose the president.

The Syrian *coup d'état* always happened very early in the morning. They announced it on the early radio broadcast at breakfast time.

As soon as you learned in Beirut about the Syrian coup, you took a portable typewriter, a notebook and a taxi and went off across the mountain to Damascus. The radio had announced that the Syrian frontiers were closed. A good deal of time was, accordingly, wasted at the frontier. It was not so much you as the taxi. Its Lebanese origin might be noticed.

By the time you got down through the winding, arid valley, the morning was drawing on toward noon. Where the road enters Damascus, the crew was already tucked in for its midday rest under a discouraged looking old armored car. At a few other spots armored-car crews slept soundly or sprawled wearily over the gun turrets. Small boys clambered up, were lazily brushed aside by the soldiers and fell off like beetles.

You then went immediately to the General Staff Headquarters, a large, rather decayed building on a clay bank near the center of the new city, where the military chiefs of the coup would be setting up the new regime. There you encountered a lieutenant. It was always the same lieutenant and by the third *coup d'état* he appeared very bored.

He said there was no one there. You asked why there was no one there. He answered that everybody was taking an early siesta. You asked why on earth they were taking a siesta when there had been a *coup d'état*. He said that everyone had been up very early. That was true.

You asked for permission to go to the office of Major So-and-So. The request was absurd since you knew he was not there, but the lieutenant was aware that you just wanted to make sure that there was really no one there. He assigned a soldier to you as a guide and guard. Most of the offices stood open, and papers were scattered on the desks. Flies buzzed vigorously.

A round of the ministries disclosed that everyone had gone home. No one knew who had good connections for the moment, and the practice of government is dependent on the civil servants' having some idea of who is influential and who is not. The wise thing for an official to do was go home until the point was cleared up.

Toward late afternoon the new strong man and his associates

appeared looking purposeful and clean-shaven. The issue was what to do about the government. A furious telephoning for elder statesmen ensued. But the elder statesmen had gone to ground like rabbits.

Most elder statesmen were absentee landlords, as was nearly everyone else who mattered. Normally, it was almost impossible to drag them out of the city, and their absenteeism as landlords was one of the much discussed problems of Syrian rural life. The first time an armored car backfired in one of those coups, however, elder statesmen were seized with a passionate longing for their ancestral acres.

A good part of the evening was taken up with the new strong man convincing elder statesmen that they were not rural gentry who had merely dabbled in politics. During the night or in the following days, they turned up again, looking not very sure of themselves.

Most interesting of the strong men was the first, Colonel Husni Zaym. He became chief of state and then president and promoted himself to general and then to field marshal.

In the Occident he achieved a sudden reputation as a progressive by giving the vote to women. I had an interview at that time with a leading Syrian suffragette. She had been one of the first women of good family to go out without a veil. She recalled that her brother would dodge down a side street when he saw her coming, in order to avoid seeing the bare naked face of his sister being exhibited to every passer-by.

Down in the old city some of the women still wore the full regalia of Moslem modesty. You knew it was a woman and not a tent because it moved.

Colonel Zaym had taken over Syria by coming down with a few armored cars from the barracks southwest of Damascus and catching President Kuwatly in bed. Four and a half months later at two-thirty in the morning the same garrison came down under a different command. President and Field Marshal Zaym was either shot down in the entrance hall of his house or executed after a drumhead court-martial. The official version is that he was court-martialed. Premier Mohsen al Barazi kissed the hands of his captors and begged for his life before they executed him. Zaym was shot because he had become a menace to his own officers. No one ever did seem to know why they shot Mohsen al Barazi.

The new head of the army was Colonel Sami Hinnawi, who had promoted himself only as far as brigadier general when, by late December, the same garrison got up early again and came down the hill. Hinnawi was only arrested.

Khaled el Azm, thrown out of the premiership nine months before by Husni Zaym, went back to work on his old problem of whether there was any way for the state to dredge up enough income to keep going. Happily, Syria had almost no foreign or internal debt. It had never had enough credit to acquire a public debt.

Three *coups d'état* had brought things right back where they had started, and that was nowhere in particular—literally nowhere. Because now an amazing development took place.

Parliament got so annoyed that it refused to bother with legislating. The deputies drifted off. Among the many things parliament was not interested in was legislation on civil servants' salaries. With price increases and this and that, civil servants had come to the point where they could barely eat. They began to wander away, looking for odd jobs or just sitting in the cafés. Finally they got together and went out on strike.

Government offices closed down. No one delivered mail, no one did anything that government usually does.

The cabinet ministers, too, had long been losing interest. The minister of national economy had not been in his office for five weeks. The minister of public health had resigned and had not been replaced. Others had simply disappeared. The premier began to spend most of his time at his house outside Damascus.

Eventually the cabinet let it be known that it had quit. You could not say it had resigned, for it did not bother to put it in writing. Anyhow, whether the cabinet had resigned or not was rather irrelevant since government had ceased altogether.

I sat there holding my breath and waiting for anarchy. It took me a couple of days to get it through my head that anarchy was this complete peace.

The Damascus population, which ordinarily had a reputation

for brawling and occasional rioting, suddenly became exceptionally polite. The Damascenes' resentment was against authority, possibly an inheritance from Ottoman times. Now there was no authority to resent.

Such routine inconveniences as the absence of mail delivery were overcome rather easily. Messengers packed local mail around town and collective taxi and bus drivers took mail to one part of the country or another and to neighboring Jordan and the Lebanon.

I think the politicians and the civil servants were a little dismayed to discover how relatively unnecessary they were. In any case they began to drift back, and in due time a new government got going again after making some minor adjustment in the matter of civil servants' salaries. Once governing was resumed, the Damascenes returned to being their old rebellious and belligerent selves.

During that period of anarchic peace, before the new government was set up, I began to feel at last the conviction of being to some degree at home and at rest among the vast wastelands and oases of the Middle East.

My life in the Middle East had been taken up with news, a thing that falls into patterns concerned with governments, crises, projects, change. I had barely noted that what was not changing was so great a part of everything. News is a very special distortion. It is either about something changing or something unusual. Life, however, is to such a large extent about something not changing and not being unusual. Follow the news diligently enough, and you will become stone blind to the greater part of reality and to most of the values of living.

My story and the news story of Syria was that it was in constant disorder. But was it? Government had ceased before my eyes, and it had apparently not mattered. You had to ask yourself why. The explanation was all around you in Southwest Asia.

It was the older reality, the intimate society within the public society that had held fast and triumphed for the time in Syria.

Modern government and modern business in the Middle East

sat like two hats crazily askew on a rugged substructure of organically grown family, tribe, clan and community life. The state—our bureaucracy with filing cabinet and ministers, parliament and elections—always underwent a metamorphosis in the East. Constitutional monarchy and republican government became exasperatingly personal. They were permeated with clan relationships, communal ties, old and diverse loyalties.

You became aware of that rooted belonging together in the village clans and in the tribalism of the people of the black tents out in the desert.

This was once more the organic society I had found in the villages of Japan, China and, to a degree, in peasant Europe. Seen against that, the lone nomadism of the modern West, our high living-standard way of life, were completely alien.

I had a hard time learning to understand the Arab East because of the poverty and physical need there. It seemed hard to grasp that they had something precious which I and mine had lost along the way—an intimate society within the public society, and an inner fortitude.

But they also had the mosque. In the seventh century the desert had spoken. The message of Mohammed concerned faith, state and society, but above all a personal settlement with the affair of life. If God spoke through Mohammed, the desert spoke also, for Mohammed was a man of the desert and he never claimed to be more than a man.

In the desert the problem is one of survival—you cannot argue with the desert. Subsistence living and acceptance of the inevitable is virtue, not vice. Islam is the religion of submission to the changeless, to the will of Allah.

There are no clergy in Islam. At its purest, it has no saints, no intermediaries and no savior. Islam is bare as the desert is bare; in the mosque there is no human or animal image.

Whatever else there may be in the Koran, the God of Mohammed is no man-God, no anthropomorphic crutch. The incessant insistence of the Prophet is that there is but One. There is possibly no other religious concept so immaculate as that concept of Oneness.

The bareness and aridness of the desert lands are, in a way, a benediction. Go up into the arid hills to the black tents. There are the coffee fires, a few rugs, goats, perhaps a camel, sun-scorched people—nothing more. In a village out in the green Damascus oasis, the water ripples slowly through an irrigation canal. There are fruit trees, a square, clay house almost without furniture, a plow, a few hoes and the like, draft oxen and water pots.

And there is something more. The father is called *Abu,* a word which means the father of his son, and the child *ibn,* something which means the son of his father. It is the man's accepted name—Abu Mohammed, or father of Mohammed, his son. The Arab is named after his son.

I recalled the Slovakian peasant who had come home from America because what you did in America did not seem to get you anywhere since your children and your grandchildren became strangers. We forget easily in our modernism that change erases not the past but the future. It makes you irrelevant in terms of the world to come. We of the modern Occident all die, in a sense, childless.

However, out of our world were coming forces benevolent to a degree but bearing the curse of our restlessness. Presumably they would in time improve standards of living but, as a whole, they were not doing it at the moment, and they were fiercely destructive.

A boy on the Euphrates was named Consolidated Pumps Inc.

I discovered he was not the only child named after the big pumps by the tribesmen of the Euphrates. Idolatry is of our nature. The river tribesmen would have been astounded to hear that Consolidated Pumps Inc. was not the name of the iron god that poured water onto the land, but of a legal device symbolized by pieces of paper that were bought and sold by men to other men seeking to gain money.

But the tribesman did know the iron god, and it was a cruel god. Because of it the tribal lands had become the sheik's lands.

At the beginning the sheik probably had not had much money, but he did have enough to buy or get the credit to buy a pump. That was enough. The tribal communal life broke down. Everyone worked for the sheik's overseers and was no better or worse off except that he was no longer free and the old equality was gone.

I met such a sheik from out on the Euphrates in a hotel. He was ordering one double whisky after another and tipping splendidly. He had on a robe that was too short for him and was displaying without inhibition his long woolen underwear and red garters. But he had arrived in a very big, very new car, and the chauffeur was waiting with it outside.

The journalistic cliché for the system was "pump feudalism."

But out on the Djezzira, the rich plain under the Taurus in eastern Syria, you could at certain places see searchlights blazing on the fields at night to light the land for the work of hurriedly imported tractors and plows. Uncultivated land brought into cultivation had doubled or tripled the cotton acreage. Production had multiplied ten times in three years. There had been both a cotton boom and a wheat boom.

Syria's wealthy families had been seized with the entrepreneur spirit of the Occidental.

As a result, it was in Syria that I saw the first signs of a serious agrarian revolt. Syria was largely a land of tenants who were serfs under another name.

But there was hope. The country had land enough, much of it free and uncultivated, to settle the greater part of the rural population on independent peasant holdings.

Now, however, the heritage of free land was going one way or another under the control of the landlords and wealthy urban speculators. They already controlled about half the cultivable area of Syria.

Their allies were tractors, gang plows, binders and the mysterious deity, credit, usually housed in the branch of a French bank. All these forces of the Occident were marshaled on the side of the privileged.

An unusual and unexpected wave of pity for the poor who

were losing their last hope had taken hold of part of the not very large middle class. In the Homs and Hama districts, seats of some of the biggest landholding families in the country, Akram Hourani and the Arab Socialist Party had aroused the tenant serfs themselves to protest. In parliament Maaruf Dawalibi, its president, had introduced a bill that would restrict landholdings to a few hundred acres. However, it applied only to newly acquired land and to land inherited in the future.

The landlord caste reacted promptly. Their agents and gangs of men armed with clubs attacked Akram Hourani's people to keep them from talking to farm workers.

An urgent conference of large Syrian landowners, the great feudal families, was called in Aleppo. The president of the Agricultural Chamber presided and the secretary was the spokesman of a family who held a famous tract of cotton land fifty miles long. The agrarian reform movement was branded as Communist and opposed to the country's progress.

The pattern was peculiarly precise on the Euphrates and in Syria. When the profit-seeking free-enterprise ideas of the West and certain of the instruments of the machine age had been introduced, they served to further the disruption of the old society, and the privileged were strengthened while the great majority were more downtrodden than before. But elsewhere much the same thing could be found. In Egypt the national income had increased by three-fifths during the postwar boom period, and the fellah, according to reasonably reliable studies, was worse off than at the beginning of the century. Cairo and Alexandria were full of new office buildings, apartment houses and villas but there was no change in the misery of the mass, urban or rural. Competitive investment in land forced up both land values and the land rent demanded of the fellah.

The cities of the Middle East were being infected in varying degrees with the chronic discontent of the new Occident. The increasing inequality and the increasing discontent kept pace.

The political catalyst had been the educated middle class. Their main wish was absolute independence from any foreign interference, in the conviction that if only they could take over a new day would dawn. Nationalism had become the great cause. It had become a profession and was to a great extent a class phenomenon. The power of the ambitious educated class was due largely to the circumstance that they were the only element that could put a protest into spoken and written words and could thus engage in politics and political agitation. The young nationalist caste was primarily worried about itself, not the mass, but it protested, and in its misery the mass felt the appeal of that protest and believed.

All through my years in the Middle East there was violence. One year I spent only one month out of the twelve in a place where there was not curfew at night and pacing patrols in the streets and martial law or the equivalent. Under such circumstances you had a special pass to get about and walked carefully in the middle of the street, not hurrying.

People who hurried got shot. In Cairo on one such night a father-to-be, and that very shortly, had found himself in the traditional predicament. There was no telephone and he could not get the doctor. If he went out in the street, the child would probably be born fatherless.

He remembered that he had a bugle. At once people came from all directions. They thought it was the signal for revolt.

I once lay huddled up on the seat of a railway coach compartment one night with a friendly Irakian's robe thrown over me, so that people climbing up at way stations between Basrah and Baghdad to look into the train would not see my Occidental face and drag me out of there. Because plane service to Baghdad was suspended, I had flown to Basrah. The governor there had forbidden me to hire a car and drive through to Baghdad. A large area was out of control for the moment.

Fortunately the mail train went through that night but at the stations in the disaffected area it would not have been wise for the mob to learn that there was an Occidental aboard.

In Baghdad the mob burned out the United States Information Service while the authorities stood by helplessly. Rashid Street, the long, cluttered highway through the center of town, was a bellowing river of furious humanity. The mob slaughtered the police in one station in the heart of the city, and was only kept from storming the British embassy by the solid resistance of the troops on the Tigris bridges.

Much of the violence in the Middle East was about the British and some of it about the Americans, and in Egypt about the nearly 300,000 foreigners living there. People always knew what they did not want. Young men of the middle class could talk for hours, reciting the Middle Eastern litany, about the British, the bazaar profiteers, the crooked, callous politicians, the landlord caste, but the conversation faltered when it came to what they wanted to do. They wanted to clean things up, they said, and were off again on the negative line of their thoughts.

Usually it was a question of the Outs trying to get rid of the Ins. The ballot box hardly served the purpose: the Ins ran elections. Unless there was some gross error in the operation, the Ins won when the ballots were counted. The only way to get the Ins out was to throw them out, but the rallying cry was habitually that the Ins were subservient to the foreigners.

You got sick of the incessant rioting and the blind violence. During a riot in Cairo I saw a tall young man in a gallabieh— the Egyptian garment which always looks like your grandfather's nightshirt—throwing a rock. He was trying to throw it through the grating pulled down in front of a jewelry store window. It always hit the grating, and in a screaming, shouting passion he kept throwing it until his face was bathed in perspiration and his eyes were jumping out of their sockets.

He could not have reached anything in the window because of the grating. It had been installed to that end. He merely wanted desperately to smash that window and smash something displayed there, for he always threw the rock at the same spot.

The man with the rock became a howling horde on January 26, 1952, when the fury against the continued presence of the British garrison at Suez, tight behind barbed wire, came to a head.

Seven hundred establishments were burned down or wrecked—13 hotels, 40 moving-picture houses, 392 stores and

117 offices and dwellings. Once it had started the reason was no longer the British at Suez, but a raging hate against the new, westernized city of Cairo. It was revolt against the perversity of the iron god in showering benefits on the powerful and the prosperous and bringing only misery and envy to the man in the gallabieh.

35

THE SPEAKER of the house was up on his feet crying at the top of his lungs that the opposition leader's father had been about the biggest thief in Persia.

Assorted deputies were standing at their seats insulting by turns the speaker and the leader of the opposition. A thickset, small, red-faced man kept rushing to the dais to proclaim that parliament was being foolish and should debate the agenda of the day. The issue being debated at the moment was an opposition charge that the speaker had been handing around checks that bounced.

The uproar had been going on in one form or another ever since the Imperial Anti-Corruption Commission brought in its report. Several members of the cabinet, a substantial part of the chamber and the speaker had been listed among five hundred men found unfit to hold public office.

I could not take my eyes off the man who wept. The tears rolled down his cheeks. He sobbed as he lay half across the dais facing the deputies. His long, sensitive face expressed utter, soul-rending despair.

Why he was so sad was not entirely clear. Obviously, it was not the circumstance that the speaker's checks were alleged to have bounced. The man who wept was not on the Anti-Corruption Commission's list. He was the most honest or, as most people claimed, the only honest politician in Iran. He was, however, overcome with grief.

Dr. Mohammed Mossadegh, leader of the opposition, bowed his head, trembled and fainted away. The chamber rose in a storm of mutual recrimination. Mossadegh was carried out by his followers. Shortly afterward, still trembling and with his clothes all awry, he was brought in again.

The majority leader led his party out of the chamber and the day's session was declared closed. Up on the dais again, Dr. Mohammed Mossadegh shouted that he would stay right there until parliament met again in three days. He would then resume his speech concerning the speaker's alleged rubber checks.

After a while, his bed arrived and he got into it. The world was to learn that when Mohammed Mossadegh went to bed, it was time to sit up and take notice.

By the time he sat in another bed stroking my hand, his country had become one of the world's danger spots, and the frustrated British were as nearly frantic as it is possible for that phlegmatic nation to get. Mossadegh was premier and a world figure, and Iran, according to the headlines, was bankrupt.

I had just arranged a working agreement between my newspaper and Iran, which was better than the Anglo-Iranian Oil Company and a hard-working British embassy could do at the time.

The premier stroked my hand and assured me of his conviction that I and my paper were friends of Iran. Under other circumstances you would have wondered what sort of man it was who would sit up in bed and stroke another man's hand. But I knew that he had once been asked to leave Switzerland because he was living quite legitimately with his plural, and presumably contented, wives.

I had gone to see him because I had already arrived in the country again while the question of whether I should be admitted was still on the agenda of the Iranian cabinet. Almost anything could get on the agenda of the Iranian cabinet. My assistant, who was actually just the other man in the area, had just been unceremoniously expelled, a common enough occurrence in those times and not to his discredit. My position was an embarrassing one, but the old man smiled at me. He smiled a hypnotically meaningful smile that said there was a secret bond of friendship between us that ordinary mortals could not grasp.

Throughout the conversation his actor's face shifted from the classic mask of comedy to the mask of tragedy. Sitting in his bed in his old bathrobe, he seemed to be continually rehearsing a novitiate actor's repertoire of emotional expressions. But Mohammed Mossadegh was no novice.

Most of the world had never understood his weeping. They did not understand that it was an element of strength, not of weakness. His grip on the Iranians was in part due to his portrayal of the passion of the nation. Iranians are a passionate people. They have emotionalized the austere monotheism of Islam into the martyrism and mysticism of the Shia Islam, mourning through the ages for Ali, Hussein, and Hassan, and they await the return in messianic glory of the invisible Imam.

Iran had been for centuries the land of the great days of mourning in which all the adherents of Shia, the national religion, joined in weeping for the lost cause of the partisans of Ali, the son-in-law of the Prophet, and his descendants. It had been the country of the flagellations. The truly devout had beaten themselves with chains until they bled, and there had been a regular toll of deaths from this merciless castigation of the flesh.

Under the old regime an ability to weep had been a source of prestige and evidence of elevated character publicly displayed on the anniversaries of the martyrdoms. A large part of the treasure of anecdote and popular stories which is the common property of the whole Iranian society is concerned with the victory of weakness over strength.

The word Shia means partisans, and Ali, Hussein and Hassan were the losing party in the early struggle for the Caliphate after the Prophet's death. The Shia are the partisans of the defeated.

That Iranian partisanship for the lost cause and a certain lack of confidence in life account, conceivably, for a literary circumstance: of all the overabundant poetry of the Near Orient, only the Persian has had universal appeal.

Whatever compromise we may make with life and whatever self-delusion we adopt as consolation, defeat, not victory, has been the lot of the vast majority of men. Self-pity is one of the most universal of emotions. The great Persian poets have given masterly expression to that emotion.

Throughout the Anglo-Iranian oil crisis the generally unspoken assumption of diplomats and of the Anglo-Iranians was that Iran's increasing weakness under Mossadegh would force it to give in. They were mistaken.

The British had a particular blind spot in regard to the phenomenon, Mossadegh. He had come as a prophet with the demand that the nation be cleansed of alien gods, in this case the Anglo-Iranian Oil Company, admittedly more Anglo than Iranian.

Prophets, as the Old Testament indicates, are notoriously difficult people to deal with. The British are peculiarly incapable of comprehending prophets or dealing with them. Mossadegh was a cultivated, many-sided Persian prophet. His mother was a Kajar princess, and he was born at the royal court. As might have been expected with a prophet in power, finances fell to pieces. Administration became even more chaotic than it had been, which was, in its fashion, no mean achievement.

Hardheaded people stood aghast. In London clubs the dashed fellow was regarded as a confounded maniac.

Weeping and hysterical, the trembling old man put through the confiscation of the vast assets of the Anglo-Iranian. Britain dared not move, for under the treaty of 1921 Russia might march into the north to counterbalance any foreign invasion. Proclaiming that he and his country were at the end of endurance, Mohammed Mossadegh expelled Britain's consuls.

The world marched through the bedroom in Teheran and left shaking its head in horror. Iranians loved it. The show was well worth the price.

The country sank into a morass of chronic disorder and economic depression. After a time the Iranian government could no longer pay its civil servants. Violence became the order of the day in that continuous self-flagellation of the weak engaged in exorcising the foreign demon.

In the course of that series of outbreaks of rioting you always asked yourself who the dead had been trying to kill when they themselves died, and why. There was no clear pattern to the violence except a seeming hypnotic need for it. On several occasions it looked as if Iran would go under and emerge as a people's democracy with the crypto-Communist Tudeh and a waiting Soviet Russia in power.

As it turned out Mossadegh himself was swept away in the final paroxysm of that national self-flagellation. The Shah had fled to Rome and the mob, completely out of control, paced the streets of Teheran. But, by that time, the great powers of the West, political and oil, were on their knees. The victory of weakness over strength had been achieved.

An instinct saved the delirious nation. The Teheran mob suddenly went royalist. The army restored order. The Shah returned. Bankrupt and prostrate, Iran dictated its terms. Britain and the Anglo-Iranian surrendered. Iran controlled Abadan. I had seen Abadan, the world's largest refinery.

After months spent in dusty villages and small-city environment of Arab Asia, I had gone in a decrepit taxi from Basrah across the plain to Abadan. Twilight had come as I saw first the high blue-green flares of escaping gases and then the soaring surrealist structures that were steel towers stretching for miles. Steam rose in clouds. The sky glowed far out into the gathering night.

As an Occidental I felt a reverent awe. These were altars. This was Baal in all his heathen glory.

The Persian Gulf is the petroleum world's Mediterranean. To the east of the Shatt al Arab up in the hills lie the great Iranian oil fields, to the north are those of Irak, Kirkuk and Mosul; a few miles to the south is the Sheikdom of Kuwait on the Gulf under which lies the richest single oil reserve known;

farther south along the west coast the Saudi Arabian reserves outrank those of any other nation; and beyond that are the developed and undeveloped oil resources of various petty coastal states and protectorates.

In all, the oil reserve of the Middle East is estimated to be seven times that of the United States, the second ranking oil area.

Christianity's Palestinian heritage and the Occident's historic links to Egypt and the Levant have made us overlook the significance of that other Middle East out beyond the Syrian and Arabian deserts.

The longer I stayed in the Middle East the more I became convinced that only Irak, Iran and the Persian Gulf mattered much in Occidental terms. The resources, such as they are in the Middle East, are concentrated there: oil, surplus irrigation water and a substantial amount of untilled land to be brought under cultivation.

The real task of both Iran and Irak was to put into practice their national programs of rehabilitation for which their formidable oil incomes had been legally earmarked. There are resources enough on that new frontier of the Middle East to do away with poverty.

Three times I had occasion to discuss this with the Shah in Iran, who was sick and weary of the spectacle of poverty. He had been educated in Switzerland, and so he understood the meaning of the community, of independence based on property and of the co-operative enterprise of neighbors. He was wrapped up in his own program of dividing the vast Imperial Estates, acquired by his father, under conditions which would guarantee a lasting freehold to the peasant and the development of sound rural communities patterned after the most modern peasant societies of Europe.

Progressive elements in Irak were pushing a similar program with state lands. Land was distributed but could be held only by those who continued to farm according to a strict, supervised program. Tools, seeds, necessities and markets were provided by co-operatives that would be turned over later to the peasants' own management. Credit was taken out of the control of the moneylenders. It was granted by a public institution working through the co-operatives.

Both the Shah and the small progressive group in Irak clearly felt the necessity to build from the bottom. Elections, parliaments and free competitive economy were getting them nowhere. There was no foundation. The centuries had reduced these societies to rubble. Nothing could be more irrelevant than the running feuds and chronic intrigues of the caste of landlords, sheiks and rapacious town notables that constitute the parliamentary system as practiced in such a society.

The new Irak was put together out of mere rubble left by history. A certain unreality has been characteristic of the Kingdom of Irak, as if no one quite meant what they did or said. Irak has been just people, chiefly Arabic-speaking, who lived in Mesopotamia. Politics have been primarily concerned with anger at the British for being so important in Mesopotamia, the need to lean on the British out of helplessness and arguments about the existence or nonexistence of a greater Arab nation. The great majority of people lived as wretchedly bad farmers, ragbags, struggling to keep enough back from the big landowner to exist.

A type of farming was practiced in Irak which can be called suitcase irrigation. You poured water onto land which was by nature saline and broiled by the sun, you took as many crops as possible and then moved on to other land. I have seen such land when it looked as if snow had fallen on it in the night. You could scoop up the salt by the handful.

The worst human habitations that I have ever seen were in a mud wallow on the outskirts of Baghdad, the town in it made up of huts constructed of grass and rubbish. The people walked around up to their knees in the slime which was also the floor of their huts. They were refugees from the rural misery of Irak who had come up to Baghdad seeking any escape from the Irakian landlord.

Mesopotamia has been a miserable spectacle since the Mongols destroyed the irrigation system in the twelfth century. Fat volumes have been written on the details of the obvious fact that the unruly Euphrates and Tigris and their tributaries can only be made to fertilize the land by an elaborate system of control, distribution and drainage. The Irakian needs to be as disciplined as the Dutch. The human community itself has to be reconstructed. Everything has to start all over again.

One afternoon, in the midst of one of those interminable riots, some American experts arrived at my hotel on Baghdad's long, cluttered Rashid Street.

Behind the hotel a few guests were sitting on the lawn, sipping their coffee and listening to the rattle of the rifle fire. Suddenly a head appeared over the balustrade from out of the Tigris, or so it seemed. The head wore a hat and an unmistakably American, red, shaven face. The guests, after the initial shock, looked reassured and watched as more heads appeared. The men were climbing out of a boat that had brought them across the Tigris from the airfield. It was immediately obvious to anyone who knew his Middle East that these were American Experts. Each of them was equipped with a brief case and a wife, and they walked single file like soldiers across the lawn and into the hotel. The accepted witticism was that America had sent its shock troops.

I had met the technical experts and I had done my bit of journalistic sniping, but nevertheless, I had faith in them. They knew the iron god and his potentialities for good and evil.

I had studied their plans closely and had come to suspect that perhaps they were unwitting heretics in the high house where the managerial and financial high priesthood ruled and which they served. With them I had dreamed their dream of the great canals and the power lines and the new villages, and of the cooperatives and hierarchies of councils tying things together. If you looked at their plans quite closely you found that the free competitive market and the entrepreneur did not have too much to do with it.

They understood that the problem of this world of oases in the sands was an old one. Man must learn to make little do and spread it thin. This was no new world with as yet unexhausted resources. In the midst of all the turmoil they alone were in fact concerned with the establishment of a hierarchy of interdependence. They alone were concerned with any conceivable future for people for whom Allah in his immeasurable wisdom had provided so meager a heritage.

Mankind had once been very young on those plains by the great rivers. Nowhere else have I felt so strongly what it must have been like at the beginning of man's venture into the civilized life.

At the time I was around Baghdad the Irakian Directorate of Antiquities was digging around in a place just beyond the date palm gardens of Baghdad. It had run across some 2,400 textbooks, clay tablets inscribed with cuneiform writing which were used by schoolboys four thousand years ago.

An archeological quarrel of some news interest arose over whether one of the tablets presented the Pythagorean theorem that the square of the hypotenuse of a right triangle is equal to the sum of the squares of the two other sides. As I remember it the argument concerned whether the tablet contained an arithmetical or a mathematical demonstration.

Whoever may have been right on that one, the discoveries in such places as that Sumerian town of Shadippur were revising the history of the human mind. The discoveries indicated that a great part of what had so long been attributed to the Greeks must have been known to the Sumerians long before there was any sign of Greek civilization.

The clay tablets of Shadippur all seemed so neat and new. They looked at you across four thousand years, and you wondered what it had been like to be young four thousand years ago and sit in Shadippur and study a clay tablet.

Shadippur had been a little town with about 500 houses and four temples and a protecting wall about four-and-a-half feet thick. It had been the local administrative center of the small Sumerian kingdom of Esthuna. Because I had become involved in that quarrel over the triangle tablet and had held those newly excavated clay books in my hands, I had a sort of civic pride in Shadippur. The big American archeological outfits had ignored my Shadippur, it seemed to me, because it had been a small place. I felt they had rather a tendency to look down their noses at the discoveries that my Irakian friends were making there.

Shadippur was not about wars or historic epochs or any great matter. The whole of the Sumerian civilization, back so close to the beginning before Babylon, had been a matter of small city-states, irrigation canals, engineering and temple scribes who discovered you could work out all manner of things inside your head.

I went alone one morning to a room in the museum of the Directorate of Antiquities to see a bust that had recently been dug up. It turned out to be that of a wry, better sort of college professor chap, the sort who would overlook a point or two and give you a C instead of a D. I very nearly said hello.

In all those Sumerian things one feels the sense of the dawn. The Sumerians were so very near the beginning. They were never an empire but remained city-states where life was evidently vivid and intimate.

The good thing about Iran and Irak is that the storms of the centuries have swept nearly everything away. The countries have lain fallow for a long time and empty of much of anything but archeology. The big landowner and bazaar-merchant caste are not an aristocracy and have no tradition. Population is relatively sparse.

Little is left out there on the new frontiers of the old Middle East. I used to think about that when I lay in my room, kept awake by the heat, and in the night silence heard the jackals crying on the naked plain that in Babylonian times had been filled with villages.

Part Six

Africa

36

I STOOD at the tip of the embankment where the strong dark stream of the Blue Nile, pouring down out of Ethiopia, cuts across and seems to dam up the more sluggish light brown waters of the White Nile, as I looked north toward Egypt and south toward black Africa. The broad stream of the White Nile came from far down in Africa where I was bound.

Here on this side was the colonial town of Khartoum. In the houses hidden back in the broad, tree-shaded British lawns lining the street that ran beside the Blue Nile lived the officials of "the blues who governed the blacks." The members of the Sudanese Service were by tradition all-around, athletic sort of men recruited from the two traditional British universities, therefore "blues," a reference to sports. It had been an elite service under the Foreign Office because the Sudan was in theory an Anglo-Egyptian condominium and not a British colony. Its members tended to regard the Colonial Office and its people with a certain condescension.

It had been a dedicated service. There had never been very many of them in that vast land which was shortly to become the largest in territory of the Arab League states. The British never got rich at it, but each member of the Service took pleasure in the fact that the peace and order of areas half the size of Great Britain depended on the character of one man, on his calmness and judgment above all else. Accordingly, entering the Sudan Service was an honor. It had been a very proud "white man's burden" sort of thing, with the flag flying over a small outpost in the brush country and long safaris through the lonely land.

Their women were of the lean, browned, horsey-looking type, the type who goes and lives in the bush and whom you think of as standing on the bungalow steps and quelling the riotous natives with an austere glance before going in to tea.

As we sat having tea on one of those broad lawns in Khartoum, the wife of the number-two man to the governor of the Sudan told of the trouble she had once with maids. She and her husband had started out down in the south with the deeply primitive people. She noticed that the new native girls who came to work in the bungalow would look shaken and sick when they served the family. After some hesitancy, the black, wrinkled old housekeeper, who had run the place for many district commissioners, came out with the explanation.

The girls were nauseated by the smell. White people gave off an odor like a corpse.

I was also told of the case of inter-female competition versus Dutch beer.

The Sudan government had an immensely successful business: the Gezira cotton operation south of Khartoum with 26,000 Sudanese families on it. Forty per cent of the profit went to the families working the land. In building the thing up the government had remembered nearly everything except the standard of living. When the profits to the families finally exceeded food, clothing and a couple of other necessities, the people were baffled. They did not know exactly what you did with that money.

At the crucial moment someone began peddling Dutch beer. That seemed to solve the problem. You raised cotton. The cotton was sold. You sat against the wall and drank Dutch beer. It amounted to a complete ideology and way of life— baled cotton and bottled beer.

Personally, I could see nothing wrong with it but I kept my opinion to myself. Experience had taught me that my quixotic attitude toward the great goddess, the living standard, always got me into trouble when there were Occidental women around.

At any rate, foreign exchange that was needed for development was pouring out of the country to buy Dutch beer.

It was a social worker who found the solution. To me it was rather a grisly solution, coming as I did from an economy based on the demand created by the greatest spender in history, the American woman. The social worker induced some women to hang curtains in their windows. I knew. They didn't have to tell me the rest. All the other women started clamoring for curtains in their windows.

The Gezira project directors were, of course, extending the operation. Other household things were being planted on other decoys. The idyllic simplicity of the Dutch-beer-for-cotton economy was being systematically undermined. It must have been a calm and joyous life, that period of innocence before the social worker snake turned up with the apple in that Garden of Eden.

However, from the standpoint of the welfare of the poor man, the Gezira development was the most successful single project in the Middle East because it was the opposite of the Garden of Eden. Its whole success was based on putting poor Adam to work.

The British administration in the Anglo-Egyptian Sudan had acquired the million acres or so of scrub land on long-term lease, resettled the population on properly laid out thirty-acre plots and dammed the Blue Nile for water.

Management and operating funds were provided by a company established by an American, Leigh Hunt, who had come out to the Sudan and built up the Sudan Plantations Syndicate early in the century. The company got twenty per cent, the farmers forty per cent and the government forty per cent. The company's rights had run to 1950.

The company could only make a profit and amortize its investment by making everyone else prosperous. The impeccable Sudan Service, the blues governing the blacks, supervised the books.

There was a key clause to the whole arrangement. Any farmer who did not do just what he was told to do by the supervisors got ousted from his land. He could not have the land taken away from him for any other reason. On one-third he grew fodder for his cattle, on another food for his family and on the final third, cotton, which was the cash crop and the company's business.

The elements that have made a success of the modern industrial and commercial society were there. In all matters that concerned production, the rule of the high priests of the pieces of paper was autocratic. The punishment for disobedience was to be thrown out into destitution and to scrabble for another livelihood. You had to obey. But there would be no libations to offer in the London temple of the pieces of paper unless the company and the peasants prospered. If the managerial high priests were corrupt or incompetent, the guardians of the inner sanctum—members of the investment marketing and banking caste—would defrock them.

Very few of those temperamental, anarchistic Sudanese, men of the scrub land and the wild, wandering life, disobeyed and were expelled from Eden. They took orders, sweating in the fierce sun of the Sudan. They probably longed for the old life, for the lost freedom that only disorder can give, but they clung to the irrigated land.

Before, they had planted as they pleased. Many, as it happened, had gone trading in the off season. They had been dependent on their own wits and energy, and they had not fared too well.

What had been lacking was not initiative. They had been able to live only by exercise of initiative of some sort. What had been lacking was the hierarchy of authority, the stream of orders coming down from above that is the life blood of the new society that provides the new standard of living.

They had needed the boss and paid the price we all pay. The price is high. They were on the way to becoming modern men in the form that modernity comes to most of us as we are transformed into eunuchs. Their lives, like most of ours, no longer were generated out of the exercise of their own judgment and capacities. Virility had become the affair of management.

The day would come when the Sudanese cotton growers too

would sit passively in front of television sets and go to the moving pictures and read publications carefully edited and pre-digested according to the techniques of easy reading. Marketing experts and advertising executives would in time also guide them on their appointed way.

In 1950 the company's concession expired. The company became superfluous. Management and the supervisors went to work for government. It was a matter of little consequence to the 26,000 families.

At that moment the Sudan was on the verge of becoming a sovereign democracy governed by an elected parliament. Once more the empire on which the sun never set was laying down the white man's burden. You thought of the melodrama of "Recessional," and of the prophesy in it. You thought of bugles calling the last retreat.

> On dune and headland sinks the fire—
> Lo, all our pomp of yesterday
> Is one with Nineveh and Tyre!

The Sudan, with its wide grasslands, the desert, the raw ragged hills, was Kipling country.

I spent a final evening at a party at one of Sayed Siddig's residences. The best of Khartoum and Omdurman society, black and white, had been there. Sayed Siddam was quite black.

The Sudan Service was not color conscious. It was a gentleman's service, and a gentleman, according to the code, was not conscious of color. Because I was an American, and they had read a few things, they watched me discreetly. They were interested to know if I was a gentleman or if I was color conscious.

From the party I went to the hotel and then to the airport. I fell asleep as we left in the night, and I woke with a start. The truculent tropic dawn came like an ill-tempered landlady jerking open the curtains.

Far away to the west the upper Nile shimmered, and to the east the foothills rose toward Ethiopia. The plane drummed stolidly southward out of all that I had known and into Africa.

37

NOTHING as North American can be found in the Euro-Asiatic-African land mass as Johannesburg in South Africa, the one large city of Africa south of the Sahara. To an American it is about as foreign as Dallas or Houston or Kansas City, although if he were drugged, and put in an airplane on a wager that he could not identify the American city in which he awakened, he would probably assume that he was somewhere south of the Mason-Dixon line because of the color bar and the Jim Crow atmosphere. He would be puzzled by a few borrowed British phrases, such as milk bar for soda fountain, but he would not suspect that he was abroad.

The neon lights, the tall square buildings reaching for the sky, the dime stores, the malted milks, the lunch counters and steaming coffee urns are all American. And it sounds like America, or at least the American south, because of the Negro laughter, the laughter that the Negro has brought to the American scene, laughter that is sudden and a little barbaric with overtones of both mockery and sadness.

Yet the city proper is a city of white immigrants, of people from overseas.

The pace and the feel of Johannesburg was that of the immigrant civilization there where I came from. They, like us, were men who had no part in tomorrow, who seemed to seek to justify themselves in the eyes of others, hastily, before a death that is so definitive. Here too there was no closeness, no being part of one another but organization, administration, management. I encountered here again the firm handclasp, the positive smile, the rapid half-fellowship that is the modern numerical society's substitute for the older life with its organic bonds of mutual obligation.

I had been born a stranger too and was to a degree at my ease there in that ready friendliness which is not really friendship. I fell readily into that pattern where the score of life is kept on the scoreboard of success or failure. Johannesburg was a city of success stories and of young men coming up, and I encountered here, as in my land, the "has-been," bearing for all to see the stigma of his failure and his shame. I knew that among the "has-beens" and the average men there were many who lay in the silence of the night pleading with their God for mercy, for something that would give them success, for they had no other recourse on the long, dreary trail of life.

These people were my people and this, in its emptiness, was home if home be where you came from. I too was only an opinion of others and a notation on the scoreboard of relative success.

This world of equal opportunity oppressed by the fear or fact of failure was, wherever you found it, my native land.

The atmosphere here was perhaps a little more characteristic of the America of my youth. Johannesburg was still near the years of the lost frontier. The eunuch civilization was only slowly emerging. The habitat of the modern eunuch, of the average man, had not been built up. The mass-communication industries were meagerly developed. The instruments of attitude engineering were very imperfect. The sciences of behavior control had not yet developed as far toward becoming an adequate substitute for the human personality.

Johannesburg constitutes a thing apart in the continent of Africa.

The greatest gold reserves in the world, far surpassing any other discovery in the history of gold, lie buried deep under the Witwatersrand and the near-by northern Orange Free State. Both the nature of the chocolate-bar ores specked with gold and the extension and depth of the strata required the building up of a major industry.

Manufacturing followed. Within the South African union are found the fifth largest coal reserves in the world, they are larger than those of Great Britain. There are also substantial iron reserves and scattered deposits of other ores.

The South African high veld lies south of the Tropic of Capricorn as Florida lies north of the Tropic of Cancer, but at elevations of five to six thousand feet it is free of tropic diseases and tropic heat. Accordingly, the whole industrial area centering on Johannesburg is about as African as Illinois.

The fame of it has spread far into the kraals of the north and the bush country, and the black man has come from deep in the tropics to work in the mines. On Sundays, when the Johannesburger was away in his car or sitting out in his suburban house, and the city was empty, the raw natives came to town to see with their own eyes the wonders of Goudi.

I found myself trailing along after the black men; perhaps I wanted to regain my own faith in these wonders by seeing them through their eyes. Men from the ancient villages must once have gazed with the same fresh joy at the towers of Babylon. The colorful displays of candies rooted them to the pavement. They observed with uncomprehending wonder the glass doors of a moving picture theater and admired gravely the toothbrush smile of an actress presented in a bigger than life-sized photograph.

You remembered when you were a child long ago and the world was so young. But that would not come back, and these were only strangers out of another age and time, asking no questions. You knew also that they were Africa, and that these were not the temples of their gods but of yours, of whom you were weary.

Coming to and going from Johannesburg during the continuous traveling that made up my years in Africa, I felt an ever increasing sense of the impermanence of this alien city. I thought of the ruined cities out in Transjordan and on the edge of desert. One felt a sense of futility when seeing the forum, the colonnades, the ruined circus and fallen temples. For a thousand years those alien Greek and Roman cities had stood in the Orient. In the end the Orient had arisen and enveloped them, swept them away and forgotten them and the alien who had built them.

One night I arrived in Johannesburg just before New Year's. The city had emptied almost completely. There was life only in the far-flung encampments of the natives—slum towns and barrack towns—the so-called locations spreading out through the veld around the high-built citadel of the "white civilization" like a besieging army.

New Year's Day was the day of the great carnival in Cape-town and the Cape Province.

The native African had little part in the main event in the south which was reserved for the 1,000,000 Cape colored, a group that had emerged out of a long period of racial miscege-nation in the early years of Dutch settlement. But, the young African Negro bands in the Johannesburg locations were begin-ning to regard it as their day too. They too would dress up and turn out with their drums, fifes and musical whistles.

I was breakfasting a little late New Year's morning in my room high up above that deserted city, for there was nothing to do.

At first I did not understand. There was a rhythm in the empty streets, the sharp staccato beat and roll of African drums. Few white men have ever mastered that rhythm which is not of their nature.

Out in the business section of that concrete and steel city, bands of young Negroes, in multicolored satin costumes or the nearest they could come to it, were floating on bare feet—mov-ing back and forth across the streets and up onto the sidewalks and back again.

One of them stepped away unexpectedly with that high, strutting step that was tribal, ecstatic, mystic and a mockery of the ostrich in flight. The drums cried out in rhythmic passion and sudden response.

They were town natives, but the town dropped from them. The drums laughed with a rhythmic laughter and the black mass swept from curb to curb carried on the ebb and flow of that laughter.

The troubled, commercial-minded British of Johannesburg

were not a laughing people. The rhythm of Africa did not appeal to them. It was too much the voice of the black man's continent. The white preferred to ignore it and shut himself off from it.

I was rather pleased to discover that with the substantial German at my command I could soon read the mother tongue of the white majority, Afrikaans. It helped to understand more rapidly that Johannesburg, and what it stands for, is as alien to the original white population of the Union of South Africa as to the black man.

The Afrikaners, or Boers, of South Africa are the smallest of the nations that resulted from the massive North European overseas emigration that began in the seventeenth century. Plymouth was established by the Pilgrim Fathers in 1620 on the shores of what is now Massachusetts. The Dutch established Nieuw Amsterdam, now New York, in 1626. The Dutch forefathers of the little Afrikaner nation arrived at Capetown to establish a cabbage patch and victualling station for ships in 1652.

No vast immigrant empire grew up around the southern African Dutch. They are today only a little nation of around 1,700,000 in a multilingual and multiracial South Africa with 1,000,000 English speaking, 1,000,000 Cape colored and some 9,500,000 native black Africans and some Indians.

They have as a nation no actual territory that they can call their own. But they have done something that no other emigrant nation has done. They have simplified and so changed their European mother tongue, Dutch, that a new language, Afrikaans, has appeared.

Something earthy and intimate in that language of a small people attracted me. It is a frank and oddly pungent tongue of people who are close to one another, talking in the farmhouse over supper or around the fire on the veld where the nights are cold.

In fifty years there has been a complete reversal in the meaning of the word Boer. In the days of the Boer War of 1899-1902, Boer meant a sort of American Minute Man. Today the Boer is regarded as a tyrant and reactionary of the darkest stripe.

Justification for both views has been present during nearly the whole history of the Afrikaner people. Afrikaner history, as I found, and you needed to be no exceptional scholar, has been the tale of a sturdy and liberty-loving people. It has also been the tale of the seizure, by violence or fraud, of the black African's lands and a persistent effort to keep him down.

It is the story of the white North American and the Indian up to the time when it became clear that the Indian would become a museum piece, or rather it is more precisely what would have been the story of my own people in a North America heavily populated with red-skinned men.

Near the southern point of Africa, Cape Agulhas, lies an island with a rocky spine and one stretch of fertile rolling land on the side toward the continent. It was long since joined to the continent by the accumulation of drifting sands in the shallow waters of the former strait.

The island is called today the Cape of Good Hope Peninsula, with the city of Capetown or Kaapstadt under Table Mountain at the northern end and the Cape of Good Hope at the southern. It is one of the loveliest places in all the world. The great waves of the South Atlantic seas break continually along its coasts, and vineyards and gardens cover its eastern slope, rising through wooded parkland toward the precipices and peaks of the mountains that drop abruptly to the western shore. To the south, beyond a sandy table land, the ocean grumbles and scolds at the foot of the upflung towering rock that is the actual Cape of Good Hope.

You stand today on the terrace of the University of Capetown, high in the wooded parkland against the mountains, and see over in Africa the ragged mysterious line of the mainland mountains. Fittingly, the University of Stellenbosch, the Oxford of the Afrikaners, is over there in a mountain valley in the Dutch town of Stellenbosch, shaded by great trees. There on the mainland the Afrikaner story began.

South Africa started with a clear-cut principle of what is called today *"apartheid,"* separation of races. The Netherlands East India Company had established its victualling station, fort and small Dutch colony on the island peninsula of the Cape of Good Hope.

The Cape of Good Hope Peninsula was to be for the Dutch, and Africa was to be for the Africans or, in this particular case, for the brown-skinned Hottentots and the Bushmen. The actual black tribes of the southern portion of Africa, roughly designated as the Bantu peoples, had never entered any part of that southernmost portion of the African continent.

Sometime about half a century after the establishment of the colony on the Cape of Good Hope, a few settlers and their grown sons, who had drifted over to the mainland and established themselves a few miles inland, began to act strangely. The Dutch barnyard ducks had hatched wild geese.

Free burghers disappeared over the Hottentots' Holland Mountains. The broad shelf of the south coast lay open before them. Others moved up inland and came into a dry land of far horizons and adopted from the wild Hottentots the life of herdsmen. The barnyard ducks, officials of the East India Company left behind in little Capetown, quacked and scolded.

Edicts were issued and boundaries set beyond which no Dutchman was to go. But out beyond the misty line of the mountains were men who no longer heard. Africa was beginning to speak to them as the far frontier of America spoke to the pioneer.

Little conscious of what he was doing, the Dutch frontiersman trekked on into freedom—that actual freedom which life offers to only a few in rare circumstances.

Civilization fell behind. He began to live in a house that was only a larger native hut. He spent little time indoors. For weeks he would wander off hunting in a country rich in game. The herds of cattle and the flocks of sheep slowly moved inland. This was a sunlit and temperate land. The fevers and insects of the tropics were not encountered.

For most of two centuries, while the Afrikaner nation was being formed, the inland Dutch led a subsistence existence. Exchange of goods was insignificant. It was not an economic society, buying and bartering, but a living together in a state of economic independence of one another.

The compromises, the adjustments and the acceptance of hierarchy and impersonal authority that are the hallmarks of civilizations did not enter into it.

That kind of living develops frugality in more than one sense. Such people come to prefer a few things to many things and a simple code to a variety of opinion.

Two peoples formed in those nearly two centuries, the Afrikaner and the mulatto Cape colored, both speaking the variation on the Netherlands tongue which has become the Afrikaans language. That land apart down under Africa, today the Cape Province or most of it, is their original homeland and place of their beginnings, and they know and acknowledge no other. Because of that the Afrikaners hold themselves to be forever a people of the African continent, a white tribe set apart from the black tribes.

Perhaps it is a love of the land of their origin that has blinded me somewhat to the widely and justly publicized faults of the Afrikaners. There are few more heart-warming portions of this earth than that country which is some 650 miles across and roughly 200 miles deep. Houses in the Dutch colonial style, vineyards, orchards and wheat fields lie in the valleys. Up beyond the ranges sheep browse on the thick cover of sweet desert herbiage. Tipped with snow in winter, the mountains stretch away to the African horizons. Bays open into the quiet land from the rock barriers against which the great waters of the southern seas break in a vast lament. You could rest there.

At the beginning of the last century, the British replaced the Dutch officials at Capetown, and trouble slowly came. The British were alien. The population grew. Slavery was abolished. On the route along the east coast, massed tribes of the black Bantu peoples, the advance guard of the battle line of Africa, were at last encountered. To the north the Boers stood on the banks of the Orange ready to trek into the high veld, the country beyond the frontiers.

The British colonial government sent an official named Donald Moodie up to the banks of the Orange to expostulate once more with those incorrigible pioneers.

In his early nineteenth-century English, he wrote to the government in Capetown, "I blamed them for making all their children graziers and ascribed to this custom many of the inconveniences to which they were subject.

"I asked them: Why not rather serve one another than accumulate stock without land.

"One of them replied: Because every child is a Boer and in what country will people serve for hire if they can live their own masters."

I was drawn to that Boer who remembered freedom—which is so much a matter of how you live and earn your living rather than of civil rights.

The freedom which the pioneer experienced was individualistic but not as the uprooted resident within the modern industrial society understands individualism. It was not an aloneness.

I soon discovered that one of the odd features of the Afrikaner community was the paucity of names. There seemed to be only a dozen or so names. Everyone was named Kruger or Burger or Malan or one of a few other things. Picnics of people of the same family name were like national conventions.

The white tribe of the Afrikaners is made up of white clans. To be more accurate, the Boers live within the world of the extended family as do the native Africans with black skins—as does so great a part of the Orient.

The God of this society is a living God, intimate and anthropomorphic. He is neither a vague ethical principle nor a philosophic abstraction.

He is there, vivid as the God of the Hebrews, in the full blaze of the African noonday, in the night and in the wide spaces of the veld. No people, except possibly the orthodox Jews themselves, are more steeped in the God of the Old Testament. He is a just and a rugged God and to a degree, like Jehovah of old, a tribal God.

This Afrikaner society has been described, usually with a touch of condescension, as a patriarchal society. The Boer's instinctive answer is doubt that the boss-ridden hierarchy of modern aloneness is better.

The Great Trek, which started soon after Donald Moodie

went to the Orange River, had brought into being sovereign Afrikaner states, the republics of Transvaal and the Orange Free State. Discovery of the gold strata of the Witwatersrand and the sudden appearance of Johannesburg, filled with *uitlanders,* foreigners, led to the Boer War. British victory brought the establishment of the Union of South Africa in 1910 with a white electorate, which meant a predominantly Afrikaner electorate.

After the Boer War the period came when it was no longer possible for every Boer's son to be his own master. Some had to serve others, generally British owners and managers of mines and factories.

The nationalism and intense racialism of the modern Afrikaners have developed out of an increasing fear as the old freedom and the old intimacy passed away. Those who could no longer find land or only land so poor that it provided no livelihood became the "poor whites" in the early decades of this century, and the poor white Afrikaners in the countryside became a national problem.

It was the increasing number of factories that in the end solved the problem by providing a livelihood for the poor white Boers. It was a solution, but it shook the Afrikaner nation. Baffled, disoriented, the sons of the free Boers had become hired men in industry. The Great Trek of the Boer people into the boundless veld now ended for so many at a workbench in a British-run factory or as a miner in a British-controlled mine. The hopes and the visions of the trapped Afrikaner were buried out there in the open veld, in his *platteland.* The dream of the pioneers was dreamed out, but the memory of it hurt like a fresh wound.

From the side of the black majority came the other threat. The demand for justice for the native African involved surrender of land by the Boers still out in the veld. Land was the very heart of their concept of security, economic and moral. The *platteland* was not only the Paradise Lost of the urban Afrikaners but the stronghold of their nation, the foundation of its hope of survival.

On the political level the Boer is equally threatened. Equality of all men in South Africa can only be obtained by the Boer nation becoming a tolerated minority in a black majority state.

Cast out of the rural community into industrial employment, the Afrikaner who was no longer a *boer*, which means rancher or farmer, became all the more passionately Afrikaner. The fear of anonymity, of the proletarian existence, was on him. He was convinced that the bosses in what was to him a still alien urban world were somehow going to force him to mix with the native workers until he became an indistinguishable part of a racially mixed proletarian mass.

The state and their control of the state as the majority of the white electorate have become the Afrikaner's weapon against extinction.

The fear for their children, for their land and their people also haunted the actual *boer* on the *platteland*. He once more began to live "kraaled in" as in the days when, in the fashion of the American western pioneers, he stood off the attacks of the savages from his circle of ox wagons.

No expression in the Afrikaans language is more charged with emotion than *ons mense*, literally "our people." It is both freedom and home.

But I envied them for that *ons mense*. Every member, good or bad, of so small a community on the defensive becomes precious. Everyone within that circle is needed. The sense of being needed is one of the most intense of human satisfactions. It is a different thing from being number 165,000,000.

My sympathy with their desire to be together in the intimacy of their smallness gave me a somewhat different attitude toward the famous word apartheid which meant in the popular concept simply that the black man should stay down in his place.

There is a difference between the eventual purpose of apartheid and the color bar as it exists in the United States South. The American color bar has been an instrument for the oppression of a minority and has included the black ghetto. It is the layer cake, white on top and chocolate on the bottom.

Apartheid is two things. For a great many white South Africans, as far as I could make out, it is also the doctrine of the black ghetto, and in this case a ghetto for the majority. But for the actual spiritual and intellectual leadership of the Afrikaner nation today, associated notably with what is called the Stellenbosch group, it is a doctrine of total territorial separation.

I was sitting with Henrik Verwoerd, the minister of native affairs in the Malan cabinet, in a big shaded office on a hot day in Capetown while parliament was in session. He drew a picture on a piece of paper. It showed the road of South Africa to date which he did not describe further. There was no need. It meant the color bar and the layer cake. Then he drew the two roads into the future. He labeled the one total racial integration. It meant obviously a South Africa of the majority and the absorption of the white minorities into the black nation. Then he drew another road off in the opposite direction and he labeled it total territorial separation.

Apartheid in that sense is the acknowledgment of the fact perfectly familiar to many Afrikaners, that the white man did not come in Africa to an empty continent. Black Africa is no America. Almost all of it is the heritage not of the man from overseas but of the black man, even as Asia is the heritage of the Asiatic.

For the Afrikaners it is a serious business. They are a little nation, no bigger than the Esthonian or the Latvian. An apartheid which attempts to leave the black majority in a minority ghetto will be swept away.

They have only two choices to make. The territory of a small white African-born nation cannot be very large. They would not have the resources that the white man now has.

It will be up to them whether they want to preserve a small homeland of their own down there in Africa or whether they will prefer to merge with the black man and participate as black men in the future of Africa.

I never became particularly interested in the long-term outlook for the English-speaking in South Africa. They had come predominantly for jobs or to make their fortunes.

Some could be absorbed into black Africa, but not many, I suspect. A certain number would become, perhaps, bilingual Afrikaners. Many will simply go away. They or their forefathers took the wrong boat, unaware that Africa was already someone else's house. Most of them have arrived since the Johannesburg gold rush late in the last century and live in cities very similar to cities they will find elsewhere. They are in any case citizens of my world, where the dead have no part in tomorrow.

38

FOR A WHILE I could not understand why I had no sense of really being in Africa. Outside the Union of South Africa, a great part of the continent had the slightly nightmarish quality of hotel lobbies suspended in a vacuum.

Then the explanation finally dawned on me. I got down out of the sky and started using the railroads, such as they were, and the roads, such as you wished they were not. It was airplane travel that created a good deal of that visual distortion. It accounts in part for the excessive importance the European in Africa comes to assume when you are traveling about. I had been merely flying from European town to European town, and for a time white man's Africa was about all that had registered with me.

The towns were scattered about in my working area which was the African Subcontinent or region south of French Equatorial Africa and the Sudan and which included the Congo, Angola, the Rhodesias, British East Africa and Mozambique as well as South Africa. Altogether, outside South Africa, there were about fourteen white man's towns of any consequence— fourteen towns in an area substantially larger than the United

States! And in that same area there are about the same number of whites as in the city of Indianapolis. That was what white man's Africa amounted to.

The Africa that I had been seeing was an optical illusion. The African emptiness was the reality, and it was only an apparent emptiness. The brooding, primitive emptiness was ages old but was not uninhabited. Primitive man in grass and brush shacks still crouched like his forefathers close to the earth in villages linked by almost indiscernible tracks.

This was older than the pyramids and older than Babylon. It was the oldest form of human life.

It could be found out a few miles from town and a little away from the rare arterial highways. The period from early Sumeria and Egypt to this day was a brief episode compared with the agelessness of the grass hut, the gourds, the pottery, the people. Theirs was by far the greater part of the human story.

They were people with another awareness; every movement in the grass and every insect buzzing across the clearing attracted their attention. They were forever exchanging glances in silent conversation, and their intimate and constant awareness of one another was the shared awareness of everything around them.

A child is aware in that fashion. Civilized man's word-thinking that distorts and cushions the dramatic impact of the presence of others and of environment, were absent.

Africa is the one great region of the world where primitive man in large numbers has lived into the modern age. It is not a phenomenon to be dealt with in terms of underdeveloped or backward nations. One cannot identify the peoples of Black Africa with the ancient civilized peoples of Asia who have shaken off European colonial control since World War II. It is childish to think of them in terms of the color bar, making comparisons with the American Negro.

Black Africa is not essentially a spectacle of the underprivileged struggling for justice. Here are the exhibits of an anthropological museum come alive.

The crisis of the African Subcontinental area arises from the fact that in the last great homeland of primitive man, modern man's presence is, in its present form, irrelevant. To the native, the white colonial out to make a fortune is irrelevant; even the native African imitating white man's way is irrelevant.

Colonial powers sought resources and markets in Africa for the home country. Business concerns wanted inexpensive labor and freedom to exploit natural resources.

The leaders of the new Asia and liberal orators everywhere have been clamoring to have Africa set free. But what does freedom mean in the context of the African Subcontinent? Conceivably it might have some meaning in West Africa, but in the Subcontinental area outside the Union of South Africa there are no citizens and no nations. In our terms primitive man has not arrived at freedom or unfreedom. Our categories based on our rationalism and convictions do not apply to him.

The organically rooted and intimately linked family, clan and tribal groups are an even more predominant pattern in indigenous Africa than in Asia. Within that pattern you find again the social device by which the curve of life goes up with age. Honor and prestige gather around a man or a woman with increase in years. Success, as we should probably call it, is guaranteed. There is no fear of the emptiness of old age and of being thrust aside; age is not something essentially shameful, lessening your value in the eyes of a dynamic world that is half-consciously eager to have done with you.

The honors could be overdone, perhaps, as was the case in a Kenya village which I visited. It was a matter of viewpoint—personally I found it the most perfect formula for growing old graciously that I had yet encountered.

We had gone up there to get pictures of their almost miniature cattle. On the hillside, among the banana groves and the garden plots, stood the huts of the village. Against their walls, in relaxed somnolence, sprawled or sat the old men and old women. Most of them wore benign expressions and despite their relaxed postures presented a very special appearance of dignity and contemplative repose.

My interpreter got nothing out of them; in their calm they merely regarded him as a minor distraction.

We finally found a younger man who rounded up the tiny

cattle. I then learned about the matter of the old men and old women. They were full of honor and high prestige due to their age, and they were full of something else. Custom dictated that no one could drink until he had achieved old age. Then, custom prescribed, they should be liberally supplied with beer, the viscous, native beer made in the huts; you could then, with liver intact, settle down to an accepted and expected alcoholic old age. The habitual alcoholic daze of the aged was held in veneration on the assumption that they were communing with the ancestors. It made you wonder what imaginative patriarch had thought that one up back in the history of the tribe.

Kenya had produced the one outstanding African personality who has appeared in the Subcontinent in this generation. The result had been the Mau Mau rebellion.

The story of Jomo Kenyatta is the story of the perilous affair of a man searching for the meaning of his existence and that of his people.

Jomo (Burning Spear) Kenyatta, a Kikuyu, had gone to Britain and the European continent and stayed seventeen years, returning to Africa after the war. He had studied anthropology at the University of London under the famous Bronislaw Malinowski, and he wrote a book, *Facing Mount Kenya.*

Of the Kikuyu tribesman he wrote: "His personal needs, physical and psychological, are satisfied incidentally while he plays his part as a member of the family group (the large African grouping of kin) and cannot be fully satisfied in any other way. Kinship is the root of Kikuyu ideas of good and evil."

That sort of thing would hardly have brought on the butcheries and wholesale terror of the Mau Mau rebellion, but the book gave merely the clues to the more dramatic message he brought back to the highlands of Kenya.

He became president of the Kenya African Union and took over the rather extensive system of African independent schools. At his Githunguri training school he began to teach his disciples.

His doctrine was that European civilization is based on a false premise and amounts to a false approach to life, superficially superior but fundamentally inferior to the African approach. He had at his disposal modern anthropology's critique of individualism.

That corner of Africa had been brewing up for some time an intellectual ferment concerned principally with religion and therefore with the meaning of life. Missionary activity had been intense, and among the Africans strange sects had appeared. Square in the middle of the turmoil stood, however, a practical matter of social justice: there were no *shambas* for the young men!

The African, living in a relatively sparsely settled continent and practicing nomad agriculture, feels that a man has a right to air, water and land.

Within the fertile highland belt—the total world that mattered to these people—sat the white reserve of 12,000 square miles, constituting thirty-five to fifty per cent—the amount varying from one authority to another—of the actual fertile land. In that reserve there were some 4,000 white settlers. The Kikuyu tribe of 1,250,000 had perhaps a fifth to a fourth as much land.

The Kenya white reserve had been created casually early in the century to provide traffic for the railway to Uganda, built under the auspices of the Foreign Office and proving beyond doubt that foreign offices should stay out of the railway business. The railway engines regularly tumbled off the track in the rainy season, and sometimes in the dry season just to keep in practice.

The little white colony in Kenya was largely made up of people seeking refuge from the social forces liquidating the Victorian Age. They sought for themselves the security of land and the manor.

The conflict between the black man's need for his *shamba* and the white man's for his manor was inevitable. That little parcel of land which the African calls a *shamba* and which will feed a family, is the social-security system on which human life has mostly been based ever since man ceased to be purely a hunter.

The black African will go out today to work in mines or factories as he went out previously to hunt. The *shamba*, however, normally worked by the woman, is the root of the tree of his existence. Life without the *shamba* does not basically make sense to the African any more than it has made sense to most men during man's affair with the world for the past milleniums.

British settlers, however, built up a planters' colony in the white reserve. Finally some 200,000 tribesmen were at work on plantations or in the two towns.

The Englishman had gone all over the world seeking to set up his manor in the form of the plantation. Nairobi is, in a fashion, another Williamsburg of colonial Virginia, where the plantation masters come in for a week end of drinking, gambling, dancing and talking politics.

The British settlers saw Africa in terms of the labor pool and not in terms of the *shamba*. Their position became largely undermined by the success of neighboring Uganda, an almost purely black state with a basic *shamba* structure. Uganda has become a substantial cotton exporter and the most important productive area in East Africa.

To the wrestling with religion that had already started and the *shamba* issue, Jomo Kenyatta brought his great critique of modern civilization. Expressed in the passionate language of a prophet among his own people, it was the final thing that opened the gates to the demonic powers rooted in primitive animism and the primitive imagination. The urgent and sudden desire to see the last of the white man and his deviltry threw everything into turmoil. The dark world of the outcast sorcerer in the bush came to the fore. In the successive massacres, more reluctant or recalcitrant Kikuyu were killed than whites.

I have not found to be convincing the evidence that Jomo Kenyatta "managed the Mau Mau rebellion," the charge on which he was sentenced to seven years in a northern desert prison camp. Whether anyone but an East African white court would have found it convincing is a question. That his teaching brought to the breaking point a passionate desire to drive the white man out seems now self-evident. But Mau Mau was not a politicians' rebellion. It was not concerned with black men in office and with native self-government.

While I was in Kenya, Peter Mbiyu Koinange, after Jomo

Kenyatta the most famous native African figure of East Africa, brought into the courts the issue of the right to educate African children in terms of the African way of life.

He and his associates in the case offered a simple argument. Kenya was full of mission schools which were the most important part of the European effort to form the mind of the African child. There was, however, an African approach and concept. Its essential values were different from the individualism and other major tenets of the European way. They had as much right, they contended, to teach an African pattern of living as a European.

The desire for an African approach, which took throughout Black Africa the form of an African interpretation of Christianity, is perhaps the most significant movement in African life, for out of it can come an ideology.

Jomo Kenyatta and Peter Koinange were intellectuals—that bad word. They had given direction to the searching of the bewildered native. To a degree they had given him faith in the value of his heritage in preference to a black-skinned imitation of the white strangers' institutions and ideas. It was a perilous affair, as the Mau Mau fury demonstrated, for it reached too deep. It was something that needed time to mature, if only the white stranger could be induced to proceed slowly and hold back his headlong rush toward what he considered progress.

While wandering through my Subcontinent I came to the Victoria Falls where the Zambesi plunges over the mile-long edge of an abyss and cries out in a sudden titanic clamor of great raging waters before it rolls away through a break in the imprisoning walls into the canyon below. Columns of vapor and spray fill the abyss and rise above the falls to form a cloud called the Smoke That Thunders.

When the sun is low in the west, the light of the late afternoon flows horizontally across the chasm and the spray and vapor. A multitude of rainbows drift through the mounting spray. That hour of the day is accordingly known as rainbow time.

At rainbow time you went down from the hotel on the hill

past the falls and the rainbows and up along the Zambesi to have tea with the monkeys.

The tea lawn was quite neat and British with chairs and tables but nothing else around except the African river-bank woodland and the bush country out beyond. Two small thatched rondavels served as kitchen and storehouse.

The monkeys lived in the wild country up river but were very regular about their teatime. It was a rather formal tea because of the monkeys' attitude in the matter of cake. It took me a considerable number of shillings to verify that you could give two pieces of cake successively to any one monkey but that he could not have three. It was clearly bad manners to take three, and the other monkeys would not tolerate it. If you came to tea—that is if you were a monkey—and sat on the grass in the proper way opposite the people in the chairs, you were evidently supposed to behave yourself and not be a pig.

A certain spirit of free enterprise was permitted, however. There was no protest when a monkey dropped from a tree and made off with all the cake in the plate. It is a point in good breeding that is possibly a little obscure to anyone but a Zambesi monkey.

For the people there was no particular rule of etiquette except that they were not to bring their dogs. The monkeys had sentinels out on the paths to the tea lawn. When one of them came chattering wildly and half the guests went up the trees, protesting furiously, you knew that a dog was coming.

In general, however, I did not find the people of the Zambesi country particularly interested in animals. The Kenya whites are the most animal-conscious people I have known.

When the Mau Mau rebellion was at its height the Kenya British got themselves into a considerable state of agitation about chilling the tender stomachs of hippopotami. There was a small lake in the dry country halfway between Nairobi and the coast. The place was off in the bush and hard to get at but it was well known.

Hippopotami had set up housekeeping there. A rough platform had been built from which you could look down into the clear water and watch them go about their business. Hippopotami are not exactly the most graceful of creatures on land, but in their own element there is a certain heavy grace to their movements like a slumberous dancing. The spectacle came to be known as the ballet of the hippopotami. Adding to it was the play of the sunlight down in the water and the small, darting blue fish that formed sudden clusters of dissolving color.

Then the government announced its intention to build a dam. Additional water supply was needed for the port town of Mombasa and the hippopotami's pool was to be turned into a reservoir. The press was outraged, and various distinguished political personages were shocked and indignant. Of course, no one intended to oust the hippopotami who, in that dry country, had no other place to go. The issue which so outraged the press was that, by raising the level of the water, the pool would become colder and would therefore chill the underparts of the hippopotami.

An embarrassed administration finally came up with a proposal to install in the pool concrete parking platforms for weary hippopotami on which they could sit and warm their chilled underparts. The proposal was greeted with disdain and for a time nothing more was heard about the Mombasa water supply.

39

THE ARAB of the empire of the dhows must have puzzled a good deal over the "discoveries" of the great British explorers in the nineteenth century. In the places the British discovered, the literate, civilized traders and slave merchants of Zanzibar and the dhow ports were going about their business as their fathers had before them; in the business houses and on the quais the explorers encountered men whose normal occupation was to go as traders to the places which the explorers intended to discover. Gamins in the streets of Zanzibar could presumably have described to them those places with considerable accuracy.

By the time the great British explorers arrived, there was no longer any particular mystery about the greater part of the eastern half of the African Subcontinent. The mystery was principally how Africa had succeeded in staying so primitive.

Hindus had been settled on the African east coast two-and-a-half milleniums before. There is a record of a presumably civilized settlement at Mombasa in the first century A.D.

The Islamic civilization, which still exists though in weakened form, came into full strength four centuries before Columbus sailed for America. A string of cities traded vigorously, maintained schools, built up wealth, practiced the arts, constructed ocean-going vessels and established farms and plantations.

The unbroken history of the civilization of the East African seafaring Arabs probably extends over a period of a thousand years or more. Before the American Pilgrim Fathers landed at Plymouth, the African coastal civilization had already gone through a period twice as long as that which has been covered by American history since that date.

Yet, in the late nineteenth century, the British moving into Kenya found the tribes inland completely primitive and unaware of the existence of the simplest devices and earliest discoveries of civilized man.

A series of historic and geographic facts explain why civilization did not infect the African and Africa: slave raiding, climate, malaria and the indifference of the Arab coastal traders toward colonial expansion inland.

However, it is not true that eastern Africa remained primitive because it had no contact with civilization.

A clue to the mystery of Africa's resistance to the spread of civilization is found in Tanganyika. Tanga in Tanganyika is a palm-shaded little port with a middle-class air of meaning well but having no sense of humor.

It is the most important world center of a low-wage and low-profit industry: the production of sisal fibre. On a green terrace above the blue tropical bay are the offices of the East African Sisal Growers associations and of the Swiss, British and Indian sisal concerns. Green, stiff, regimented square miles of sisal looking like something by a futuristic painter stretch for leagues inland and down the coast.

At the time one-third of the native Tanganyikan wage-earners worked in the sisal industry.

Sisal perversely thrives on soils and in climatic conditions where most commercially valuable vegetation will not grow at all. Its stiff, pointed leaves are razor sharp. That this self-willed misfit should be turned into binder twine seems only just.

The sisal industry is a triumph of frugal men and a frugal plant over natural poverty. Soil experts and agricultural specialists have consistently emphasized the fact that Africa is a poor man's continent and must develop on the basis of its essential agricultural poverty, not pretend to be a new Eldorado.

Geologists have found great parts of Tanganyika eroded to the bare bones and incapable of sustaining any useful vegetable life. What is true of Tanganyika is, in varying degrees, true in the rest of Africa.

You do not have to go all the way with the theory of the "dying continent," but there is obviously something wrong with Africa. It often seems to be merely an area covered with dry, stiff, heat-and-drought-resisting bush.

Africa has formidable weapons against anyone attempting to civilize it. The most formidable is the interplay of sun, water and soil. Chemical and physical action due to the heat, a vast superfluity of microscopic life in the soil and the drenching tropic rains keep the soils poor. Great expanses are covered with or underlaid with laterite, a stone leprosy that attacks tropic soils. It either forms an impermeable shield on the surface or is covered by only a thin layer of actual soil.

Cultivation not only speeds up the processes which destroy

the humus in the soil and bring about a deterioration of its chemical substance, but it bares the soil to the extreme erosion typical of tropical rain areas.

Once the soil is fully exposed to the sun, without forest or brush cover, the humus is burned out and the chemical furies let loose.

Only one complete answer has been found to overcome the hostility of the soil. That is to let the soil cover itself up and rest for some twenty years after being cultivated for a period. And that is precisely what primitive man had been doing.

He cleared an area in the forest or burned out a plot in the bush. He planted in the land enriched by vegetable ash. In due time the soil lost its fertility, and he moved on and let it rest. In his old age he or his sons would come back to it again.

You cannot build up elaborate civilizations on this basis where life must be simple and concerned with simple matters, and where there cannot be a crowd around.

Part of the irrelevancy of white man's presence in Africa has been the fact that he has refused to accept Africa. In clubs and on hotel porches and in offices I sat and listened to them insisting on the agricultural wealth and the potential wealth. Their own government experts merely shook their heads.

Basically there is a question whether there is actually a place for the white settler farmer as well as the black man's *shamba* in East Africa.

In the system set up by Belgium in the Congo a more fruitful approach to Africa seems to exist. Once over the snow-capped Ruwenzori Mountains, you found yourself in the Congo, freed from that eternal, nagging problem of race that haunts British Africa and South Africa. The Congo is a business concern with a policy of the open door for everyone in the company, irrespective of color. After the South African, it is the biggest economy in the African Subcontinent.

The black Congolese was not only permitted to learn any sort of skill and rise to any sort of job—he was urged, prodded and trained. In the banks were native African bank clerks; there were Negro engineers, Negro machinists and Negro pharmacists.

But there were at the time neither Negro politicians nor white politicians. There were no politicians at all.

The Congo was frankly a trusteeship vested in the Belgian government in Brussels and more specifically the Colonial Council. It was not a partnership between black and white. The Belgians drew a handsome profit from their trusteeship through the great trusts in which a good part of the savings of the Belgian people were invested. The triple trustees which controlled the Congo—the Colonial Council in Brussels, the great trusts and the Roman Catholic Church—worked on a basis of common principles.

First of these was that the 12,000,000 native Africans must be capable of judging their own interests and producing more or less on a European level before self-government could be considered. The emergence of a native African political class was not to be permitted until the mass was educated.

Second principle and corollary to the first was that Belgium is obligated to provide every opportunity for the native African to acquire skills, enter every branch of activity and improve his agriculture. That was known as the principle of the open door.

The third principle was that Belgium was obligated to provide increasing educational facilities but with emphasis on the primary education of the masses.

The fourth was that Belgium must create a native middle class equal in status to the white settler.

The fifth was that the white settler should not be permitted a role in politics and should not be given the franchise until the native masses were sufficiently advanced to use the franchise intelligently. By that time it would not actually matter much whether the white man had the franchise or not, for it could be presumed that the government of the country would be taken over by the Africans.

The Congo was unblushingly colonial, an investment to be protected as long as possible. In that colony which pretended to be nothing else, where there was neither freedom of the press in any real sense nor the franchise, primitive man had been brought along to deal with a steam shovel, a lathe, a locomotive, a urine specimen in a test tube—but not the ballot. Considerably more important was that there was an elaborate operation under way to teach him to use land and water, to shade his land from the full heat of the sun with proper vegetation and combat the chemical furies that break loose in tropic soils.

Because the men who controlled the Belgian investment were convinced that someday the Congolese must govern himself, he was patiently and slowly being introduced to self-government at the township level.

Whether in order to keep control as long as possible or for other, better reasons, the Belgians were set on building slowly from the bottom. They would leave the black lawyer and politician to the last.

I was not sure that the reason mattered as much as the method. The slow way seemed to be the better one because it respected the circumstance that Africa is neither Harlem nor Alabama nor Asia. It is older and stranger. Primitive man in the vastness of his continent down under the Sahara is outside all other experience of modern man.

Why rush them into what we are? If there is one thing about us that is clear, it is that we are only en route. They will be forced to jump so many centuries. One could conceive that they might, with advantage, jump us.

Possibly further along the road, those who follow after us will find again what had been accomplished in all those primitive milleniums when man had made his fundamental adaptations to the tragicomic affair of living. We, too, might return by a different way to the ancient intimacy.

40

DURING THE PERIOD I was in Africa I also made a visit to Bahia and Rio de Janeiro in Brazil.

Brazil has been the nightmare of the race-conscious South African whites. I have heard them say many times, "We don't want this country to be another Brazil."

The Republic of Brazil was a creation of the Latin peoples within a Portuguese context, and Africa is present there as a vital force that I had never encountered among American Negroes. It is not only present but interwoven with the texture of what makes up the Brazilian's concept of life. That concept could best be called the coffee-colored approach, and it involves more than the existence of the mulatto. The coffee-colored approach is a physical, intellectual and spiritual complex. It is an interpenetration of the life forms of the European and the dark tropical peoples. Involved in it is a strong element of Latin Catholicism, of that conviction of universality which is the heritage of Rome.

I thought about this on an afternoon when I had crossed from Rio de Janeiro over to the other shore and walked for hours until I came to a deserted beach on a bay. I did not know its name but on one end on a small hill there was a shrine and church dedicated to the Virgin. As the sun went down I sat there alone listening to the words of the Ave Maria that came gently down from the hill.

Far over on the other side, above Rio de Janeiro, on the high peak of the Corcovado, stood the Cristo Redentor with arms

318

outstretched in the gathering night. There was a strangeness to that great statue of the Christ on the mountain peak. At that moment, with the darkness about to fall and the mists rising from the ocean and the bay, it seemed to stand alone and unsupported, lifted and carried in the clouds as on the day of resurrection.

I was not sure that the vast gesture of the Cristo Redentor, suspended over the suffering and the failures in living, offering the consolation of divine love to the humble and the contrite, was wholly comprehensible within the context of my people's civilization.

Later that night, seeking a theater in the hot, older portion of Rio de Janeiro, I blundered into a competition of black Samba schools in preparation for the carnival. They danced to the tempestuous roar of drum bands that stretch full across the stage. You could not have been in Africa and not know that this was again the passion and sudden response of African drums, the rooted tribal symbolism and release of the dance that is inherent in the African spirit.

This was no nostalgic lament of the slave and of men inwardly abhorring the fate that had given them black skins. These were not American Negroes, and there was nothing in this music to soothe, with tones of complaint and subjection, the neuroses of my overwrought countrymen.

Yet there was misery among the black people in Brazil, and slavery had lasted a quarter of a century longer there than in the United States. The black man in slavery in Brazil had encountered brutality and the black woman dishonor and the lust of her masters. There had been rebellion. What they had not encountered was the shame of total rejection. The mulatto had not always come to life out of nuptials blessed by the church and recognized by society, but he was regarded with affection and normal parental pride. There was in the Portuguese nothing of the cantankerous introverted arrogance of North-American and northern European; absent was the narcissistic nastiness of the cult of the white skin which made sexual relations of the northern white and the woman of color an obscenity.

The European had come to Africa as a master or as a caste apart, or had evolved, as in the single case of the Afrikaner, into a small white nation. Only one thing had not been tried, that he should come as an immigrant.

The Brazilian coffee-colored approach is not rejected by the Latin, and the Portuguese have been extreme examples of Latins.

The Portuguese Governor General of Mozambique, Gabriel Texeira, told me, "The end result which we seek is Brazil."

We had been in his study discussing the Portuguese policy of an integrated state of Portugal in which the two great African colonies were regarded as simply provinces within the Portuguese Republic. The Portuguese colony of Mozambique was the oldest in Africa south of the equator, its settlement started shortly after Columbus discovered America. The Portuguese had, however, always been thin on the ground.

Now, after drifting far in the direction of the white-reserve system prevailing in neighboring South Africa, Mozambique was in the process of making a new start. The Governor General granted that in time the native Africans must come to full citizenship, and I had pointed out that this would mean Portugal would have a native African majority of citizens and voters.

He accepted that with the greatest equanimity and with a trace of a smile that said I was rather painfully obvious. It would, and so what of it? The point, he said, was that the Africans, by the time they became the majority, would all be *civilizados*.

Mozambique has an institution of the legal status of *civilizados*. They vote and under the law are to be recognized as fully equal in all ways to white Portuguese. There were at the moment only four thousand of them, partly because Mozambique had a totally inadequate school system outside the main centers and partly because you had to pay only a very small tax if you were not *civilizado*. It would be a long time before the Portuguese Republic had an electoral majority of *civilizado* Africans.

The Governor General, a relatively young man who was also a naval officer, explained, "We do not believe in superior and inferior races. The black man in Africa is simply where the white man began thousands of years ago. You cannot rush that sort of thing.

"You must have a balance between a moral advance and a material advance. Too sudden contact of advanced material civilization with primitive peoples destroys primitive people. On the other hand, if the material advance falls behind the moral advance, you have hatred and disorder. The problem is to keep a balance between the moral advance and material advance."

He went on to explain that the new policy of the government called for the settlement of white colonists among Africans, but never to the exclusion of the Africans.

Throughout the African Subcontinent various administrations were at work trying to bring the black man from the primitive into the peasant stage of the human story. He needed the example and assistance of the peasant.

It was possible that the European had a contribution to make to a new Africa if the landless peasant, seeking with great difficulty to be his own master, could find his way there and with proper aid and direction become a companion to the African in dealing with Africa's strange and perilous soils.

This was not the whole story of the coffee-colored approach, of course, though I began to feel it was the most important one. There would be a place anywhere in the Africa of the Africans for the white man who became indifferent to his famous skin and was prepared to find fulfillment in his mulatto children. There would be those who would find escape from the numerical society in the intimacy of the African clan society. It would always be a black man's continent, but it could do with a touch of Brazil.

Part Seven

Homeward

41

I WAS GOING back to Germany after so many years, and I was not sure there would be much happiness in it. What I did look forward to was a stopover leave on Gran Canaria in the Canary Islands.

Gran Canaria is both Africa and Spain. In the south there is a miniature Sahara where you see camels plodding about. Inland is an arid sierra, and in the folds of the mountains are green and watered valleys. The northern coast is a country of abrupt cliffs and terraced banana plots, and there is a long, walled valley running up from the sea in the west.

In all there are 758 square miles of it, and 300,000 people live there. It is dotted with large, round, cement water cisterns from which small irrigation channels run to garden farms.

Half the people live in Las Palmas, a dumbbell shaped area with the old town and cathedral at one end, and at the other the Porte de La Luz where you sit on the large square with its rather dusty trees and innumerable little tables as they bring you black coffee from cafés across the street. The important thing about Porte de La Luz is a mole one-and-five-eighths miles long always filled with liners and freighters in to take oil. Nearly all the ships on the African and South American runs come in for fuel, and it is the grand junction of shipping lanes of the South Atlantic. The tonnage in and out of port every day makes it statistically one of the major Atlantic ocean ports.

The Gran Canaria is possibly the world's most complete museum of the history of the motor car. High-wheeled red Win-

325

tons, the millionaire's car when I was a boy in the Middle West, go coughing up the mountainsides along with the British luxury vehicles of long-dead dukes. They are all there, all the models, demonstrating that in the old days they built them to last.

The museum pieces are operated by unshaven gentlemen known as pirates or pirates-on-the-line, the latter referring to the fact that they operate regularly up and down the routes into the villages and towns in the mountains. It is not quite fair to call them pirates, for they charge very little per passenger although they do squeeze them in. The cars are a great convenience, for they leave with the frequency of subway trains in the rush hour.

Pirates must be peculiarly talented mechanics, for they have to manufacture their repair parts for cars long since off the market.

I stayed at a hotel five miles straight up out of town, at the sort of price which causes otherwise inoffensive hotels to be overrun with jobless journalists and public-relations men who are writing novels. There were three things to do—go to the *jai alai,* do not go to the *jai alai,* and hate the football team at Santa Cruz de Tenerife. Someday in Las Palmas they are going to massacre the Santa Cruz de Tenerife football team—the only way the Canary Island will ever get in the news.

Also the locusts fly over from Africa and the whole island is out beating pans and lashing around wildly with palm branches. The locusts don't seem to mind, apparently presuming that Canary Islanders normally spend their time beating pans. After the wind from Africa has changed, the high officials receive messages of congratulation for beating off the locusts.

In certain districts the faces of the cliffs are dotted with house fronts—just the fronts. The rest of the houses are inside the cliffs. The British tourists from the ships can't remember how you spell troglodyte and say it is terrible to be so poor. It is not guaranteed that all troglodytes are poor. They like to live in cliffs.

The Guanches, the original inhabitants, had lived in caves

principally and, as their skeletons show, were as close to literal giants as people get. They were exterminated or got married to Spaniards around the time Columbus sailed for America, and now and then you meet people with immense hands, which is what is left of the Gaunches.

In Las Palmas there is a beautiful old Spanish house where Columbus stayed—and you cannot prove he did not—while he was refitting his ships and carrying on a love affair. Incidentally, he sailed for America from the Canaries and not from Spain. People who say he sailed from Spain for America can go and drink their black coffee all by themselves at their own table and be ignored by the waiter if they want another.

Columbus knew a lot about that ocean. Yachtsmen come down to the Canaries to make the Atlantic crossing in calmer waters approximately on the route that Columbus took in those yacht-sized boats of his.

If you look at the map of Columbus' first journey you will note that he was heading more or less straight for Miami Beach and then suddenly swung south. Did a prophetic vision disclose 'the future? The thought that he might have landed at Miami Beach is horrible. You can visualize the Christopher Columbus shrine at Miami, with lighting effects and the world's largest organ with built-in chimes playing under the world's largest dome.

Gran Canaria is a great place to talk about the Iberian world. The whole Iberian community of nations is within the network of the Asturians and Galicians from the north of Spain and the Canarienses. They have their clubs and they hang together like glue. People are poor and save up their money to go to Buenos Aires, Santiago, Caracas, Cuba and places you never heard of in Latin America, or they may go just to Madrid or Barcelona. When they get there they save up their money to come home again. The popular thing to do is to arrive barefoot and end up with a department store, but it cannot always be arranged.

I sat with my feet up on a chair and smoked Canary cigars, which are worth approximately what they cost, and that isn't

328

much. I listened to the exchange of tales and anecdotes from the world that lies between the Rio Grande at El Paso, the Pyrenees and Patagonia. That crossroads in the sea is the place to realize that there is a unity in that which has nothing to do with political principles or perhaps any particular principles, but is concerned with a pattern and feel for living. The Iberian pattern is, in its way, sound.

I went north through Cádiz, Seville and Granada, and, feeling nostalgia for my lost youth, back across Europe.

42

RUNNING FOR the Rhine, the Rome express emerged from the high tunnel in the Alps into the mists and clouds of the winter just starting in northern Europe.

I had come aboard at Lugano in the clarity of an early Italian morning after a day there and a few spent walking the hills above San Remo on the Riviera dei Fiori where the florist peasants' terraced gardens had been blooming under the sun of a belated summer. A sudden urge came over me to turn back into the lands of the sun for in the north of Germany I was afraid of finding again that egomaniac indifference to living life for its own sake that was inherent in the nature of the great civilization of our times.

The feeling passed away under the influence of the wet, green meadows and the quiet villages of the Swiss countryside seen through the window. The train rushed northward as if eager to reach the cities of that other Europe.

All that day on the long trip down the Rhine valley, mist swirled about us, cleared and closed in again like battle smoke, reminding one of this continent's too numerous battlefields. That swirling mist gave a sense of impermanence to the cities and the German countryside, as if there were nothing sure and solid here. If you pressed your face against the glass when the fast-moving mist became opaque, it made you a little dizzy. Such a dizziness amid swirling vapor must have been the last experience of the four million who had died in German gas chambers.

I turned from the window to look at the stolid, florid Germans who had entered the compartment after we crossed the German frontier, and they baffled me. This first sense of bafflement did not decrease as the months went by.

I have few definite impressions of the early period of that return to Germany. For a time I lived largely in the artificial atmosphere of Bonn, the new capital about which still hung a feeling of occupation rule. Bonn was so accustomed to the predominance of the victorious allies that even after sovereignty had been restored its people were like prisoners who no longer feel at home outside jail and away from the warders.

As a citizen of one of the great Allied Powers you were thrust completely into a sterilized world of your own. It was not really intentional on their part, or hypocritical, but an ingrained habit after the years of occupation rule.

All who could insisted on speaking English. Most of them employed an overgrammatical but rather elementary English that made them sound as if they were explaining something to a not too clever child. Jokes sounded like those the language teacher tells slowly and punctiliously to relieve the monotony of memorizing verbs. Germans who had to use their own German tongue with you succeeded in employing a similar beginners' type of German—elementary, sterilized and expurgated for teenagers. Because of your citizenship not only the language used but all thoughts expressed seemed to assume that expurgated, oversimplified, cheerful but not jovial character. You felt that there was an unspoken agreement that you were well intentioned but only understood very simple things and must not be upset.

I do not think the Bonn political people and civil servants were hiding anything. It was rather, if I got the point, that they had a feeling that any careless word might set off a chain reaction of clichés in your head and you would start riding your red-white-and-blue hobbyhorse in all directions simultaneously.

As I went about I kept running into more and more former National Socialists in official positions. If I raised the question, the answer was that they had had to be party members, by which was meant that they would otherwise have lost their careers. The idea seemed to be that it was all right if you had done it for the sake of your career. I had known in my time some sincere National Socialists. You wondered if it had not been somehow cleaner and more decent to have been one by conviction.

None of those things were probably too important. National Socialism had been totalitarian, and a whole generation could not be banished into ineffectiveness and go unused because it had been swept up into a totalitarian system. But I wondered about this Germany.

It was only when I got away from Bonn and began to travel about the country fairly regularly that I got a somewhat broader picture.

The Germans themselves, more than the economic miracle of recovery, were the German miracle. They were so intact, so unscarred. They were not ashamed. The concentration camps and the gas chambers had left no mark. If you chose to be tactless, you talked to them about those things. They told you what the Russians did. If the point were pressed, they lost interest. Oh, they would agree with you that it was all very bad. You could even call it sinful to their faces. They were not resentful.

The cry, *"Sieg Heil, Sieg Heil!"* of the vibrant, thunderous throngs echoed only as a whispered memory within your own mind. You could still recall mistily the massed swastika banners, the rows of shining faces, the man Hitler. But it was like some private memory of your own, and unreal.

You could remember the Jew in the dark bedroom of that courtyard in East Berlin coughing blood and the children pulling at his nightshirt and what it must have meant to him that he must leave them fatherless. The sobs and desperation of the wife of that other man who was taken out of your apartment house before dawn came back to you.

But all that, and what followed, seemed to have made no impact on Germans. Hitler was dead and therefore, apparently, all this was dead with him, as far as they were concerned. The years of that great catastrophe had passed out of sight like a set on a revolving stage.

You talked with them in terms of our common interests, meaning the postwar allies' interests, which were real enough. It seemed discourteous to remember the long agony and the last agony of those other millions. It was all just one of those things.

I struggled a little against that "we," remembering the pictures of the stacked naked corpses.

But, were they necessarily the same Germans? I had a sense of both knowing them and not having ever encountered them before. Who were they?

Superficially there was something that made them, in West Germany at least, similar to the German Swiss, the Dutch and the Danes, those notoriously small, healthy, progressive peoples whose very existence is based on their having made their compromise with life. It had always been there along with the other thing in the Germans. The plump, scrubbed German and his plump wife, with cuckoo clock and goldfish bowl, almost caricatures of domestication, were not new. There never seemed to be any explanation in the old days for the presence in the same people of a burgher stodginess that came close to the grotesque, and a seemingly unbridled romanticism, chronic melancholia, an incorrigible philosophical wrestling with life, a primitive fleshy sense of humor and a sort of brass-band militarism and heavy-witted belligerence.

These Germans I saw now were not only intact, seemingly

untouched by the war; in some ways they were more intact than they had been in the last years of the Weimar Republic and during the National Socialist regime. It is probably fair to guess that they had not been this way since the quieter years of the Hohenzollern epoch. Perhaps they had not been this way since the Hohenzollern Reich was established and did away with the other Germany of small states that Goethe knew.

The small peoples of predominantly Germanic character such as the Dutch, the Swiss and the Danes had long ceased trying to challenge fate and had made a satisfactory best of not very much. They shared with the Germans the most evident and widely advertised characteristic of this Germany: they liked to work.

With the martial romanticism of the Reich gone, German energy had poured into the channel of creative work. This had become a businessman's society, an indefatigably industrious society. The German nerve cure that accounted for the fact that they were so intact and unbroken was, before everything else, an apparently boundless enthusiasm for hard work. The Germans had worked themselves back to health.

They functioned under the orders and leadership of a managerial caste that possibly had no equal in the modern world. The trains in which the members and representatives of that managerial caste constantly criss-crossed the republic had built-in offices. When there was not room in the office compartment, they turned every compartment into an office. Their secretaries traveled with them. They dictated without break, pawing around in their armfuls of brief cases for accounts and documents. At their destination they rushed to taxis or cars waiting for them and hurried away to other offices.

That managerial caste was the extreme example of what the Germans themselves, with a rather deprecatory shrug, called their work-fanaticism. Another expression was that work was the German opiate. Work was less a means to an end than an end in itself. When you tried to find out where they thought they were going, their responses were blurred. It seemed as if they did not actually know and, in a sense, did not care.

I wondered if a man who uses work as an opiate is cured, and if the Germans had, in fact, made their compromise with life.

Talk to those apparently sound, unscarred and unbroken people who were so busy and you begin to be assailed by doubts and uncertainty as to who they really are.

Living in that Germany was too much like living in a hotel. The universal feeling was that it was all provisional, an elaborate economy balanced on the tightrope of international trade. Germany's eastern agrarian provinces, which had helped to balance out the economy, were gone.

Your surprise over those so normal, unshaken Germans slowly began to wear off. You began to notice the little things again.

The girl who came into the bookshop in Munich said, "I was *draussen* and just came back." Her way of saying that she had been abroad rang a bell. She had been *draussen,* which is to say, outside. They all say the same thing. They said it then and they were saying it now.

There are speech habits that have an inescapable connotation, a significance that is in the usage and the feel of them. The use of *draussen* for abroad, with its implications of a people caged in, is the partner of that other famous German expression, *Lebensraum,* or space to live in. Two wars had been fought for *Lebensraum.* For a long time it had been one of the main themes of German political thought.

I wondered if you say that you have been outside when you mean abroad, if you have made your compromise with life. An American or a Frenchman or an Englishman does not say that he has been outside when he has been in another country. A German does. Was the expression now only a habit, with the old implications gone? Perhaps.

In those days before the war there could be no mistake. It was clear then that the German nation had not made its compromise with life. Long before, Clemenceau had said of the Germans, "They do not love life."

Friedrich Sieburg, critic and writer, said it a little differently. After the war he wrote, "Germany is the German's fate but it is not a way of life."

I recalled the sense of urgency before the war, the feeling

that Germany had been born late and that time was running out. The Germans that I had known in those first years had been filled with the subtle fear that they could not fulfill themselves before it was too late in history.

Their breakdown in the early thirties, when not only they but the world stood still and stagnant, had come of that sense of urgency, of time slipping away from them until it would be forever too late. Hitler had been borne to his dictatorship by that neurotic fear—or was it a sense of a dynamic reality?—that time was running out on them.

The second defeat had been more overwhelming than that of 1918. About a third of the territory of what had been the German Reich lay east of the Oder-Neisse line in what had become postwar Poland or Russia. Millions of refugees from the lost east lived scattered among the population of the west.

You asked yourself whether any nation had ever surrendered an irredenta making up a third of its former territory. For most Germans it was the same thing as if the Japanese had conquered and occupied permanently the western third of the United States. After all, the lost territories had been German long before a United States existed.

That was part of the impermanence, the provisional, living-in-a-hotel feeling of this Germany. But there was more. The postwar German spoke of democracy, representative government, the free world and all the rest of the litany of the post-defeat era, in the fashion of someone reciting something. They were not aware of it. You felt they were neither sincere nor insincere but walking in the dark. There was a sense of groping, of not belonging quite anywhere but doing what the others were doing.

Yet in spite of the provisional character of the life of this people who used work as an opiate against the desperate frustrations arising out of the collapse of their towering ambitions there was in this twice-defeated Germany perhaps a conviction that a decision had been reached, notably in the long struggle between German and Slav. The odd intactness and health of these Germans could be related to acceptance of the fact of defeat. The blood-red banners of the new Rome flying on the eastern horizon answered perhaps one of the questions which the German people had put to history.

Looking westward they seemed to have become convinced that the center of gravity had passed from Europe to what the Europeans call the overseas world. Jealousy had been woven through the history of the Reich. But it was jealousy of other members of the intimate European family. The breakdown of colonial empires and spheres of interest overseas was easing that jealousy. They insisted on the new relative unimportance of Europe and dwelt on the weakness of Europe and its waning prestige. It made things easier for them, and they comforted themselves with it.

However that humbleness or near humbleness was somehow a little ominous. They dwelt also on their doctrine of "killed the wrong pig," meaning that Russia, not Germany, had been the real enemy of America. The National Socialist regime in its death agony had clung to the belief that Russia and America would clash, and the Reich would regain its place but as one of the western allies.

These postwar Germans hung to that idea, and you heard the "wrong pig" phrase a good deal.

Still and all, the old urgency was gone.

The Germans might at last be about to find such peace of mind as they could in the acceptance of the fact that the race with time was over. They might be preparing now to make their compromise with life, sadly, rather bitterly, but also with a sense of relief.

Perhaps, and perhaps not.

Among the exceptions to the work-for-the-sake-of-working pattern of life, with the wherefore put aside for the moment, the small neo-Nazi groups were quickly identifiable. I was looking for them. They were, as far as I could make out, merely tiresome, a political reflex action after death.

More intriguing was another exception—the people who kept busy but did not want jobs.

They had of course been investigated and catalogued. After

all, this was Germany. Their habitat, typically, was in the far-spread colonies of little, rather primitive houses that surround every German city. The colonies, half suburb and half squatters' camp, are a familiar and puzzling feature of the German landscape. Originally they had grown up as garden plots of people living in the towns. Then a considerable population moved in, expanded them and settled down.

The inevitable systematic investigation had been made by the Institute of Sociographic Studies in Frankfurt, and the director, Professor Hans Neuendorfer, had described the phenomenon as a new way of life—*Lebensform*. He had suggested there was something to say for it.

Up to forty per cent of those people were receiving some sort of pension. A large proportion of them were found not to be near the retiring age.

Several studies had indicated that among the 4,000,000 pension receivers under usual retiring age was a large number of able-bodied who had simply found means to evade regular employment although industry was, at the time, scraping the barrel for man power.

I found most of these people fairly neat and orderly. They worked at odd jobs of which there was a fair supply and carried on part-time businesses on a huckster basis. A substantial part of their food they grew themselves on owned or leased land, and they usually built their little houses with some aid from a carpenter. They were always busy, and it was a type of living that required considerable initiative and adaptability.

The psychology of the phenomenon was described as escapism. Their incomes were well below what they would have earned in regular jobs open to them.

They were tired of the boss, of the factory pattern of living. They had sacrificed everything else, according to the studies made of them, for a degree of personal independence.

I recalled the Bantu and his *shamba,* and that he was always going back to it, to the annoyance of the white employer. I remembered the Afrikaner and that "no man will serve another for hire if he may be his own master." These people in the new

Germany were heretics as they would have been in my country. They were little interested in material things and possessions, or in purchasable services and purchasing power.

It was quite the opposite tendency in postwar Germany which the American observers, who were a regular corps, had entered on the moral-assets side of the ledger. Great satisfaction was evidenced because interest in acquiring material possessions seemed to have replaced the ideological movements that had long been so important and so dangerous in Germany. The American observers called the new thing individualism. It was, apparently, the concept of the individual as it was coming to be understood in America. The individual was the customer, the man who purchased life.

That had not been, as I recalled it, the America and the individualism of my father, who had outlived his generation and would perhaps have fitted even better into an older one than his own. It was not my America, or at least what I had at one time in boyhood thought of as America, for my father had in some way infected me with his concept.

That America had become, by my time, more a memory than a reality. Yet I sometimes wondered if that memory of an America that I had never seen was not the only home that I had ever known. That, I was reminded, was perhaps my problem and possibly that of others of my nationality, likewise born into exile.

Accordingly, those Germans who had chosen to escape into little houses and frugality without even status, which means so much to the German, interested me perhaps more than they should have.

There was no frontier here in this country and they had created an odd one of their own in little houses and garden plots outside the towns. They in their way, to cite the title of a famous book, had chosen freedom.

After a time I went again to Berlin, which I had not seen since the days when Hitler's armies were bringing to a triumphant close the short Polish war. There I became aware that I had in a sense come back to Germany in search of my youth. A great part of my young manhood had been spent in Germany, and I was getting close to the half-century mark.

But it meant nothing to me now, this postwar Berlin. Much of the city that I had known had been destroyed, but it was not so much that as what struck me as its fraudulence. There was no longer any sound reason for the existence of what had been the second largest city on the European continent. It was almost on the Oder, the eastern frontier of this Germany. For half a century or more it had been what the Germans called a *Wasserkopf,* or water head, a swollen abnormal growth beyond the Elbe. Now it had become almost totally useless.

Little was left of either the hangman's humor or the air of defiance that had characterized it. This Berlin was querulous and self-important. Conversation had the character of a burlesque on the platitudes of the West and the East, but it was not intended as burlesque. The whole attitude was that the world owed Berlin a debt. That attitude had apparently originated back in the time of the Allied Powers airlift. The world, you gathered, owed the people of Berlin something for having been there, caught in the trap.

In Munich the bomb crater had been filled in and the ground smoothed out where once had been the student pension in which I had learned to say *Gabel* and *Loeffel* under the stern tutelage of Frau Major. Otherwise a great deal of my Munich was still there, and the trains ran out in the misty mornings to the mountains.

One Saturday morning before I left Germany, perplexed and defeated, I watched the students, boys and girls, getting a scalding milk at the Milchstube in the station as I had on such mornings a quarter of a century before. They ran for the trains to sit on the hard benches and unbuckled their knapsacks as they ran. After overnighting in a mountain hostel some of them would stand in the morning and watch the dawn wash over the distant Dolomites as I had in that spring long ago.

But the full knowledge had come to me, as it has come to others, that there is no road back from afternoon into morning.

43

The lights of San Miguel blink on in the late afternoon. The waters of the Caribbean to the south and the distant bay on the Atlantic coast to the north, are turning dark. Shadows gather among the palms on the ridges around the little town. Here and there along rocky paths men ride toward town on their small horses. Through a gap in the hills I can see the green expanse of sugar cane out on the plain, shimmering in the last light of the day.

I sit on the hill under the tall statue of Christ, looking down the flights of stone steps to the road that winds toward San Miguel. Women down there in the nondescript barrio walk in and out of *cabañas*. Children play in the dust.

I remember another eventide spent across the bay from Rio de Janeiro, and the outspread arms of the distant Christ of the Corcovado, symbol of love, the ultimate human aspiration.

Now I know. Somewhere in this far-flung Iberian world— perhaps in these islands—I shall find home. I need the heart-warming, histrionic language of Spain or its Portuguese brother tongue that has been, since the days of Camoëns' epic of the sea empire, saturated with the rhythms of the mounting and falling waters.

Words, the savor of them, have always meant so much. They are the most human of human things. Marriage has been called a life-long conversation. The same can be said for life itself, the brief period of a man's marriage with humanity.

The people here in San Miguel are great talkers, *habladores*.

339

They mock themselves for it, but among them, as among certain other "backward foreigners" with whom I have lived, a restraint is lifted from me. So much of what goes for conversation back there in the centers of the world's progress is merely indifference clothed in words, reiteration of passionless conformity, vocalized reflexes. Words used in earnest are increasingly restricted to the business of selling oneself or things, or to getting things done.

There is another need, similar to that of wanting to be among these *habladores;* I want soil and growing things.

This, when it comes, will be a compromise. It will be another inadequate solution but relevant to my need and not impossible to accomplish. The world of the peasant and the peon on both sides of the Atlantic, in the Spanish- and Portuguese-speaking lands, is still in many places and in varying degrees intact. The kernel of the matter is that intactness.

I shall go down now and eat with these people who are my friends, and I shall take the small *bailador* on my lap. He will laugh and slip away to engage in a silent, dancing conversation with himself, imitating or symbolizing with his quick body what he has found in his child's world. For that reason he is known to the family as "the dancer."

The feeling will be there of that cell of all that has come after, the family clan. I will be reminded of the old men and women asleep in the sun, leaning against the walls of their African huts. I will remember that night in San Gigminiano delle belle Torre.

The soup will be hot and fragrant and the wines perhaps a little sour but comforting. Afterward, we shall sit outside in the tropic night, and the lawyer who was once a member of the cabinet will talk about co-operatives and new peasant land schemes and the care of pregnant women in the villages. He is a born orator and, using that dramatic tongue with its cadences of vowels come down from classic Rome, he makes these matters seem exciting. There must have been something of that drama in the conversation of Cicero when he sat with his friends at Formia and talked of common things.

The stout, big-breasted matrons will be a little malicious,

lowering their voices when the young girls come by. They know all about who is related to whom. Like the authors of Genesis, they know who begat whom through generations past.

The refugee priest, who sat in the Republican parliament in Madrid, will come, and we will hear his aspirate consonants, heritage from the Moors. He will bring that other element necessary to good living: talk of books and the meaning of things, with references to the poets.

The people here are not building the world to come. Not they. These—let us say it frankly—lesser and in some ways second-rate Latins have nothing special to contribute, but then neither do I. The great world out there will get on without us. What matters is that here is something, in a form that I can digest, of what I saw and felt in Asia and in the African bush. It is, at least, livable. It is hard to get at the simple matter of living in this world.

This refuge will not be a solution for others or even for its own people. There is physical misery here, and there is injustice.

This has a great deal to do with what matters in life, but it is not a solution for that homelessness of mankind in our world which is the final heritage of the Renaissance. It is no real solution even for me. There will be no solution for my generation, there is only a groping toward home.

Humanity has made the old blunder. It has mistaken the means for the end. Freedom is a means, an essential means, but not an end. Science, techniques and the possession of things are means, not ends.

Life in our world has become a badly staged play. The scenery, the furnishings and the lighting effects have got in the way. Human relationships are all that the drama is really about, and accomplishments or possessions are only means to that end. The plot is about living with oneself and living with others.

Life is the business of living together with others. It is not merely a co-existence. It is not that life lived together is better that way or more ethical or necessarily more pleasant. Life is that and nothing else. It is, in a sense to which Nietzsche has only partially referred, beyond good and evil.

Most of the human story is made up of tribal and clan life in the milleniums which we disparagingly call primitive. Man became man in that environment. He was a social creature, an aspect of a living whole, begotten and brought forth and formed in those fruitful primitive milleniums. The rest of his story has been a brief postlude compared with those milleniums. That was, for me, the lesson of Africa.

The pattern of the village community has prevailed through most of the seventy centuries of recorded history for the vast majority of men. The ancient form of human wholeness in good or evil, fortune or misfortune, has remained intact. That was, for me, the lesson of the Middle East and the Far East.

The period since the Renaissance was only one-fourteenth of the period of recorded history, of what we call, roughly, civilization. How slowly the forces which the Renaissance loosed came to prevail over the ancient patterns that emerged out of the necessities of the nature of man—this I came to realize in Europe.

Compared with what has gone before, the period since the technological revolution in the last century is infinitesimally short. And a second, far more potent, technological revolution has taken place since I was a child. This I have seen in both Europe and America.

The fantasies of the ages—the stuff of fairy tales both gruesome and glorious—have become realities. As never before in his story, man has lost control of his environment as his physical mastery of it increased.

The pattern is becoming dehumanized. Man, swimming in the maelstrom, may become no longer man. The fabric of the ancient human community, of which he is only a thread woven in, is unraveling.

Population has swept upward, and man is becoming an anonymous creature in an anonymous mob, alone as one is alone in a mob.

The miraculous devices of the mass-communications industry, operating on the principle of the lowest common denominator and searching the multitude at all costs, have become instruments of mob living. Man, more often than not, has come to live bathed in banality.

Humanity in the modern environment is becoming sterile, not in ideas or devices, but in the capacity to generate wisdom and inner fortitude and serenity. Man now has the means to overcome the plagues of ignorance, poverty and disease, but he has abandoned or is about to abandon the intimate communion with others which is the form and essence of his being.

The individual lives increasingly outside of and without experience of that ancient institution, the actual community. By a coincidence only superficially strange, he is becoming more than ever dependent on outward circumstances and the opinion of others. He is coming to value himself and the content of life itself only in terms of his position in the hierarchy of success. He seeks in the possession of things and in so-called pleasures to assuage the grief of his essential aloneness.

Competition has become a way of living as if the good life were a prize in a horse race. Purchasing power has become a dogma as if the full life could be bought in a store.

The competitive society is, beneath an enforced self-discipline, a way of life saturated with hidden, perhaps semiconscious hostility. It is a world of rivalry bordering on enmity. It is a world of victory and defeat in which the defeated sink too easily and too often in the estimation of others into a bottomless abyss of worthlessness, and in their own estimation into the void of self-contempt.

The human being is constantly looking outside himself for reassurance as to how his battle with life is going. It is to a degree life lived as if life itself were civil war.

The vast storms of our century carried within themselves a vital element of this war of man against himself, of his flight from a freedom that had become his master and of his revolt against an aloneness that was becoming intolerable.

Men have sought unity passionately. They have seemed to hurl themselves with blind fervor into anything that would draw them closer together. In their panic, they raised the nation-state to the status of the supreme loyalty and supreme value, and they

344

groveled in a new idolatry before the blood-stained altars of nationalism.

The torment and frustration of the German spirit brought forth the ultimate insult to human dignity, waging a relentless crusade in the name of a mystic nihilism and a deified maniac.

Communism was the legitimate offspring of the age, conceived in the nineteenth century with the appearance of double heresies against humanity—the individualist doctrine of "economic man" and the collectivist doctrine of "economic determinism," two sides of the same coin. It became another and more virulent form of the disease of the times, evolving a mystic imperialism and idolatry of its own.

All of this is true. I lived, and we did live, in such an age.

There is no going back. Yet that is what I am trying to do and, if that mercy is granted me, shall do. I want the slow peace of that other, older world in which you are born into your place in life and change is reckoned in centuries.

I have been searching all my life to escape from the twentieth century, to escape from the predicament of modern mankind. I want the old lost intimacy of a dead or dying world and will try to find the best substitute for it that I can.

In that I am not alone. So many want to go home again into the lost past even if they do not know specifically that that is what they seek. They want, as I want, a place to hide in.

But mankind cannot hide from itself.

Coincidence or fate has taken me by the hand and led me step by step through the confusing years deeper into the past. I have gone from Europe, where the past is little more than memory, first to the Far East and then to the Middle East. From that world, more ancient than Europe, I crossed the final divide and found myself before primitive man.

Each step increased a nostalgia and longing that I could never fully understand. We are so many things, and atavistic voices speak within us. Homelessness is the predicament of modern man. We are lost, cut off from what we have been for so long.

Yes, there are serene people, a good many of them who keep alive, even in the centers of the most fanatical and banal forms of the modern competitive civilization, their marriage with humanity. It is harder to do now, especially in places like "back there" where I was born and reared. It is beyond the strength of people like myself—and there are a good many of us—some living what Thoreau called "lives of quiet desperation" and others becoming clods or escaping from the actual business of living into "busyness." Some of us, a few, are roaming the earth.

The old peace has been the peace of the slow flow of stagnant waters. It has been a mold and a life to which a man belonged intimately and organically. But what contentment existed there was the contentment of ignorance and, in a sense, the absence of that unsettling thing, hope, and the possibility of new achievement.

Those who can raise that real need of belonging together to a new level in this new kind of world will build the future. Belonging, solidarity, is a necessity to humans. It will have to take new and different forms in this environment created by modern man and be clothed in new and different institutions. During the half century that I lived through, the full force of the disruptive, second technological revolution has broken over mankind with shocking violence. There has been political revolution on top of political revolution, empires breaking up, liberation of nations and those two major outbreaks of sheer senseless slaughter.

Yet, in the course of all that, one thing has begun to go out of this world, one thing that was still there in my youth: the belief that life is a kind of free-for-all in which the strong rise to the top and the others sink to the bottom, the creed of every-man-for-himself; the idea is still there, deeply ingrained in the society. But the conviction that it is right and moral and that it will be the way of the future, is gone.

Everywhere men's interdependence is being increasingly emphasized. The instrument of the state is being used more and more as a mutual insurance by the members of the society against the risks of life. There is still a good deal of protest against the welfare state, but it has become a protest without conviction, mostly just a critique of mistakes and exaggerations. The opinion that it is sinful for workers to band together and sell intelligently their merchandise—labor—on the labor marketplace has now become restricted to querulous old men.

The actual great issue of our times has become how to live dependent on one another—free not to stumble into the complete dependence of the governed on a governing caste. The new freedom will be a freedom of clearly recognized and gladly accepted interdependence.

The old world of the ancient communal fashion of living that still haunts the minds and emotions of so many of us did not require that men make so great an effort.

True, we have not really tackled the question of finding something to replace the intimate, living face-to-face community unit. It will have to be done. Men require it and life is about men and not what has been regarded as "progress." The enormous cities that rear their grotesque bulk here and there are products of the first technological revolution and are a hindrance that must be removed.

Man's new home must be found at a higher level than the old world of the milleniums, or this one. It will be a long hard journey into those peaceful highlands. I and so many others in my lifetime could not find the road. It will be left to others in a time to come to find their way forward, not backward—to find their way home.

They must do it who are small children now, like that child so many years ago in his bed back there in Ohio, listening in that half dream before sleeping to the express passing and, as it whistled for a distant crossing, to that lonely far cry that was a summons to far places. It will be for little children like the small *bailador* in the town of San Miguel who sits in my lap in the evening—the *bailador* who looks up puzzled, half-smiling and half-afraid.

He does not understand why I suddenly press him close against me.